Public Relations and Nation Building

All public relations emerges from particular environments, but the specific conditions of Israel offer an exceptional study of the accelerators and inhibitors of professional development in the history of a nation.

Documenting and analyzing the contribution of one profession to building one specific nation, this book tells the previously untold story of Israeli public relations practitioners. It illustrates their often unseen, often unacknowledged, and often strategic shaping of the events, narratives, and symbols of Israel over time and their promotion of Israel to the world. It links the profession's genesis – including the role of the Diaspora and early Zionist activists – to today's private- and public-sector professionals by identifying their roots in Israel's cultural, economic, media, political, and social systems. It reveals how professional communicators and leaders nurtured and valued collectivism, strong consensus, solidarity, and unity over democracy and free speech. It investigates such key underpinning concepts as Hasbara and criticizes non-democratic and sometimes unethical propaganda practices. It highlights unprecedented fundraising and lobbying campaigns that forged Israeli identity internally and internationally.

In situating Israeli ideas on democracy in the context of contemporary public relations theory, *Public Relations and Nation Building* seeks to point ways forward for that theory, for Israel and for the public relations of many other nations.

Margalit Toledano is Senior Lecturer in the Department of Management Communication at the University of Waikato, New Zealand. She holds an accreditation in public relations (APR), is a Fellow of the PRSA and PRiNZ, and is former President of the Israeli Public Relations Association. Margalit is currently on the editorial board of *Public Relations Review* and *Public Relations Inquiry*.

David McKie is Professor in the Department of Management Communication at the University of Waikato, New Zealand. He has published or co-published four books (including the 2007 NCA prize winner *Reconfiguring Public Relations*), 22 book chapters, and 55 refereed journal articles. As CEO of RAM International Consulting, David works in leadership and strategic communication in Asia, Europe, and the United States.

Routledge New Directions in Public Relations and Communication Research
Edited by Kevin Moloney

Routledge New Directions in Public Relations and Communication Research is a new forum for the publication of books of original research in PR and related types of communication. Its remit is to publish critical and challenging responses to continuities and fractures in contemporary PR thinking and practice, and its essential yet contested role in market-oriented, capitalist liberal democracies around the world. The series reflects the multiple and interdisciplinary forms PR takes in a post-Grunigian world, the expanding roles which it performs, and the increasing number of countries in which it is practised.

The series will examine current trends and explore new thinking on the key questions which impact upon PR and communications, including:

- Is the evolution of persuasive communications in Central and Eastern Europe, China, Latin America, Japan, the Middle East, and South-East Asia developing new forms or following Western models?
- What has been the impact of postmodern sociologies, cultural studies, and methodologies that are often critical of the traditional, conservative role of PR in capitalist political economies and in patriarchy, gender, and ethnic roles?
- What is the impact of digital social media on politics, individual privacy, and PR practice? Is new technology changing the nature of content communicated, or simply reaching bigger audiences faster? Is digital PR a cause or a consequence of political and cultural change?

Books in this series will be of interest to academics and researchers involved in these expanding fields of study, as well as students undertaking advanced studies in this area.

Public Relations and Nation Building
Influencing Israel
Margalit Toledano and David McKie

Public Relations and Nation Building
Influencing Israel

Margalit Toledano and David McKie

LONDON AND NEW YORK

First published 2013
by Routledge
2 Park Square, Milton Park, Abingdon, Oxon OX14 4RN

Simultaneously published in the USA and Canada
by Routledge
711 Third Avenue, New York, NY 10017

Routledge is an imprint of the Taylor & Francis Group, an informa business

© 2013 Margalit Toledano and David McKie

The right of Margalit Toledano and David McKie to be identified as authors of this work has been asserted by them in accordance with sections 77 and 78 of the Copyright, Designs and Patents Act 1988.

All rights reserved. No part of this book may be reprinted or reproduced or utilized in any form or by any electronic, mechanical, or other means, now known or hereafter invented, including photocopying and recording, or in any information storage or retrieval system, without permission in writing from the publishers.

Trademark notice: Product or corporate names may be trademarks or registered trademarks, and are used only for identification and explanation without intent to infringe.

British Library Cataloguing in Publication Data
A catalogue record for this book is available from the British Library

Library of Congress Cataloging-in-Publication Data
Toledano, Margalit.
Public relations and nation building : influencing Israel / Margalit Toledano and David McKie.
p. cm. – (Routledge new directions in public relations and communications research)
Includes bibliographical references and index.
1. Public relations and politics–Israel. 2. Nation-building–Israel.
3. Nationalism–Israel. 4. Propaganda, Israeli. 5. Israel–Foreign public opinion. I. McKie, David, 1947– II. Title.
JQ1830.A69P858 2013
352.7'48095694–dc23
2012035798

ISBN: 978-0-415-69892-4 (hbk)
ISBN: 978-0-203-78697-0 (ebk)

Typeset in Times New Roman
by Keystroke, Station Road, Codsall, Wolverhampton

Contents

	Preface	vi
	Acknowledgements	viii
1	Explaining the nation: Israel, Hasbara, and public relations	1
2	Public relations, history, and nation building	13
3	Shaping communication: Diaspora life and the Jewish public sphere	25
4	Determining identity: Zionist leaders as forerunners	39
5	Shaping factors: the political and media environment	56
6	Early Zionist institutions and communication practitioners	69
7	Emissaries, fundraising, and nation building	84
8	Economics, market changes, and major campaigns	104
9	Speaking on behalf of government (1): government practitioners and Hasbara	121
10	Speaking on behalf of government (2): other civil servants and military spokespeople	135
11	The emergence of private consultants	149
12	Conclusion: representing nations and influencing Israel	168
	References	180
	Index	193

Preface

Oscar Wilde is reputed to have answered the standard customs officer's question about anything to declare by stating, "I have nothing to declare but my genius." Authors in public relations tend to imply that they have nothing to declare but their objectivity. This book doesn't. Instead, it is more informed than most by L'Etang's (2008a) insight that "the position of the researcher is central to the nature of the story-telling and that requires more reflexivity than is common or conventional in much academic writing" (p. 324). Recognizing that we can't be objective about this topic in particular, we offer these disclosures and background up front to lay out at least some formative factors.

The book is the fruit of powerful feelings: our passion for the discipline of public relations; a wish to share the story of its role in Israel's nation building; and our fear for the future of Israel and Israeli public relations. We wrote it partly to work out how public relations contributed to the shaping of Israel and how Israel was shaped by the same experience. We wrote it to tell the story of how public relations evolved in Israel's complex culture and history. We wanted to research and relate significant stories and people who were not known to the academic community and to capture the actual reflections of prominent Israeli practitioners on the page while we could. We wrote it partly because the complexity of this nation's building is part of our lives, but also partly in the hope that it is both similar enough, and different enough, to give perspectives to other citizens in other nations.

Backgrounds

Margalit is an Israeli with over 20 years' experience as a public relations practitioner in Israel, including service as the President of the Israeli Public Relations Association from 1993 to 1995. Not that her professional experience is limited to Israel. She is an active member of the Public Relations Society of America (PRSA) and the Public Relations Institute of New Zealand (PRiNZ), and was inducted into the College of Fellows of both organizations. She has managed communication on behalf of business and public organizations, including political movements that promoted peace negotiations with the Palestinians during the Oslo period of the 1990s. She is the daughter of an active Zionist father who migrated to Israel in 1934 from Lithuania and a Lithuanian Jewish mother who, although she lived in Israel most of her adult life, remained more interested in Impressionist art in Europe than in the Zionist movement in Israel. Almost all the members of Margalit's parents' families were slaughtered or shot by the Nazis and their Lithuanian collaborators in 1941. She went through a socialist-Zionist indoctrination in her formative years, still cares deeply for Israel, and supports organizations that promote dialogue with Palestinians and call for the end of Israeli occupation of Palestinian territory and control over Palestinian lives.

David teaches and studies leadership and strategic communication and runs his own international consultancy. Born in Scotland, he used to think that Scots had a black belt in guilt until he learned more about Jewish people and realized they were rank amateurs. As a Catalonian-loving Celt, he has a keen interest in stateless nations and found that studying Israel helped him to understand how nations evolve, how imagined communities become realities, and how the public relations of nations still matters locally and globally. Being married to an Israeli meant that he shared the house with a culture as well as a woman, and learning about it became a matter of survival. He also came to appreciate the importance of such a small nation to the future of so many non-Israelis and non-Jews, and how peace in that region would be a giant step for humankind.

Joint

Both of us live in New Zealand and teach at the Department of Management Communication of the University of Waikato. In doing work on life values with students, New Zealanders tend not to rate peace that highly since they have come to take it for granted. This is a gift, while any news report from Israel causes a tightening of the chest until we know all are safe. We often travel to Israel and spend time there with family and friends who help us gain deeper understanding of the dramatic daily events on the Israeli news. While we treasure Tel Aviv – Israel's secular capital – and other Israeli experiences, we are also conscious of political developments undermining democracy and future relationships. Writing this book helped us to understand the evolution and roots of Israel's current situation and to identify the public relations practitioners who were part of its development. Nevertheless, we have tried to present things as they are – albeit through lenses that we acknowledge are tinted with personal experiences: "Transparency enables the historian to explain their assumptions as clearly as they are able, which may subsequently add to the defensibility of an analysis" (L'Etang, 2008a, p. 324).

We would like to pay tribute to Di Gowland and Tony Nichols for their generous hospitality in Neuvicq-le-Château when we really needed it for writing, and the University of Waikato for having the foresight to buy, and for letting us use, the house of the late historian Michael King in Opoutere. It was a peaceful and inspiring setting. Sitting by his desk and hearing the birds sing, while looking out over the green bush to the estuary, allowed us distance while writing about the more turbulent times and public relations of a distant land.

Acknowledgements

Margalit wrote this book to her beloved children Yonatan and Doria, to Galit and Tomer, and to her grandchildren and to other family members, Ilana, Dana and her family, and Murray and his family. She has been inspired by her cousin Shirley Adelson and her friend Ayala Malach Pines, who, with her usual generosity, sent suggestions for this preface only a month before her death. The book was written to help scholars and laypeople in Israel and elsewhere understand the history of public relations and its role in the history of Israel. Margalit dedicates the book to the future of Israeli public relations with the hope that knowing the origins will motivate high professionalism combined with democratic and responsible practice.

David would like to dedicate this to his inspirational daughter Anna, wonderful granddaughters Abbie and Mhairi, and his parents. He gratefully acknowledges his University of Waikato Students (especially the 111, 133, 583, and MBA leadership classes, Vanessa, Lloyd, and Malcolm), the MComrades Department, WMS CEE team, family – especially Nimrod, Gilad, Zohar, Noga, and Dror (all beautiful on the inside as well) – and friends in Israel and international mates and colleagues (usually the two are inseparable), with special mention to Debashish and Priya (and Akanksha and Alya), Juliet, Jordi, Bob and Ginger, Anne G., Paul W., Kevin M., Diana, Jacquie and Deek, Vikram and Aasha, Ros and George, Tim and Sherry, Vince, and Sriramesh. Special thanks also to the Waikato Hospital Coronary Unit's intervention – without it, my part of this book would not have been written.

We both acknowledge Professor Ray Hiebert and *Public Relations Review*, and Professors Dejan Verčič and Krishnamurthy Sriramesh for publishing previous versions of some of the chapters and for giving us permission to use the material here.

1 Explaining the nation
Israel, Hasbara, and public relations

In April 2010, before boarding a plane at Ben Gurion Airport to fly out of Israel, we picked up a brochure called "Masbirim Israel" [Explaining Israel]. It was provided by the Israeli Ministry of Public Diplomacy or, to give it its Hebrew name, the Ministry of Hasbara and Diaspora. The ministry's brochure invited its readers to serve as ambassadors and to "change the [negative] picture" foreigners have of Israel. Its brochure in Hebrew, as well as an internet site, www.masbirim.gov.il (in Hebrew and English), along with social media interventions and other public relations and advertising activities, formed part of the ministry's public relations campaign to improve Israel's image in the world. It focused on motivating Israelis who travel abroad to explain the Israeli government's official narratives and to present Israel in a positive light to people they encounter on their travels.

The campaign presented "facts" to refute negative "myths" about Israel. It advised travellers how to be effective in their communication: by telling personal stories, by offering new perspectives, by being concise and clear, by listening to the people they meet, by using humour, and by presenting visuals (for example, a map of the Middle East showing how the tiny State of Israel sits surrounded by the larger lands of Arab countries). As an Israeli living abroad, and a Scotsman who can't read Hebrew, we were not the target audience for the campaign but were struck by the open recruitment of citizens as public relations advocates. The ministry's attempt to enlist a whole nation to serve as voluntary ambassadors for the State of Israel is a contemporary campaign with a long history. The Masbirim Israel campaign is not only an expression of an Israeli longing for international recognition but also a demonstration of how deeply public relations is embedded in the Israeli experience and continues to play a vital role in nation building. The Masbirim campaign at the airport introduces one of this book's key contentions: that Israel's past and its nation-building activities are a major part of the formation and values of the contemporary practice of public relations in the second decade of the 21st century.

2 *Explaining the nation*

Background and context

> If all writing about the past is partly an effort to understand the present, a confusing and contradictory present would seem to call more insistently for historical analysis and explanation. This is particularly true for the professional and academic discipline of public relations.
>
> (Pearson, 1992, p. 111)

In line with Pearson's (1992) observations, this book aims to understand the roots of Israeli public relations and its development as a profession within the context of building the State of Israel. In the process, it seeks to shed light both on the history and philosophy of public relations and on the development of Israel. It contends that the story of the Israeli public relations practitioners – and their role in shaping the narratives, the discourse, the symbols, and the events of Israel's history – has never been told. In addition, it considers how the specific nation-building challenge affected their professional identity. This is even more true of Palestinian public relations and nation building, but although that story is even less documented, it is not part of this project. Instead, see Zaharna et al. (2009).

By tracking Israeli public relations practitioners' work within major institutions in the public and the private sectors, the book also contributes to the professional and academic field of public relations in general; to contextual research into the role of public relations in nation building; to the understanding of the different functions of public relations in different cultures; to the historical construction of public relations identities; and to considerations of the different roles public relations plays in different environments.

Explaining the nation

Hasbara and Israel

Hasbara is a Hebrew noun form of the verb *le'hasbir*, which means "to explain" or "to account for." In *The Lexicon of the State of Israel* (Shatz & Ariel, 1998), the editors relate to Hasbara under the item "Taamula" [Propaganda] and explain it as the government of Israel's attempt to deal with unique internal and external challenges. From this perspective, Hasbara describes a persuasive communication effort, either by the State of Israel in defence of its image externally, or in attempts to promote social integration within its borders, or to convey a social marketing message. Its usage comes from a paternalistic attitude towards a population who are assumed to require explanations to be able to understand the place of Israel in the world and the associated meaning of news items and their fit with official narratives. Hasbara stresses positive messages and unifying issues that help create a national consensus.

Shatz and Ariel (1998) identify some of the complicated tensions in Israeli society that fostered the nation's special Hasbara system:

Explaining the nation 3

The security focus ... The constant threat to the physical existence of the state obliges the individual to always trust the power of the state and its ability to deal with the challenge, not only in the state's physical power but also in its moral justification....

Absorbing the immigration ... The values and symbols that the immigrants brought with them were diverse, according to their countries of origin.... The need to create a unified system of symbols, while undermining the previous system, demanded lots of flexibility ... the integration of different values ... is essential for the creation of national consolidation and identification with the state's goals.

(p. 1209) [Author translation from the Hebrew, hereafter ATH]

One of *The Lexicon*'s two editors, Yakov Shatz, worked for the Israeli Hasbara services for over 38 years, including 18 years as the head of the Israeli Hasbara Center [Merkaz ha-Hasbara]. In an interview, Shatz (2002) made a list of all the official Israeli Hasbara institutions: the broadcasting authority (TV channel One and the radio channel Kol Israel); the Hasbara Center, the Israeli Films Service, and the educational TV channel as part of the Ministry of Education; the Government Press Office in the Prime Minister's Office; the Government Advertising Office in the Ministry of Finance; the Hasbara division in the Ministry of Foreign Affairs and Israel's diplomatic services abroad; the Hasbara division in the Ministry of Tourism; the government spokespeople; the Israel Defense Forces (IDF) spokesperson; and the IDF Chief Education Officer. This is a formidable persuasion apparatus, and the length and scope of Shatz's list indicates the importance Hasbara was accorded in the life of the nation and gives an idea of the amount of resources allocated to it.

In addition, many non-governmental institutions, such as the World Zionist Organization and the Jewish Agency, the Histadrut [the Federation of Trade Unions], political parties, the youth movements and many non-profit organizations, use Hasbara departments to communicate with internal and external publics.

However, as demonstrated in the Masbirim Israel example, Hasbara is not the exclusive domain of organizations. Israelis have strong concerns as individuals about the image of the state and its legitimization by the world. The need to be understood and approved of is demonstrated by the Israeli television reality show *Hashagrir* [the Ambassador] in which in each season, during the 2005 and 2006 shows, 14 young candidates competed on a Hasbara job in the United States, and later around the world, sponsored by a non-profit Hasbara organization based in New York (www.israelatheart.com). The candidates had to prove their ability to represent Israel well abroad in realistic confrontational situations with critical audience members.

Less credulous about the impact of persuasion, in a theme that will recur throughout this book, Neiger (2005) raises the crucial question: is Israeli public relations not up to the job, or is it an identity problem rather than an image problem? Neiger (2005) suggests that "not through Hasbara – even if its spokespeople were to be good-looking and eloquent like the [young candidates of

4 *Explaining the nation*

Hashagrir] – but rather through policy and action it would be possible to change the image of Israel" [ATH]. His perspective aligns with Kunczik's (1997) conclusion that "from the research findings and the experiences of the practitioners ... clearly the best form of image cultivation for states is for them to be democratic, to observe human rights, and to pursue policies of openness" (p. 282).

Regardless of where it is practised, public relations "emerges from a specific social hierarchy, or field of power" (Edwards, 2010, p. 205), and that context "profoundly marks the nature and identity of public relations through the interests the profession supports and the share of voice it generates for those on whose behalf it is employed" (p. 205). Best practice in image cultivation, therefore, poses problems for a nation in multiple conflicts – often entailing violence – with Arab populations within and outside Israel. This situation is compounded by over 45 years of military occupation of Palestinian territory and the denial of human rights to its Palestinian inhabitants. Moreover, in Sand's (2009) view, "Israel cannot be described as a democratic state while it sees itself as the state of the 'Jewish people,' rather than as a body representing all the citizens within its recognized boundaries" (p. vii). In short, the Israeli government and Israelis struggle to sustain their claim that Israel is a democratic nation in the Middle East. These internal and external challenges to presenting Israel in a positive light contribute to the intense interest of Israelis in Hasbara, propaganda, and public relations.

Hasbara and public relations

In documenting how, over time, one specific professional community of public relations practitioners contributed to the building of one nation, we examine some distinctive features and some particular implications for the profession. Many of the implications emerged from the profession being an integral part of Israel's nation-building endeavours; many of the features emerged from practitioner deployment of certain discourses and key words. "Hasbara" – a word often used to describe public relations – is probably the single most important term; it is both a unique feature and embodies important implications.

Few Hebrew dictionaries even mention the term "public relations" [*yahasei zibur*]. Shvika (1997), in *Rav-Milim: The Complete New Hebrew Dictionary*, explains it as follows: "Public relations: Hasbara, advertising, and propaganda on behalf of someone (a state, an institution, a public entity, public figure, and suchlike) that is intended to create positive image in public opinion" (p. 776) [ATH]. Similarly, Yatziv's (2002) *Social Lexicon* refers to the term "public relations" as including "spokespeople, Hasbara, propaganda, advertising, and sometimes even various marketing tactics" (p. 83) [ATH] and continues that "[i]t is all intended to persuade the public that the product or the personality for whom public relations is being performed are preferred compared to the alternative" (p. 83). In contrast, *The Hebrew–Hebrew Concise Sapir Dictionary* (Avnion, 1997, p. 90), without mentioning public relations, defines the term Hasbara as:

1   providing an explanation;
2   clear, simple, easy-to-understand presentation;
3   a lecture on political position. [ATH]

The same dictionary includes the term "*yahtzan*" [public relations practitioner, an abbreviation that rhymes with the Hebrew word "noble," "aristocratic"/"arrogant" (*yahsan*) and carries negative connotations] (Avnion, 1997, p. 362) but not "*yahsai tzibur*," which is the literal translation of "public relations."

The negative connotations may partly be attributed to simple ignorance. Many dictionaries do not include the term "public relations," and the distinguished Academy for the Hebrew Language never discussed the term (K. Cohen, 2002). The neglect is reflected in the wider public consciousness. As late as 1993 a public opinion survey of the Israeli general population found that almost 50% of the Israelis had never heard the words "*yahsei tzibur*" [public relations] or "*yahtzan*" [public relations practitioner]. The survey performed by the Brendman Institute for Public Opinion Research was commissioned by *Otot*, the Israeli Advertising Association's monthly magazine, and included 521 men and women aged over 18 within the Jewish population. Only 5% of the respondents knew that the public relations practitioner [*yahtzan*] connects companies with the media, 6% said it is about events and parties, 19.7% had heard the term but did not know what it stood for (summarized from Ganor, 1993, p. 10) [ATH].

Hasbara and public relations in Europe

That cultural context has commonalities with, as well as differences from, other places. The origins of the term "Hasbara," for example, might lie in Europe: more specifically, in Germany and the Netherlands. According to scholars from those countries, the term "public relations" is used simultaneously with local terminology meaning an effort to explain.

In the Netherlands, van Ruler (2004) traces the roots of public relations to the term "*voorlichting*," which is a literal translation of "enlightenment," and notices that although the "administration as well as civil society organizations started to introduce *voorlichters*, specialists who travelled around to give information about health, good farming, housekeeping, education, politics, etc. . . . the elite remained sceptic[al] about this full enlightening of ordinary people" (p. 264). For van Ruler (2004), this explains why for "most of the time *voorlichting* was also used to show people how to conduct themselves as good citizens and to control them" (p. 264).

Van Ruler (2004) goes so far as to see the history of public relations in the Netherlands "as a history of the battle between information and emancipation on the one hand, and education and persuasion on the other hand" (pp. 264–265). Although this is "always under the ('Dutch uncle') dogma of 'knowing what is best'" (p. 265), she concludes that in "theories of *voorlichting* the rather pedantic premise is, that it is given for the benefit of the person or group to be enlightened, even when the 'victims' did not want to be enlightened at all – or at least not in that way" (p. 265).

For van Ruler, the term "*voorlichting*" characterizes the profession of public relations in the Netherlands as "soft-selling 'persuasion'," but at the same time, "dialogue, negotiation and consensus-building are natural exponents of Dutch culture, which for centuries has relied on the practice of consultation and the involvement of as many people as possible in decision-making" (p. 265). Discussing the Dutch-influenced Afrikaans term for public relations, "*openbare skakelwese*," Holtzhausen (2012, p. 97) also sees a distinction with the United States, where "public relations practice is increasingly interpreted as public relationships, whereas a translation of the German, Dutch, and Afrikaans terms implies *work that takes place in the public sphere* or *work in service of the public*" (p. 97; italics in the original). It is significant that this democratic part of the Dutch and other national traditions did not exist in the Jewish public sphere and was not inherited by practitioners in the State of Israel.

The German term used to describe public relations from the 1920s is *Öffentlichkeitsarbeit*, which means "work for the public sphere" (Bentele & Junghänel, 2004, p. 162). The word relates to a broader type of communication that goes beyond media relations. The use of *Öffentlichkeitsarbeit* differs from both Hasbara and *voorlichting* by putting less emphasis on a one-way persuasion process and by relating to the profession as serving the public sphere. According to German histories of public relations, it was not until 1937, in the Nazi period, that Germany imported the term "public relations" from the United States. Since then, both terms have been used by public relations practitioners in ways similar to Israeli usage: "Economists and PR-consultants also prefer the English term, whereas political organisations, municipal administrators, and associations more often apply the term *öffentlichkeitsarbeit*" (Bentele & Junghänel, 2004, p. 162).

Practitioner-centred history and questions of method

This book uses practitioner interviews to help tell the story of public relations in Israel. It reveals how practitioners adapted to challenges and used public relations concepts and techniques to mobilize Israelis to enlist in creating, defending, and maintaining the state.

The book is also constructed from sources such as previously uncited letters and archive documents, and draws from already existing interpretations published as institutional stories, histories, cultural studies, literature, economic analyses, media coverage, and social studies. We integrate these with original semi-structured interviews of key public relations practitioners across different generations and from diverse roles and institutions. By using purposive sampling of these rich sources of information and by conducting "empathetic interviews" (Fontana & Frey, 2005, p. 696), we gathered unique insights into significant historical developments from key players.

Fontana and Frey (2005) observe that many qualitative researchers advocate these methods to create "a partnership between the researcher and respondents who should work together to create a narrative – the interview – that could be beneficial to the group studied" (p. 697). Certainly, the narratives of the individuals in this research emerged from partnership discussion, and those who were interviewed often occupy the intersection between personal and collective experiences. In doing so, they extend the limits of individual stories and enable conclusions to be drawn about the profession, not only as personal experiences but also as a part of shared socio-national history, and a part of the larger cultural context.

Influencing Israel

Questions of professionalization

In its very uniqueness, Israel's public relations history can serve as a laboratory to help illustrate the impact of environment on the evolution of public relations. In addition to our investigation on the role played by Hasbara/public relations practitioners in Israel's nation building, we examine the impact of the Israeli environment on the process of professionalization of public relations and identify stimulants and inhibitors to its development.

The conditions for the emergence of public relations as a profession are contested theoretically as well as geographically. According to Sharpe and Pritchard (2004, p. 15):

> A convergence of three factors contributed to the emergence of public relations as a profession: a growth in the global acceptance of democratic principles, growing global social interdependence, and the emergence of direct instantaneous communication abilities. These factors have now empowered public opinion to a degree that public relations is no longer a choice.

Others have offered different accounts of the process. The public relations literature tends to concentrate on ethical codes as one pillar for supporting a claim to professional status (see Curtin & Boynton, 2001; Day et al., 2001). While such research has generated interesting material, its focus can be narrowly functionalist and inward-looking (see McKie & Munshi, 2007), and other public relations theorists (e.g. Davis, 2002; L'Etang, 2004; Piezcka & L'Etang, 2001) tackle the question of professionalism from a broader sociological perspective.

Such approaches are valuable since definitions of professions, and descriptions of the process of professionalization, have long been prominent in sociology. Social theorists, such as Max Webber, Karl Marx, and Émile Durkheim, are known for their contribution to the subject in their discussions about the division of labour. According to Abbott (1988), early studies that attempted to distinguish professions from occupations developed a list of properties that informed the core of later definitions:

> Professions were organized bodies of experts who applied esoteric knowledge to particular cases. They had elaborate system of instruction and training,

together with entry by examination and other formal prerequisites. They normally possess and enforce a code of ethics or behavior.

(p. 4)

If it were assessed according to these traditional prerequisites, public relations would always struggle to be acknowledged as a profession. The role public relations plays in the democratic free flow of information means that any restriction on entry to the field would imply a restriction on the freedom of speech.

This book, therefore, draws on Abbott's (1988) later approach in *The System of Professions*. Sceptical that a list of characteristics could define how occupations gain professional status, he analyzes the process by which occupations gain, and maintain, an exclusive jurisdiction over particular tasks. Focusing on the relations between occupations, Abbott's (1988) "central phenomenon" (p. 20) is the link between "a profession and its work, a link I shall call jurisdiction. To analyze professional development is to analyze how this link is created in work and how the interplay of jurisdictional links between professions determines the history of the individual professions" (p. 20).

This approach explains the emergence and disappearance of professions in relation to the competition between them. The major factor Abbott (1988) sees is interprofessional competition, which is subject to social changes that create new spaces for evolving jurisdictions. In an example that is highly relevant to public relations, he uses journalism to argue that the professional identity for journalists emerged from their competition with public relations practitioners:

> Whether journalism's inability to monopolize makes it "not a profession" is not particularly interesting. What matters is that interprofessional competition in fact shaped it decisively. The clearest force driving reporters toward a formal conception of their jurisdiction was in fact competition with hired publicity agents. Journalists of the 1920s were amazed to discover that about 50 percent of the stories in the *New York Times* originated in the work of publicity agents. Reporters saw such stories (correctly) as little better than advertising, and their reaction led on the one hand to a renewed drive for formal professional structures, and on the other to a frank recognition of subjectivity in reporting.
>
> (pp. 225–226)

Abbott (1988) concludes that "[c]ompetition provides the key to occupational development" (p. 226). Building on Abbott's work, this book charts the professional development of Israeli public relations through its relations with such other professions as journalism and advertising. It seeks evidence for cooperation and competition between them as a key to understanding the professionalization process.

According to Abbott, journalism "crystallized" its professional identity by divorcing itself from public relations. In a mirror reflection, public relations scholars describe the emergence of public relations as a consequence of its divorce

Explaining the nation 9

from journalism and advertising. This book examines how the process unfolded in the Israeli context.

External and internal explanations

As the play on words in our book's subtitle, *Influencing Israel*, suggests, Israel is both influenced and influential. Such two-way influence also applies to explanation efforts. Hasbara is used to describe not only the function of international public diplomacy, but actually the attempt to influence internal publics (that is, Israelis being enlisted for nation building through persuasive communication by public relations practitioners working for national institutions and movements). Thus, the Masbirim Israel campaign, officially designed to influence non-Israelis around the world, also acts to persuade the inhabitants of Israel that the Minister and the Ministry serve their country's interests well, and to encourage Israeli citizens to volunteer their voices in support.

The Masbirim Israel campaign is one illustration of how the ministry took initiatives to improve Israel's image internationally. However, communication directed abroad, but available at home, can also impact on local citizens, since in practice it is impossible to make distinctions between external and internal audiences. This emerges clearly in comments about the Masbirim Israel campaign by Professor Dan Caspi (2010):

> It is well known that what we tell ourselves is not less important than what we tell the world. Thus the site towards which [Israeli] residents are referred [by the Masbirim Israel campaign] is built and edited according to the best Bolshevik propaganda.

However, although Caspi (2010) found the ministry and the campaign to be typical of totalitarian Soviet systems, the process of nation building, by its nature, is not "synonymous with creating democracy" (Bendix, 1996, p. xii). For example, in the building of nations in other parts of the world, the process clearly contributes to specific Hasbara-type campaigns that would be described as non-democratic. Indeed, in some ways the Israeli experience resembles those of post-colonial societies struggling to create a national identity, and to protect their markets, in the post-World War II context of emerging democracies. The State of Israel came into existence in 1948 following 25 years of British rule under the UN Mandate over Palestine. In other ways, Israel seems like a unique experience within the post-1945 emergence of former colonized nations. Israel, for example, revived an old language, Hebrew, as part of a planned communication campaign to unite its diverse community and forge a modern nation. At the same time, it integrated a society that had been dispersed across the world for 2,000 years.

While this book's focus is mainly on the unique Israeli environment and the changes experienced since the early days of the Zionist movement in Europe and America, it also considers the even earlier but still influential Jewish public sphere. It describes the efforts to mobilize world and Jewish public opinion from the pre-state period through the establishment of a state in 1948, and on to subsequent nation building, as well as more recent developments in the Israeli economy and society.

The specific conditions of Israel offer an exceptional study of the accelerators and inhibitors of professional development in the history of a nation. We will argue that the values of collectivism arising from generations of Diaspora experience, and the propaganda traditions in the Zionist movement, carried over into strong fundraising and lobbying traditions. At the same time, the function of media relations was underdeveloped by reason of the fact that the media were voluntarily supporting the national establishment and the agendas of the political parties that sponsored them. This proximity between journalists and politicians inhibited the development of public relations as a professional service with a separate identity.

Current cases in Israel's communication industry show continuities with the pre-state community of journalists who were enlisted for the nation-building mission and who functioned as promoters of the Zionist idea. Even as recently as 2012, journalists and editors were found to be invoicing the Prime Minister's Office for speech-writing services. In spite of this clear breach of the Israeli journalists' code of ethics, the national Press Council did not find any wrongdoing in the specific conduct of these journalists (Barak, 2012; Golan, 2012). Moreover, we describe how strong state economic interventions "distorted" conventional commercial and public relations development and how the Israel Defense Forces (IDF) managed strategic communications during war situations.

On the basis of the Israeli experience, it might be argued that in an environment which supports the idea of state-enlisted media for the sake of nation building, and which nourishes cultural values of unity and solidarity above individual human freedoms, the public relations role is closer to earlier, and now widely discredited, ideas of "engineering consent" (Bernays, 1947, p. 113). Nor would Israel rate very highly on the influential four-phase model. Grunig and Hunt (1984) rank the phases – in ascending order of effectiveness, ethics, and status – from one to four as follows:

1 "press agentry/publicity," whose "purpose" was "propaganda" and whose communication nature was "one-way," with "complete truth not essential";
2 "public information," whose "purpose" was "dissemination of information" and whose nature was "one-way," with "truth important";
3 "two-way asymmetric," whose "purpose" was "scientific persuasion" and whose nature was "two-way," with "imbalanced effects";
4 "two-way symmetrical," whose "purpose" was "mutual understanding," with "balanced effects" (summarized from Grunig & Hunt, 1984, p. 22).

The Israeli experience certainly differs not only from two-way symmetrical communication but also from more recent conceptions of public relations as a profession that builds relationships and understanding through dialogue and that "will increasingly help make society more fully functional" (Heath, 2006, p. 94) and develop civil society (Taylor, 2010). Israeli practice does not align with current

Explaining the nation 11

theories that call for the field to function as the builder of mutually beneficial relationships between organizations and their stakeholders and currently disenfranchized stakeseekers (e.g. Heath, 2010; Coombs & Holladay, 2010). This book exposes the roots of public relations in Israel to account for the link between the profession and its specific environment, and to identify the influence it had on a challenging nation-building process, and the way it was shaped by the political, socio-cultural, and economic circumstances of this environment.

Organizing the rest of the story

Chapter 2, "Public relations, history, and nation building," looks at history and nation building in the light of public relations literature. In mapping the surge of interest in these areas, and their interrelationships, especially since the turn of the century, this chapter situates our book's position among recent theories inside and outside the field. It pays particular attention to debates about how US theory and practice, including attempts to segregate public relations from propaganda, have shaped the field.

Chapter 3, "Shaping communication: Diaspora life and the Jewish public sphere," outlines the holistic approach of the book. It argues that the development of Israeli public relations is interwoven with the history of the Jewish people as well as with the establishment of Israel as a Jewish state. It focuses on the impact of the Diaspora experiences on public discourse and how the Zionist movement mobilized values from that Diaspora to promote the idea of a Jewish state in the land of ancient Israel.

Chapter 4, "Determining identity: Zionist leaders as forerunners," tells a tale of two revolutions and contends that just as public relations in the United States was forged by the American Revolution and its protagonists, so public relations in Israel was forged by the Zionist revolution and its protagonists.

Chapter 5, "Shaping factors: the political and media environment," follows Sriramesh and Verčič's (2009) call "to make a linkage between environmental variables and the profession" (p. 3). It does so by setting Israeli public relations in the Israeli socio-political environment, the media, and the relationship between them.

Chapter 6, "Early Zionist institutions and communication practitioners," considers practice during the pre-state "Organised Yishuv" period (1917–1948), when propaganda was high on the agenda of the first official Zionist institutions in Palestine. It analyzes the work of several generations of practitioners who served two official departments called "Propaganda and Hasbara" and "Public Relations/Public Connections."

Chapter 7, "Emissaries, fundraising, and nation building," identifies fundraising as a distinctive feature of Israeli public relations. It goes back in time to explore deep roots reaching to the first century and the dispersion of the Jewish people among other nations. It documents the substantial work of later fundraisers and public relations practitioners working for four key Zionist fundraising organizations.

12 *Explaining the nation*

Chapter 8, "Economics, market changes, and major campaigns," follows the "abnormal" development process of Israel's economy, motivated by the national ideological drive to "conquer the land" for Jews. It examines sources of national narratives in important communication campaigns involved in the rivalry between agriculture, industry and commerce in Israel. Finally, it looks at the development of consumer affairs and marketing activities as part of the Israeli market process of opening to world markets and increasing global competition from the 1980s.

Chapter 9, "Speaking on behalf of government (1): government practitioners and Hasbara," analyzes how the Israeli government incorporated public relations into its newly established agencies and became an important employer of practitioners. It also considers, in turn, how these practitioners helped in the forging of the new Israeli state.

Chapter 10, "Speaking on behalf of government (2): other civil servants and military spokespeople," shifts from the more direct propaganda and public relations of Hasbara departments to look at how other government practitioners were influenced by nation building and politics. It also examines the high-intensity environment of military spokespeople – their unique challenges and their professional values.

Chapter 11, "The emergence of private consultants," studies the emergence of private public relations firms as an indicator of the stage reached in the professionalization process. This chapter's examination of the way these firms were established and how they functioned in Israel provides insight into the evolution of public relations as a profession in general and the specific aspects of Israel's political economic and social developments in particular.

Chapter 12, "Conclusion: representing nations and influencing Israel," connects with the concepts of public diplomacy and nation branding in the Israeli context. It also identifies the impact of long-standing cultural features that continue to inhibit the growth of a strong public relations presence able to contribute in a professional way to the strengthening of liberal democracy and the creation of an open society in Israel.

2 Public relations, history, and nation building

For over a decade, publications and research about public relations, history, and nations have expanded rapidly. This chapter maps some of that expansion and locates this book's place within it, mainly in relation to history and nation building but with attention to the associated issue of public relations and propaganda. While the field's growth includes more international research than ever before, the literature remains skewed geographically and politically, and a "central challenge" (Freitag & Stokes, 2009, p. 35) remains "the fact that the overwhelming bulk of public relations research originated in the United States" (p. 35), so that "in most cases . . . the theories we have come to rely on in our understanding of the practice are based on research involving US populations, US media, and so on" (p. 35).

Other American authors, Sharpe and Pritchard (2004), accord similar primacy to US developments: because "the public relations profession in the United States is larger and more developed than in any other country" (p. 15); because there is more "documentation available from scholars and library resources" (p. 15) in the United States; and "because the democratic model is more closely identified with the United States than with any other country" (p. 15).

Distinguishing propaganda and public relations

Having aggregated attention around the US democratic model, the public relations literature tends to assume that the profession can function only within a certain kind of democratic system. As one consequence, propaganda is not seen as part of public relations and is regarded as the tool of totalitarian regimes and dictatorships. Despite the well-known moves of the US Congress to investigate Ivy Lee's propaganda work in Nazi Germany, this is more marked in the United States than anywhere else.

Brown (2006) sees this distinction as stemming from "Bernays' well-known attempt after World War I to cleanse the emerging PR industry from its damaging associations with wartime propaganda" (p. 207). See http://www.youtube.com/watch?v=s18vu5tCzsc for a film of Bernays explaining his idea that "if propaganda could be used for war, it could certainly be used for peace" and his decision to change the name of his role to "public relations counsel" to avoid the negative post-war connotations of propaganda.

Yet despite the US success of Bernays' "rebranding," theorists outside of the United States perceive propaganda as part of the same promotional family as public relations. More bluntly, in the words of one critical public relations scholar, "One person's PR is another's propaganda depending on what side you take in the debate" (L'Etang, 2008b, p. 34).

Other critics of an absolute split between propaganda and public relations make more fine-grained distinctions. Weaver et al. (2006), for example, argue that while critical theory perspectives find "no substantive difference between propaganda and public relations, this is as a consequence of a rejection of the notion that propaganda *necessarily* operates counter to the public interest, and that public relations necessarily works *for* the public interest" (p. 21; italics in the original) and conclude that the "merits of propaganda and public relations practice can only be judged in terms of the context and the ends to which they were used" (p. 21). Given the unusual circumstances of the State of Israel's creation, and its ongoing wars with surrounding countries, it faces serious difficulties in quarantining public relations from propaganda.

Jacques Ellul's book *Propaganda: The Formation of Men's Attitudes* (1962) offers a practical approach that takes account of shifting attitudes over time that has relevance to Israel. Unlike Bernays' image-based solution of switching the name from propagandist to public relations counsel, Ellul, as Kellen (1962) notes in his introduction to *Propaganda*, addresses the issues directly: "Propaganda is usually regarded as an *evil*" (p. x) mainly made up of "'*tall stories*,' disseminated by means of lies" (p. x; italics in the original). Ellul rejects these conventions because, while they might make for a comforting distinction to avoid negative associations, they prevent one from "understanding anything about the actual phenomenon, which is very different from what it was in the past" (see Kellen, 1962, p. ix).

Reconciling propaganda and public relations

For the Israeli situation, Ellul (1962) makes a more practical distinction between the "propaganda of agitation" (p. 71), which seeks rebellion or war, and nourishes revolutionary movements, and the "propaganda of integration – the propaganda of developed nations and characteristic of our civilization . . . [which] is propaganda of conformity . . . [aiming] at making the individual participate in a society in every way" (pp. 74–75). Ellul's distinction aids, first, in distinguishing the "propaganda of agitation" in the Zionist revolutionary movement's effort to persuade different publics to support its ideology, because "when a revolutionary movement is launched, it operates, as we have said, with agitation propaganda" (Ellul, 1962, p. 76).

Second, Ellul's distinction of the "propaganda of integration" can be seen in the effort of the Zionist institutions and, later, the Israeli government to build social integration and to unite the people in a new culture, because "once the revolutionary party has taken power, it must begin immediately to operate with integration propaganda. . . . That is the way to balance its power and stabilize the situation" (p. 76).

Ellul (1962) perceives modern propaganda as producing "a progressive adaptation to a certain order of things, a certain concept of human relations, which unconsciously molds individuals and makes them conform to society" (p. 64). In tracing this adaptation across different forms, such as "in advertising, [and] in the movies (commercial and non-political films)" (p. 64), Ellul observes that while such influences "seem a far cry from Hitler's great propaganda setup" (p. 64), they "are expressed through the same media as propaganda" (p. 64). For Ellul (1962), a government, as well as making propaganda, "will have its own public relations" (p. 65) whose "influences follow the same stereotypes and prejudices as propaganda" (p. 65) that "stir up the same feelings and act on the individual in the same fashion" (p. 65) and "are propaganda to the extent that the combination of advertising, public relations, social welfare, and so on produces a certain conception of society, a particular way of life" (p. 65).

Thus, public relations activities are considered part of the system that supports the "propaganda of integration" to integrate the individual into the collective in a form of social engineering akin to Bernays' (1947) "engineering of consent." From Ellul's (1962) standpoint, attributions of morality tend to confuse the analysis of different kinds of propaganda in action (p. vi). In practice, simplistic notions of propaganda as bad, and public relations as good, are no more helpful than simple equations of public relations and propaganda as equally deplorable manipulation. In partially adapting Ellul's standpoint, we look more to analyze than to moralize, especially around the key Hebrew term "Hasbara" (explanation, or propaganda).

Many European theorists follow Ellul in having no problem linking propaganda and public relations. Moloney (2006) simply characterizes public relations as "weak propaganda" (p. x) and gets on with analyzing what happens. In equally straightforward fashion, Pieczka and L'Etang (2001) observe how "central government peacetime propaganda" (p. 203) was an "important influence" (p. 230) in Britain. In addition, L'Etang (2004) notes that the association of British public relations with propaganda is clear from "the historical evidence" (p. 228), and states unequivocally that "its continuing activities for and on behalf of a variety of governments means [*sic*] that this connection cannot be consigned to the history books" (p. 228).

Public relations beyond the United States after 2000

Attitudes did not just differ over propaganda. After 2000, more scholars questioned the universality of US-based accounts of public relations. Moss et al. (2003), for example, claim that "public relations has begun to assume significant importance as a recognized business function within Western European countries" (p. xvi) over the past 20 years even if "still at a comparatively nascent stage in its development within many parts of Europe" (p. xvi). Moss et al. (2003) further recognize "a need for some counter-balance . . . to promote the development of a distinctive European body of knowledge in this field, rather than relying primarily on the work of US scholars" (p. xvi).

For the 2002 symposium "The Status of Public Relations Knowledge in Europe and around the World," held at Lake Bled in Slovenia, van Ruler and Verčič, in conjunction with the European Public Relations Education and Research Association (EUPRERA), prepared *The Bled Manifesto on Public Relations*. Based on a Delphi study of public relations academics and practitioners in 25 European countries, the *Manifesto* sought "an answer to the question whether public relations is just an Anglo-American concept or whether there is (also) a European authenticity of public relations" (van Ruler & Verčič, 2002, p. 1).

From 2000 onwards, public relations scholars and practitioners in other parts of the world – from Australia through Kazakhstan (Terry, 2005) to Zambia and Zimbabwe (Smythe, 2001) – are also increasingly exploring the emergence and state of play of public relations as a profession. In telling individual stories of different paths to the profession, they contest ideas of a simple US primacy and reject the "assumption in much of the literature that public relations was first developed in the United States and was then exported elsewhere" (L'Etang, 2004, p. 5).

In van Ruler and Verčič's (2004a) edited collection of histories of the profession and its development in 27 European countries, the editors explain that European forms of practice similar to US public relations might have been widespread but were rarely known by that name. Van Ruler and Verčič (2004b) also cite early signs of the profession in European business through German references to "Krups as the first company with a department dedicated to press relations set up in 1870" (p. 1), and van Ruler (2004) shows that despite the fact that the first Dutch public relations departments emerged at the beginning of the twentieth century, the industry in that country is also much older.

Sriramesh and Verčič's (2003a) *The Global Public Relations Handbook* took major steps towards balancing the limited accounts of public relations history and practices outside of the United States. Along with their revised and expanded edition of that *Global Handbook* (Sriramesh & Verčič, 2009), they provide accounts of the state of the profession within specific political, social, economic, media, and activism contexts in around 30 countries as well as perspectives from all continents and some transnational organizations. Editorially, they encouraged scholars "to build a global theory of public relations by taking into account the *native's point of view*" (Sriramesh, 2009, p. 51; italics in the original). They extend this to theory by identifying a "dire need" not only to describe "various public relations practices across all regions of the world . . . [but also] to contextualize such practice by linking public relations practices with socio-cultural variables" (Sriramesh, 2003, p. xxiii). We ourselves contributed a chapter on public relations in Israel (Toledano & McKie, 2009), and this book deepens and extends that chapter by adding other dimensions to public relations history and knowledge in a more thickly contextualized study of Israeli public relations.

Public relations history since 2000

Nations, nation building, and history are deeply interconnected. In the public relations literature, research on history is the most developed of the three. Before

2000, however, few scholars questioned the use of 20th-century US business and war public relations as underwriting the major historical narrative and "establishing the origins" of contemporary public relations. The geography and timing of those origins positioned the rest of the world's public relations practices as derivative versions. In addition, most major public relations histories (see McKie & Munshi, 2007, ch. 9) identified the field's development as the evolutionary four-phase model described in Chapter 1 that ascends to better practice from press agency/publicity to two-way symmetrical communication (Grunig & Hunt, 1984, p. 22). For much of the 20th century, few questioned either this account or the methods and motives of the people who generated it.

However, in line with a period of globalization, the post-2000 growth in the quantity, quality and variety of public relations historical writings also brought in waves of different perspectives. In a contribution entitled "The evolving face of public relations in Malaysia," Venkataswaran (2004) warned of the dangers of imposing US perspectives – "molded within a framework of Western ideals of democracy and a free-market economy" (p. 405) – on other countries with different frameworks. By the time of writing, the change had become evident not just in the content but in the confidence of Holtzhausen's (2012) dismissal of the logic of the whole four-phase model project: "Looking at international public relations practice through the appropriation of historical data from the United States is reductionist to the extent that it is illogical" (p. 94).

In establishing this new state of affairs, L'Etang's (2004) *Public Relations in Britain: A History of Professional Practice in the Twentieth Century* was seminal. Using detailed evidence from the distinct evolution of British public relations, she established a very different development trajectory that effectively demolished the notion that the United States was the prototype for the British story. By implication, she opened the possibility of other historical pathways for other parts of the world. In less depth for each individual contribution than L'Etang (2004), but with an impressive global spread, the contributors to Sriramesh and Verčič's (2009) *Global Public Relations Handbook* similarly provide a wide range of different national contexts and pathways to the development of public relations.

More path-breaking research is likely, given the expansion in volume of varied outputs. Tom Watson's (2012) retrospective summary of the 2011 International History of Public Relations Conference, for instance, highlights the increasing quantity and diversity of authors and content in that historical arena:

> Since it was launched in 2009, the International History of Public Relations Conference has become the international hub of research and scholarship in the field of public relations history. In that period, two conferences have been attended by more than 130 delegates, well over 100 abstracts received and more than 60 papers published in online proceedings at http://historyofpr.com. The third conference . . . attracted a record submission of abstracts from authors in 28 countries.
>
> (p. 339)

The increase is not restricted to content and geography. Historiography as a term can be crudely broken into two broad areas. The first is as the description of the body of work on history around a subject (e.g. the historiography of the Roman Catholic Church), and it is this body of work that has mainly concerned historians of public relations (see Lamme & Russell, 2010). The second concerns the historical method or methods used to produce history, reflections on the history of history (i.e. metahistory), and the process of writing history (see Chen, 2012). That second sense has received scant attention in the field.

Emerging perspectives

Public relations and plural histories

Critics argue that this neglect matters and that public relations history needs to move beyond implied objectivity or from "innocence to [acknowledged] interests" (McKie & Munshi, 2007, p. 207) and to question taken for granted assumptions. Observing that "[h]istorical narrative is not benign and can have significant consequences" (p. 67), Holtzhausen (2012) deconstructs the dominant historical role of the four-phase model. Since 2000, there have been other significant breaks. Gower's (2007) succinct summary reframes the four-phase US model and links the phases to the writers who promoted them rather than to their content. In doing so, she also raises doubts about the interested, rather than neutral, agenda of the theorists and about their model's validity:

> [P]ublic relations was viewed as progressing through a linear evolution from press agency, to publicity, to two-way communication. According to business historian Alan Raucher, that description was first enunciated by Edward Bernays in 1941. It was followed by Eric Golman's expanded version of the evolution in his 1984 book, *Two-Way Street: The Emergence of the Public Relations Counsel*. In 1984, James E. Grunig and Todd Hunt identified each step in two-way symmetrical communication. The progression was now accepted as fact, but it is a progression fraught with problems and personal agendas.
>
> (p. i)

Other scholars also drilled deeper into the historiography – in the sense of interrogating the theory informing the history – of this tale of progress. Brown (2006) identified its pseudo-evolutionary underpinnings. Rather than a credible account of the survival of the fittest form of public relations practice, he found that the theorists were more concerned with bidding for status for their viewpoints. Brown (2006; 2010) rejects the model's historical evolution story and its promotion of linear progress. Rather than accepting it as neutral history, he positions it as a continuation of loaded agendas from Bernays' attempt to disassociate public relations from propaganda through to Grunig et al.'s multiple attempts to situate two-way symmetrical public relations as the field's pinnacle achievement (Brown, 2006, p. 207). McKie and Munshi (2007) are similarly concerned that the four-phase model's projection of evolutionary inevitability is theoretically and "historically flawed" (p. 225).

The relative longevity of the four-phase model's history offers an excellent example of how "the past gains significance because someone has ordered it in a certain way" (Holtzhausen, 2012, p. 71) and how to establish "a single truth by presenting this history as rational and objective knowledge" (p. 80). For Holtzhausen (2012), it is "actually quite amazing that this U.S. history to this day is being applied in different ways in countries that do not have a Western cultural heritage" (p. 80), and she lays the blame "at the feet of scholars in those countries ... making themselves and their own cultures invisible" (p. 80).

In their thorough survey, Lamme and Russell (2010) observe the "absence of a general theory that describes the rise and growth of public relations" (p. 281) and lament the results: "[S]cholars have tended to organize public relations and its antecedents into time periods that present a progressive evolution from unsophisticated and unethical early roots to planned, strategic, and ethical campaigns of the current day" (p. 281). Lamme and Russell (2010) conclude that "such attempts at periodization have obscured our understanding of public relations and its history" (p. 281).

Accordingly, Lamme and Russell's (2010) research "seeks to break away from the misleading dependence on linear interpretations of the field's past and construct a broad, long-term view of the development and institutionalization of persuasive organizational communication strategies and techniques" (p. 281). We support these new scholarly directions that advocate less insular, less business-focused, and more context-rich public relations histories. We also advocate a move away from constructing a monolithic public relations history (singular) in favour of diverse public relations histories (plural) that feature many voices, neglected areas, and openly interested perspectives – see, for example, Straughan's (2007) *Women's Use of Public Relations for Progressive-Era Reform: Rousing the Conscience of a Nation*. In this kind of research, comprehending public relations will mean considerable work in comprehending the history and culture that practitioners both serve and help to mould. This is also the kind of history we recommend for better understanding nation building and public relations.

Nation building and public relations

Pre-2000 work in the nation-building literature outside of the United States includes Kunczik's (1997) *Images of Nations and International Public Relations* and Van Leuven's (1996) analysis of public relations going from "nation-building to regional independence" (p. 207) in South-East Asian countries. A 21st-century resurgence of interest includes more different voices: post-colonial and subaltern (e.g. Munshi & Kurian, 2005), and stateless nations (Xifra & McKie, 2012), and outward-focused US work (e.g. Curtin & Gaither, 2007; Freitag & Stokes, 2009; Taylor, 2000). In their book chapter on nation building and public relations, Taylor and Kent (2006) see public relations as having "the unique potential to create, maintain, and change relationships between citizens and governments" (p. 302). They also suggest how public relations campaigns "can be used to improve citizens' lives and to promote democracy in the developing world. For instance, literacy campaigns using public relations strategies and tactics can empower the uneducated and offer them opportunities to participate in the political process" (p. 302).

However, as their own example shows, this concept of public relations' role in nation building is identified as one-way communication and they express reservations about it: "Indeed, the assumption of the top-down approach presupposes that a small group of decision makers, often from the elite class, knows what is best for all citizens" (Taylor & Kent, 2006, p. 308). Unfortunately, our research confirms negative aspects when official Israeli institutions apply Hasbara by taking a top-down approach that assumes citizens are ignorant and need guidance to be able to understand "reality" in the context or frame sought by the government.

For nation building, Taylor and Kent advocate a public relations approach that emphasizes the importance of stable interpersonal and intergroup relationships, and the need "to foster trust in the nation state as a viable and responsive social entity" (p. 308). They offer three guiding theories: *coorientation theory* to inspire understanding of others and tolerance via "efforts to come to honest or objective understanding of other groups or organizations' position and to understand how other groups think about one's own group or organization" (p. 308); *dialogic theory* to foster "honest and mutually beneficial relationships with individuals rather than groups . . . [via] forums and open decision making practices as a means to provide the framework for public participation" (p. 309); and *civil society theory*, which describes "a system whereby groups and organizations mediate the relationships between citizens and government" (p. 310).

Taylor and Kent (2006) conclude that "coorientation, dialogue and civil society theories of nation building" (p. 311) offer better models "because of their ability to create solidarity, tolerance, and mutual understanding among citizens, governments, groups, organizations, and international publics" (p. 356). The evidence from Israel does not demonstrate such a relational approach. The public relations practice that emerged there gave voice to dominant political ideology, and not to civil society. The government did not initiate dialogues and did not promote tolerance towards the significant group (20%) of Israeli Palestinians who are citizens of the state, let alone to the Palestinians under Israeli occupation since 1967. The values on which Israel is built as a Jewish state resulted in an emphasis on ethnic national identity rather than on civil identity. This fact shaped Israeli society and limited its democracy. As Taylor and Kent (2006) remind us, "nation building is linked to the creation and maintenance of national values" (p. 304).

In fact, our analysis of the Israeli developments suggests that when practised in an environment that is going through an intense nation-building process, public relations runs a high risk of being enlisted, and being involved in enlisting others, to meet national challenges. Along with the rest of the nation, practitioners in such periods tend to serve the interest of newly established national organizations and their leaders. In the process of nation building, governments mainly seek to mobilize support for their policies and to promote unity rather than pluralism. Neither the enabling of diverse voices nor the promotion of dialogue is likely to feature prominently on the agendas of such governments. Along with acknowledging the many positives listed by Taylor and Kent (2006), nation building in public relations also needs to be self-critical and to recognize its involvement on the dark side of top-down and exclusionary nation building.

History, nations, and nation building

Despite the growth in the complexity and range of public relations history, and the new work on nation building and public relations, the field still lags behind developments elsewhere in history, historiography, and political science. Geary (2003), for example, self-reflects on the bias of his whole field of history by situating the origins of modern history as "conceived and developed as an instrument of European nationalism" (p. 15). Retrospectively, Geary (2003) records modern history's success in the world as "a tool of nationalist ideology" (p. 15), but acknowledges that this turned knowledge of the past into "a toxic waste dump, filled with the poison of ethnic nationalism" (p. 15).

Public relations lacks the same sensitivity to issues of power (Edwards, 2010) as political science. However, as Geary's (2003) research shows, history-fuelled drives for power include the racist National Front's nonsensical claim – since there wasn't an ethnic French people at the time – to champion "the French people born with the baptism of Clovis in 496" (p. 7) and Slobodan Milošević's citation of early "Serbian" history to lay claim to territory held by other ethnic groups. Consideration of public relations in Israel, and in any nation, cannot afford to omit the dark sides of some historical nationalisms from the resurgence of interest in nation building.

A less frightening trend is the "invention/reinvention" of history as a field that properly involves a substantial imagined and created dimension. Geary's (2003) book on the medieval origins of Europe, for example, is entitled *The Myth of Nations* because it examines the constructed nature of European nations (and their ethnic make-up) in line with a recent "rash of books and articles" (p. 16) that argue for imagined histories "from national identities to Scottish plaids . . . [as] recent and cynical invention" (p. 16). Even theological history has its inventors. The authors in Raheb's (2011) edited collection *The Invention of History: A Century of Interplay between Theology and Politics in Palestine* look at how churches use competing historical narratives to justify their positions in relation to Israel and Palestine, and Khoury (2011) acknowledges that "every interpretation includes a kind of invention" (p. 136).

This "reinvention" of history shifts historiographic emphasis away from history as recorded events (and the search for one overarching narrative) and towards history as multiple stories constructed through creative imagining and language. This is partially captured in Berkhofer's (1995) title *Beyond the Great Story: History as Text and Discourse*, although the increasing emphasis on construction emerges even more clearly in his later title *Fashioning History: Current Practices and Principles* (Berkhofer, 2008).

In discussing how history has fashions, and is fashioned by historians, Berkhofer (2008) opens up very different ideas of objectivity in historical method. For example, he cites Lemisch's claim that "sympathy for the powerless" is what "brings us closer to objectivity" (Berkhofer, 2008, p. 59) and offers a useful reminder of how "[o]ral historians query workers, soldiers, women, minorities, and other members of the subordinated and exploited for the view 'from the bottom up' or 'from below' in order to get a glimpse of a past otherwise undocumented" (p. 41). This is important to remember in public relations history in general and also in this book. While we restore the stories of Israeli public relations practitioners, we acknowledge severely limited access to sources and voices consistently marginalized or excluded (most notably in relation to Palestinian voices).

Nations as imagined communities

Writings on the new plasticity of invented histories combine well with new theorizations of the constructed nature of nations. This emerged strongly through the impact of Benedict Anderson's (1991) work on the nation as an "imagined community": "*imagined* because the members of even the smallest nation will never know most of their fellow-members, meet them, or even hear of them, yet in the minds of each lives the image of their communion" (p. 6; italics in the original). Anderson also positions the imagined nation in three key ways: as "*limited* because even the largest of them . . . has finite, if elastic, boundaries beyond which other nations lie" (p. 7); "*sovereign* because . . . the legitimacy of the divinely-ordained, hierarchical dynastic realm . . . [gave way to] the sovereign state" (p. 7) so that monarchs and religion no longer commanded the same respect as the state gained greater power and its population's allegiances; and

> Finally, it is imagined as a *community*, because, regardless of the actual inequality and exploitation that may prevail in each, the nation is always conceived as a deep and horizontal comradeship. Ultimately it is this fraternity that makes it possible, over the past two centuries, for so many people, not so much as to kill, as willingly to die for such limited imaginings.
>
> (p. 7)

As Anderson's concluding sentence makes clear, even when histories and nations are seen to be partly imaginings, the stakes can still be high in terms of human lives. Moreover, a large cast of agents can take part in imagining their particular communities and using memories of the past to underwrite their legitimacy (e.g. the racist policies of a Le Pen or a Milošević). These need not always be negative. Indeed, in many different part of the world, as the eminent historian Eric Hobsbawm (1990) notes: "[S]tates and national movements could mobilize certain variants of feelings of collective belonging which already existed and which could operate, as it were, potentially on the macro-political scale which could fit in with modern states and nations" (p. 47).

In identifying what he calls this "proto-national" (p. 47) state, Hobsbawm (1990) offers a useful augmentation to Curtin and Gaither's (2007) view on nation building "as *a concentrated government effort to achieve domestic and international goals*" (p. 9; italics in the original) where at home "governments might strive for national unity or consensus for a national cause or effort" (p. 9) and internationally use nation-building efforts "to bring a country into a global stream of credibility and awareness, often for economic support from other governments or aid organizations" (p. 9).

Hobsbawm's (1990) "proto-national" concept lends support to our decision to start the discussion on Israeli public relations and nation building prior to Israel's becoming a nation. We follow Hobsbawm's approach to nationalism by confirming that nation building does not necessarily start with governments and is not limited to government organizations. Curtin and Gaither (2007) further note that nation building is actually an ongoing process, and well-established nations such as the United States had many years of independence that were used by the government to "initiate and refine its nation building strategies" (p. 9). Israel, as a younger nation facing serious international opposition and internal challenges, is under heavier pressure than the United States. The nature of the Israeli experience as less established, and more precarious, helps to explain its different approaches to communication and public relations, inasmuch as "National unity most often emerges when there is some kind of threat to a people who share common identifications" (Taylor & Kent, 2006, p. 300).

Sand (2009) has argued that "[t]o promote a homogeneous collective [memory] in modern times, it was necessary to provide . . . a long narrative suggesting a connection in time and space between the fathers and the 'forefathers' of all the members of the present community" (p. 15). Moreover, he continues by saying that since such an intimate connection "has never actually existed in any society, the agents of memory worked hard to invent it . . . [using] archaeologists, historians, and anthropologists" (p. 15). In turn, those findings were subjected to "major cosmetic improvements carried out by essayists, journalists, and the authors of historical novels. From this surgically improved past emerged the proud and handsome portrait of the nation" (p. 15).

If Sand and other contemporary historians and theorists of nationality are correct in identifying the interconnectedness of history and nations, and the relative plasticity of the history-writing and nation-making processes, then public relations has much to take from them; and if Sand and company are correct, public relations also has much to give to them. Specifically, while Sand's (2009) acknowledged agents include essayists, journalists, and authors, he excludes public relations practitioners and their practices. This book hopes to show how much public relations participated in the "inventing," and sustaining, of the Israeli nation.

Even though the Zionist movement was secular by definition, the Jewish religion became a major mobilizing force for the Zionist movement to help persuade Jews all over the world to join it. Religion is still used by government and organizations across society to enlist support for policies and demand personal sacrifices. When Hobsbawm (1990) is discussing the issue of "fundamentalism" (p. 167) and fundamentalist groups' intolerance and their need to create a common enemy for the sake of unifying the group members, he observes similarities with a number of other ethnic and nationalist phenomena, "especially where these are themselves linked with, or seek to re-establish links with, a group-specific religious faith – as among (Christian) Armenian opposing (Muslim) Azeri Turks, or in the recent Old Testament phase of Likud Zionism in Israel" (p. 168). Hobsbawm (1990) specifically notes how this religious linkage is "so different from the aggressive secularist, and even anti-religious ideology of the [Zionist] movement's founders" (p. 168).

The following chapters will demonstrate how Israel's government, which celebrated the 66th birthday of the state in 2012, uses intensive communication and Hasbara tools to communicate internally and externally. However, we identify the nation-building effort much earlier in the "proto-national" (p. 47) history of the Jewish people. Chapter 3 sees the Jewish Diaspora experience as the proto-national condition for the Zionist movement and as one that helped shape its discourse. Zionist communication, for example, keeps framing its messages in relation to the Jewish religion (e.g. the choice of the Menorah) because this was (and is) a major component of the individual and community identity.

3 Shaping communication
Diaspora life and the Jewish public sphere

> Every history contains myths, but those that lurk within national historiography are especially brazen. The histories of peoples and nations have been designed like the statues in city squares – they must be grand, towering, heroic. Until the final quarter of the twentieth century, reading a national history was like reading the sports page in the local paper: "Us" and "All the Others" was the usual, almost the natural, division. For more than a century, the production of Us was the life's work of the national historians and archaeologists, the authoritative priesthood of memory.
>
> (Sand, 2009, p. 15)

The development of Israeli public relations is interwoven not only with the history of the Jewish people but also with the establishment of Israel as a Jewish state. This chapter focuses on the underpinning values of the Jewish people in general – including the communicative role and political consequences that surround the selection of cultural symbols – and the impact of 2,000 years of Diaspora experience on its public discourse in particular. It looks at how the Zionist movement mobilized values from the Jewish Diaspora to promote the idea of a Jewish state in the land of ancient Israel.

Jewish Diaspora communities lived as a minority dispersed among other nations without a territorial concentration, and they were dependent on the mercy of the host countries and on the internal solidarity of the community. The unique public sphere that resulted helps to explain the late development of public relations in the State of Israel and to account for the prominence of the fundraising and lobbying functions. Hobsbawm (1990) usefully presents the Jewish Diaspora as an example of a "popular pre-national" (p. 47) condition that preceded the nation building of the Zionist movement:

> While the Jews, scattered throughout the world for some millennia, never ceased to identify themselves, wherever they were, as members of a special people quite distinct from the various brands of non-believers amongst whom they lived, at no stage, at least from the Babylonian captivity, does this seem to have implied a serious desire for a Jewish political state, let alone territorial state, until a Jewish nationalism was invented at the very end of the nineteenth century by analogy with the newfangled western nationalism.
>
> (p. 47)

Similar arguments had been made earlier by others. Kohn (1965), for example, associated strong components of Jewish identity with a cultural mission rather than a national ideal. He attributed some fundamental traits of nationalism to them and to the Greeks because both "had a clearly defined consciousness of being different from all other people. The Hebrew from the Gentiles, the Greeks from the Barbarians" (p. 11) and concluded: "It is because their cultural continuity proved stronger than racial, political, or geographical continuity, that they live on today. The idea of the nation-state was unknown to them but they had the strong consciousness of a cultural mission" (p. 11).

One example highlights both continuity and connections between the traditional Jewish public sphere, its cultural identity, and modern Zionist discourse. The Menorah, the Jerusalem Temple's seven-branched candlestick, was carried to Rome in a triumphal procession by Roman soldiers after the conquest of Jerusalem in 70 CE. Its adoption as the official emblem of the State of Israel in 1949 offers a good example of nation building through symbols. A committee set up to develop an emblem for the new state by the temporary government two months after the 1948 establishment of Israel selected the Menorah as a distinctive Jewish icon because it represents

> the connection of the nation with its glorious past in its own land, the return of the state to its original location (via the metaphor of the return of the Menorah from Titus Arch to its original place in Israel), and indirectly for the beginning of the process of ending the Jewish Diaspora.
> (Mishori, 2000, p. 156) [ATH]

The Menorah served as the Jewish symbol, with the Star of David, through 2,000 years of Jewish existence in the Diaspora, as an ornament in synagogues, Jewish cemeteries, holy books, documents, and anything – private or public – that had to signify a connection with the Jewish people. Originally a religious tool in ritual, the Menorah also symbolizes the hope for the reconstruction of the Temple upon the arrival of the Messiah, which, for religious Jews, is an actual concrete aspiration. Thus, the Menorah came to symbolize the continuity of the Jewish people and the revolutionary effort of the Zionist movement to turn the humiliation of Jews in the Diaspora into a triumphant settlement in their ancestral land.

Selecting the Menorah as the unifying visual aligned well with the concept and the political agenda of the Zionist founders of the State of Israel as the first prime minister, David Ben-Gurion, "sought to erase the memory of the Diaspora by linking the Jewish state with ancient Israel" (Abadi, 1993, p. 42). To attract Jews to the Zionist revolution, the leaders of the movement framed the Zionist message with the cultural symbol of the Menorah, which is associated with the synagogue and religious rituals. This frame was part of a series of Zionist concessions to the religious Jews from the early days of the state. It had significant consequences for future cultural and social confusion around "Who is an Israeli?" and "Who is a Jew?" The influence of the religious sector on the definition of Zionism and the shaping of the Jewish state continues to the present day. The selection of the

Menorah provided both a concise narrative of the Zionist vision and a unifying strategic communication. Without any verbal text, the Menorah carries a powerful message able to resonate emotionally with all Jews and religiously with religious Jews who cared about that part of their identity as Israelis.

Identity, the Diaspora, and Zionism

According to Eisenstadt (1985), the collective identity of the Jewish people was exclusive of other nations from biblical times, as "it was the first monotheistic religion, in its attempt to separate itself from its neighbouring pagan nations" (p. 17). This distinctive demarcation of boundaries enabled it to maintain its continuity over centuries. That began to change in the 18th century with the European Enlightenment movement and emancipation, followed by the Zionist movement's call at the end of the 19th century for "the establishment of a modern Jewish community where Jews would live among themselves as a normal – economically and politically – modern nation" (p. 106).

The issue of continuity of the Jewish historical patterns within the Israeli society was, in 1977, a subject for an academic discussion led by Eisenstadt and sponsored by the president of Israel, Ephraim Katzir. The report about this "study circle of scholars" in the president's home quotes Eisenstadt about the way Jewish history, and its specific situation as a minority group living within a hostile society, shaped the values of Israeli society:

> One central aspect here is the struggle and efforts the Jewish people, from their early crystallization, to find clear definitions that would separate them from other people on the one hand, and lack of consensus about the clear content of the separation, and of the unique collective identity and our culture, on the other hand.
>
> (Eisenstadt, 1997, p. 25) [ATH]

Eisenstadt (1977) identifies the historical coincidence of the loss of political independence and the acceptance of the Hallaha, the Jewish religious legal system, as a defining moment. That coincidence shaped the boundaries of the Jewish collective life in the Diaspora as the "Hallaha took over . . . as the single definer of the identity boundaries when independent political government did not exist" (p. 29). For Eisenstadt (1977), the Jewish public consensus was based not on opinions and beliefs but on acceptance of the Jewish religious court, Beth Hadin, or the public decisions. The relationships that developed between the leaders of the Jewish community and the general Jewish public in the Diaspora are responsible for the intolerance towards any dissident idea or behaviour, which sometimes developed radical "'witch-hunting' and 'vigilante' aspects" (p. 20) [ATH].

The intolerance of dissidents carries on in Israel in the second decade of the 21st century. It surfaces in the right-wing government's anti-democratic legislation initiatives. These initiatives were intended both to limit and to delegitimize civil groups who criticize government policies and to prevent unfavourable publicity.

28 Shaping communication

They became a topic of discussion on an Israeli television show that featured Ophir Akunis, a member of the Israeli parliament (the Knesset) and former communication adviser of the leading right-wing party, the Likud (as well as a former spokesperson of the Ministry of Justice). During the show, Akunis said that the notorious US senator Joseph McCarthy was actually right in his (now historically discredited) persecution of so-called Soviet spies during the 1950s (Lis, 2011).

The climate that encourages such extremism has its own history. Writing on Diaspora culture in general, Hua (2003) identifies it as a response to the cultural trauma involved in the dispersion of an uprooted nation:

> Thus diasporic culture involves socio-economic, political and cultural transnational exchanges among and between the separated populations of the diaspora. . . . There manifests a collective memory, myth and vision of their [diasporic people's] homeland, shared diasporic identities, diasporic consciousness and solidarity . . . [D]iaspora communities and networks are not exempted from racism . . . and other discrepancies and prejudices.

While the Jews were living precariously among "Gentiles," Jewish identity anxieties were often as strong as the anxiety about physical survival. Accordingly, the Diaspora placed the values of unity and solidarity high above individual rights even when, following the French Revolution, Jews were tolerated and received political rights. In fact, the emancipation increased the worry of the Jewish community about possible assimilation among non-Jews. This threat did not exist before the emancipation, when Jews were excluded from such political participation in the societies in which they lived.

Identity, the Jewish public sphere, and Zionism

That identity crisis of the 18th century, caused by the transition in the status of European Jews in their countries, has had a long-term effect on the Jewish public sphere. The new freedoms enabled a separation between the religious component and the national component of the Jewish identity and instigated an internal debate between the orthodox and the Maskilim [Educated or Enlightened]. Katz's (1963) *Traditions and Crisis: Jewish Society at the End of the Middle Ages* analyzed the situation in the following terms:

> The approach to the historical religion in the traditional Jewish society included a national affinity, which meant an awareness of belonging to the Jewish public, its past and future, and a feeling of solidarity with the people of this religion in the present. The disintegration of the traditional society separated between the religious approach and the national approach. The development here is very different from the parallel process in the non-Jewish society. . . . Radicals from other religions, even when they disengaged with the religion and the church, were not excluded from their national culture . . . yet the Jewish nationalism was built mainly on conscious replacements for

real givens: an affinity to a non-spoken language, affinity to memory and hope for a country that was not lived in, and historical religious awareness-connections that were managed via channels of tradition, literature and institutions. Whoever exceeded the framework of the Jewish status, and whoever stepped out from the authority of the belief and the Jewish religion, got rid also of the attachment symbols of nationality.

(p. 308) [ATH]

The strong connection between religion and national identity restricted options for the individual. In traditional Jewish society, the community leaders had the power to punish and exclude dissidents by proclaiming a "Herem" [boycott]. Even during the 17th and 18th centuries, according to Katz, the boycott was a common discipline enforcement tool used by the rabbis of the Jewish communities. Proclaiming a Herem meant that no member of the community, including family, was allowed to have any contact with the subject of the Herem. Thus, the boycotted Jew could not receive community and religious services, and actually lost his or her world. The emotional power of this tool was enhanced by the symbols of its proclamation: "the opening of the Ark, the blowing of the Shofar [Ram's Horn], the lighting of black candles, etc." (Katz, 1963, p. 125) [ATH].

The strong collective identity and the blurring of the private and public realms that characterized the Jewish public sphere in the Diaspora continued to be a major feature of the Zionist movement and the State of Israel. Amos Elon (1983), in his book *The Israelis: Founders and Sons*, describes the Jewish *shtetl* [a semi-urban Jewish community, a kind of market-centre where Jews used to live in Eastern Europe] as a place where "life was with people. Simple human solidarity was the shtetl's source of strength to survive as an island culture surrounded by hostility. A ghost of the shtetl lingers on in the modern living institutions of Israel" (p. 47).

The individual, the collective, and the media

The unique relationship between the individual and the collective in the Jewish Diaspora community was carried over into the State of Israel. Shalit's (2004) *The Hero and His Shadow: Psychological Aspects of Myth and Reality in Israel* offered a psychological analysis of the collective process that underlies the creation and the development of the state. In identifying what he called an unusual "close proximity" between the individual and the collective, Shalit (2004) found that "the State of Israel came into being by the materialization of an idea, the implementation of which necessitated the merger of single individuals into a collective" (p. 169). The Israeli public sphere was influenced, much like the Diaspora Jewish public sphere, by permanent crises and existential anxiety. That the state was established following a traumatic experience of near-annihilation during the Holocaust and World War II made the intense relationship inescapable:

> The collective processes of Israel – state-building, war, mass-immigration, rapid social change, changing borders, tension between society's subgroups –

are all-encompassing. Hardly anyone, no family, can refrain from active involvement.... The individual's identification with the *Collective Idea* forms the core of Israeli society.

(Shalit, 2004, p. xvii)

Zionist thinking about the role of the media shows a clear continuity with the need for Jewish solidarity and reflects the close proximity of the individual and the collective. The resulting intolerance towards discourses that were perceived to present a threat to unity impacted on Jewish and Israeli journalists and editors. The emphasis on solidarity, unity, and collectivist discourse dominated the public sphere, including the young Hebrew media. Studying the history of the European Jewish Hebrew press, Kouts (1998b) finds that "the model of 'national responsibility' adopted by the Zionist establishment is an important key to the understanding of the long path and numerous hesitations of the Israeli press in its move towards greater 'freedom' (and 'irresponsibility')" (pp. 99–100) [ATH].

The importance of solidarity and unity in the Jewish value system continues into the Zionist movement's model of "national responsibility" for the Hebrew media: "The eternal argument about the attempt to reconcile the 'freedom' of the press with the 'responsibility' of the press has a unique significance in the Jewish and the Israeli context" (Kouts, 1998b, p. 199). Kouts concluded that "the responsibility of the press precedes its 'freedom' of expression, at least in our case and our situation" (p. 211) [ATH]. In this case, "responsibility" means supporting the community's collective interests as decided by the political leaders and avoiding criticism that might lead to open controversy.

That kind of responsibility assigned to Jewish Diaspora newspapers, and later to the Israeli media, helps explain the environment in which Israeli public relations developed. "Responsible journalists" functioned as spokespeople for the leadership and actually fulfilled the role of public relations practitioners or spokespeople or propagandists, while employed as journalists. The pattern influenced the realities of media and the public discourse for over a hundred years and is still alive in Israel today.

Kouts' (1999) history of the Jewish Hebrew press identifies several unique characteristics that also helped to shape the development of Israeli public relations:

- Jewish society encouraged learning, reading, and writing as a means of ensuring cultural and national survival. Journalists who wrote Hebrew were called "writers" and enjoyed the respect usually endowed to those dealing with the holy books . . .
- Jewish journalists were often frustrated politicians who could not fulfil their ambitions because of the Jews' low status in the societies in which they lived. The press served as substitute for institutionalized political activity and played a much wider role in the public sphere of the Jewish community, and also between the community and the non-Jewish government.

- The activity of the Jewish press had cross national aspects because the Jewish communities were dispersed (and belonged to different national states) . . . the Jewish newspapers conducted public solidarity campaigns, international fundraising campaigns for communities in distress, or for the establishment of charities and medical services. They [the Jewish press] and, later, the Israeli press, served as fora for discussions about communities' issues, such as religious reforms, that crossed national boundaries.

   (pp. 75–76) [ATH]

Journalists as propagandists

In another work, Kouts (1998a) made a significant contribution to the understanding of Israeli public relations through his analysis of the key figure of Nahum Sokolow, "the journalist and Zionist leader who was a major producer of the Zionist propaganda, the 'Hasbara' . . . in current terminology, the first 'professional' in this field in Zionist politics" (p. 199). Ironically, Sokolow (1859–1936), who was a politician and a senior leader in the World Zionist Organization, is considered the father of Israeli journalism. The present Journalists' Association house in Tel Aviv and the Journalists' Association's annual award are both named after him.

The journalistic honours are ironic since, while using the media to promote the Zionist agenda, Sokolow abolished demarcation lines between the roles of politicians, journalists, and propagandists in the Israeli public sphere. His contribution to Hasbara is no less important than his journalistic work: Sokolow designed the model of "guided" journalism. After setting up a Hebrew newspaper, the *Hamevaser* [*The Herald*], in Turkey in 1908, Sokolow writes, "[A]ll my observations have led me to recognize that we can't act here but via the press. Anywhere else the press did not have that much influence on public opinion" (cited in Kouts, 1998a, p. 204). Later, Sokolow also recognized the importance of personal contact and public meetings, and he published "guides" for the Zionist propagandist [Madrich Lamasbir].

Sokolow defined the role of the Hebrew press as responsible for Zionist education and national unification. He saw this as fair and accurate journalism. On the other hand, he criticized the more diverse Yiddish press for representing too many parties and arguments, sensationalism, and "false democracy" (Kouts, 1998a, p. 209). Sokolow represents the official Zionist leadership's expectations that the Hebrew press should foster national responsibility and promote the movement's political goals. These expectations did not meet with media opposition. Instead, editors and journalists were keen to be involved and serve the movement. Not surprisingly, strong collaboration evolved between the press and the political system, and their close cooperation continued to influence the Israeli public sphere many years after the establishment of the state.

In effect, editors and journalists felt part of the political system. They were motivated not only by their professional views but also by their involvement as contributors to a community that was building a Zionist nation. As one rare report, based on the admission of the photographers who filmed the news programmes screened in movie theatres in the 1950s and 1960s, reveals: "We were programmed. The government controlled all the photography" (Shamgar, 1999, p. 10). In the report published in *Maariv*, Shamgar (1999) called the programmes "the Israeli version of *Pravda*": "The viewers thought they were watching news; in reality this was entirely propaganda: the institutions commissioned the reportage, decided what would be filmed, what the speaker would say and they even paid for the job" (p. 10) [ATH].

Mobilizing stories: news, writing, and the culture of enlistment

According to Shamgar's (1999) report, the opposition never received exposure in the news programmes, while presentations of Zionist events were always positive and enthusiastic. The content was selected by the politicians, the government offices, and the Jewish National Fund (JNF), and they usually paid for the news report. The style was heroic and was influenced by Soviet movies of the 1920s: "Though things were done unconsciously, the photographers felt that they were part of the Zionist renaissance" (p. 10) [ATH].

The compliance and collaboration of journalists with the political leadership represents a major dimension of the Jewish-Zionist public sphere that originated in traditions of putting solidarity and unity above all. A similar situation was identified in Hebrew literature. Hever (2002) described prominent Hebrew writers as promoters of Zionist rhetoric. His book *Producing the Modern Hebrew Canon: Nation Building and Minority Discourse* argues that "Zionist principles of the negation of the Diaspora and the creation of a national majority culture became the central criteria for the aesthetic that dominated Hebrew literature and culture" (2002, p. 6).

Hebrew fiction writers and journalists alike felt themselves part of building the Zionist nation and helped create the hegemonic Zionist narrative. The infrastructure for a wide national consensus was provided from the early days of the Zionist movement, but it was a natural continuation of the values and worldviews developed in the Jewish communities as a result of their unique situation in the Diaspora. The same national consensus helped the leaders of the State of Israel to mobilize Israelis for challenging missions such as extensive army service, the absorption of mass immigration, and sacrificing life, and quality of life, for the sake of the state. The leading "socialist Zionist" parties' alliance, which governed the State of Israel in its first three decades, was able to enlist Israeli support thanks to a wide national consensus. This covered such major issues as the Jewish nature of the state, the use of Hebrew as its first language, and the prioritizing of Jewish immigration, settlement, and the army.

Consensus and solidarity: evidence from the later 20th century

The strength of Israeli solidarity and consensus emerges in the results of extensive research performed by the Gutman Institute for Applied Social Research and commissioned by Israel's Ministry of Education. Entitled "Leisure Patterns in Israel: Changes in Cultural Activity 1970–1990," the research identified, among other things, the needs of Israelis and their expectations as consumers of cultural products such as media, literature, and arts. The results showed that

> [t]he needs that Israeli society identifies as most important in 1990 are the connection with the family and the identification with the state and the Jewish people. At the top of the list was the need to "spend time with the family" (89%), and following: "to feel proud about having a state" (84%), "to feel that I'm part of the Jewish people" (83%), "to understand what is going on in Israel and in the world" (82%) and "to feel close to the IDF [Israel Defense Forces]" (80%).
>
> (Katz et al., 2000, p. 313) [ATH]

This list of preferred needs showed some change, with a slight increase in individual needs and slight decrease in collective needs, between 1970 and 1990. Personal needs such as relaxation increased from 61% to 74%, entertainment increased from 34% to 68% (Katz et al., 2000, p. 314), but in general the research concluded that "most of the Israeli public keeps frequent relationship with family and friends, gives significant importance to the Jewish and national holidays, and keeps the holiday rituals that strengthen the connection with family, the Jewish nation and the state" (p. 314) [ATH]. Over that 20-year period, the collective desire that creates solidarity stayed at the top of Israelis' list of needs, and escapist individual desires stayed at the bottom.

The expectations for connectedness to the nation were met by the providers of culture and by the media, which served, at least till the 1970s, as a unifying force promoting the Zionist agenda. Radio broadcasts were a monopolistic service controlled by the government till the introduction of semi-commercial broadcasts in the 1990s. In 1965 the broadcasting authority, following the model of the BBC, was established as a public service governed by a political board. Israeli television broadcasts started as late as 1968 as part of the monopoly of the broadcasting authority. Only as recently as the 1990s could Israelis connect to cable and select alternative broadcasts.

Interestingly, the Katz research group appreciated the benefits of the monopolistic situation when Israelis could watch only one TV news programme:

> In its best times the news programme at 9 p.m. attracted, in an average evening, 70% of the population. The critics and the supporters of multi-channels system opposed it, arguing that a society can't call itself democratic if it has only one TV channel and one news programme. But nevertheless, the

evidence shows that this highly politicized society gathered every evening to watch the evening news, and accepted willingly whatever it presented on the political public agenda . . . it is possible to state that the news programme at 9 p.m. became a civil ritual that consisted of a discourse of the society with itself.

(Katz et al., 2000, p. 392) [ATH]

The Katz research group concluded in 1990 that "if the citizens gather in one public sphere, which is devoted to the absorption of credible reports about the current issues, and to discussions about them, this promotes rather than suppresses active democracy" (Katz et al., 2000, p. 392) [ATH].

In preferring a restricted public sphere, Katz et al.'s (2000) position parallels what Fraser (1992) identifies as Habermas's earlier emphasis both on "the singularity of the bourgeois conception of the public sphere, its claim to be the public arena" (p. 123) and his casting of "the emergence of additional publics as a late development signalling fragmentation and decline" (p. 123) and perceiving "the proliferation of a multiplicity of publics" as "a departure from, rather than an advance toward, democracy" (p. 123).

Israel's immigrant society brought together people from all over the world, with different cultures and languages, and with diverse traditions and political orientations. It is not surprising that the level of desire for connectedness to the nation is exceptionally strong. The differences and conflicts between the many groups living in Israel existed in the public sphere and found their expression in radical arguments and extreme rivalries. Above the struggle, however, there was a strong consensus on the agenda of basic national issues as set by one group: the veteran political leadership that immigrated from Europe during the pre-state period and later. Mass immigration from North Africa and Asia after the state was established was not included in the cultural identity of the new Israeli.

Early pioneers of public relations: lobbyists and fundraisers

The prominence and legitimacy of Hasbara and the high level of collaboration between Israeli journalists and the political leaders inhibited the development of Israeli public relations. In the absence of public dialogue prior to decision making, the practitioners operated with a very one-sided communication process: from the government, and government-controlled companies, towards the general public. On the other hand, the same Jewish-Israeli public sphere supported the emergence of two major public relations functions that had deep roots in the traditional Jewish communities in the Diaspora. These were the function of the lobbyist and the function of the fundraiser. In the Jewish-Israeli context, these two functions were performed by professionals who were appointed and recognized by the community at a much earlier stage than they appear in current histories of public relations in Europe and America.

There are good reasons for this. The traditional Jewish society of the Diaspora was an organized subculture living within a non-Jewish culture, struggling to survive and to maintain its identity. It had its own religious court and its own social institutions, but it also had to communicate with the non-Jewish authorities and obey their laws. Jews were totally dependent on the authorities that granted them the right to settle in a certain location. That right could be taken away at any time, even when they had been born and lived in the location for generations. Zhut Hayeshiva [the Right to Settle] meant that if Jews were not needed, then they could be expelled from their homes, and from the countries that hosted them, with no right to protest.

During the 16th to 18th centuries the go-between who communicated with the Jewish community and the authorities developed into a professional institution. In Eastern Europe this function became a paid job, a part of the community leadership team, and was sometimes rewarded as much as, or more than, the judge [Av Beth Din] and the rabbi. In Hebrew, the go-between was called the *shtadlan*, someone who makes the effort and does the soliciting:

> The community shtadlan has to deal with the authorities that sit somewhere else. Moreover, unlike the rest of the public servants, the Shtadlan needs to have knowledge that is not available to the rest of the community: the language of the non-Jewish authorities, the legal system, the political and legal environment, flexibility in negotiations and more.
>
> (Katz, 1963, p. 105) [ATH]

In effect, the shtadlan performed the role of a lobbyist who had to commit all his time to the community, and to represent its interests to the authorities. The role also involved travelling and risk. But because the service was so essential to the community, it was well paid through Jewish community taxes and was highly appreciated.

In this way, the realities of life of the Jewish Diaspora community laid the infrastructure for the expertise of the lobbyist, who is part and parcel of public relations. The Zionist movement used the expertise it inherited from the traditional Jewish community in its lobbyists' activities around the world and in its effort to persuade international public opinion to support Zionist goals. The lobbyist was not a stranger to Israeli culture. But professional lobbyism in specialized consultancies – as in the United States – developed in the State of Israel only in the 1990s following dramatic political changes that resulted in a growing movement of decentralization of political power and of activism.

Although detailed analysis is outside the scope of a book on Israeli public relations, Mearsheimer and Walt's *The Israel lobby and U.S. Foreign Policy* (2007) acted as kind of lightning rod for contemporary controversies and lobby power. They exposed "the political power of the Israel lobby, a loose coalition of individuals and groups that seeks to influence American foreign policy in ways that will benefit Israel" (Mearsheimer & Walt, 2007, p. 112). Moreover, Mearsheimer and Walt (2006) argue that no other ethnic lobby has been so successful, to the extent that since 1973 "Washington has provided Israel with a level of support dwarfing that given to any other state . . . and [Israel] is the largest recipient in total since World War Two, to the tune of well over $140 billion (in 2004 dollars)" and "receives about $3 billion in direct assistance each year, roughly one-fifth of the foreign aid budget" (Mearsheimer & Walt, 2006).

The controversy around these claims raged, with the two US professors being at the receiving end of what Ben-Ami (2011) calls "smears and personal attacks" (p. 26) that are calls "all too familiar" (p. 26), with Alan Dershowitz – not surprisingly since he is named as one of the "apologists for Israel" (Mearsheimer & Walt, 2007, p. 98), used their book to prime an emotional debate about what constitutes "antisemitic conspiracy" theories – and others were similarly derogatory (see http://en.wikipedia.org/wiki/The_Israel_Lobby_and_U.S._Foreign_Policy).

While disagreeing with Mearsheimer and Walt about the power of the lobby (and especially AIPAC'S role), Ben-Ami (2011) testifies to its efficacy in setting out its accomplishments: "It has solidified the U.S.–Israel alliance, locked in broad partisan support for a generous military aid package and helped to ensure that Israel has a qualitative military edge over its neighboring enemies" (p. 92) and forms "a near-perfect case study on the effective accumulation and deployment of political power in Washington" (p. 92).

Despite this recent achievement, professional fundraising was not just an innovation brought in from the United States. It has been part of Jewish history since the destruction of the Second Temple, when a small Jewish community that remained in Eretz Israel [the name of the territory since the first century and before the State of Israel was established] sent emissaries to raise funds from Jews in the Diaspora. Shluhei Eretz Israel [Emissaries of Eretz Israel] was the name given to official messengers that were sent abroad from Jerusalem, Hebron, Safed, and Tiberia as emissaries to raise funds. They reached Jewish communities all over the world and were wandering for three to ten years, bringing messages from the Jewish towns and yeshivas [religious academic institutions] in Eretz Israel to the Jewish communities in Europe, North Africa, and the Middle East.

The history of the emissaries has been well documented from the first century to the 19th century in a two-volume book by Avraham Yaari (1997). In a chapter on "the propaganda tools of Eretz Israel emissaries" (pp. 68–103), Yaari describes the methods used by the emissaries:

> The emissary was accustomed to preach on the first Sabbath of his arrival in the community. . . . Sometimes he brought with him some soil from the holy land for the communal worthies, drawings of the holy places and the graves of the Zadikim [Pious Men], or scrolls of Ester and amulets from Eretz Israel. An important medium utilized for publicity was the printing of various books about Erez Israel. . . . Sometimes the emissaries printed books describing the immediate events which gave rise to their mission . . . the difficult conditions of Jerusalem in 1625 . . . the resettlement of Jews in Tiberias in 1740 . . . the riots against the Jews of Safed . . . in 1834, and of the Safed earthquake in 1837.
>
> (pp. 68–103) [ATH]

Shaping communication 37

The use of news media as a persuasive communication method in fundraising thus has a long history of success in the Jewish world. According to Yaari (1997), "the emissaries from Eretz Israel to the Diaspora are an institution that survived uninterrupted for almost one thousand nine hundred years" (p. 11) [ATH]. The mission of the emissaries was not only to collect funds and take from the Diaspora community but also to give to the community – news from Eretz Israel, consultation, arbitrations and such (p. 11) [ATH].

The emissaries were accepted by the Jewish communities abroad with respect, and they raised large sums of money by approaching the community in general and some wealthy members in particular. They were the major source of income for the small Jewish community in Eretz Israel. If not treated with dignity, the emissary reported the fact to the community's religious leaders, and "if they found no other way to gain their ends, they made use of the power of Herem [Boycott], which was proclaimed in Jerusalem in front of the Western Wall" (Yaari, 1997, p. 43) [ATH].

Each emissary was empowered by letters, for example Iggeret Klalit [General Letter] and Iggeret Le-Nedivim [Letter to Philanthropists], describing the mission and signed by the rabbis and leaders of his community or institution. These were in addition to power of attorney and other documents supporting his credibility. The tradition of fundraising substituted for the fiscal tax paid by the Jews for temple sacrifices after the destruction of the Second Temple and enabled Diaspora Jews to identify with, and connect with, their nation and lost land. Fundraising was, and still is, part of the social ritual in synagogues, on major holidays, and just before prayers. Funds were raised not only for the small community in Eretz Israel but also for Diaspora Jewish communities.

Thus, the roots of key public relations functions in Israel can be found in well-established and legitimized traditions of fundraising and lobbying that were performed by professionals in persuasive communication. Widely accepted by the Jewish community, the fundraising function is another aspect of the unique Jewish public sphere and another expression of solidarity. The fundraising efforts of Zionist institutions in Israel are described in detail in Chapter 7 and contemporary lobbying campaigns are described in Chapter 11.

Conclusion

The traditional Jewish society of the Diaspora developed unique social structures that were needed for coping with stressful – often dangerous and life-threatening – situations. The daily challenge of surviving as a dependent minority in an often hostile non-Jewish environment developed a public sphere favouring the values of internal consensus and solidarity above individual rights. This emphasis determined the role of the Jewish media in the Diaspora and carried over into the role of the Israeli media. In the first three decades of the state, journalists functioned as servants of the political leadership and promoted the leadership's interests. The consensus and solidarity that dominated Jewish and Israeli public discourse until the 1970s inhibited the development of professional public relations. This is simply because, under such conditions, there was no need to employ professional communicators to deal with the media. Thus, a basic skill of public relations practitioners, media relations, did not develop. As long as the media were in direct contact with, and shared a common understanding with, the political system, few media relations skills were required. As we will show in later chapters, the few practitioners who were employed, initially by the pre-state institutions and later by the government, did not face big media challenges.

On the other hand, the history of the Jews and their social institutions inspired early professionalism in the public relations practices of lobbying and fundraising. A long tradition of hardships in the Diaspora, and the worldwide dispersion of the Jewish people, established these two functions and allowed them the recognition and appreciation that provided cultural capital and infrastructure for future practitioners.

By looking back in history, this chapter has established specific characteristics and core values of Israeli society as grounded in the long exile of the Jewish people. It has tracked how the Zionist movement mobilized these Jewish Diaspora values in support of its campaign, begun in the mid-1880s, to promote the idea of a Jewish state in the land of ancient Israel. The next chapter describes the role of Zionist leaders and the way they used public relations tools to persuade and enlist support for the movement's goal of building a nation in that land.

4 Determining identity
Zionist leaders as forerunners

> An analyst in 1900, asked about the likelihood of a Jewish state, would have replied: "Don't be absurd! Even Herzl admitted that the idea of a Jewish state, if proclaimed publicly, would be met with "universal laughter." The Arabs derisively call the Jews "the penniless of the weakest of people, whom all governments are expelling." The Jews, without a state in over 1,800 years, have no idea how to be soldiers, farmers or government officials. Lacking any international power, they think the idea is a mirage. Over 99 percent of them don't live in Palestine or want to live in such a backwater. Those few who live there are dependent on *halukah* [foreign charity]. They are a drop in the sea of 600,000 Palestinian Arabs and 20 million Arabs."
>
> (Adelman, 2008, p. 3)

Just as public relations in the United States was forged by the American Revolution and its protagonists, so this chapter argues that public relations in Israel was forged by the Zionist revolution and its protagonists. We retell this tale of two revolutions in order to explore sources of distinctiveness in Israeli public relations development.

The American Revolution is taken as a key event because "today's patterns of public relations practice were shaped by innovations in mobilizing public opinion developed by Adams and his fellow revolutionaries" (Broom, 2009, p. 104), and it is still seen as formative for current principles of public opinion and persuasion. Samuel Adams, Thomas Jefferson, Alexander Hamilton, Tom Paine, and other political heroes of the revolution are foregrounded as communication experts who "understood the importance of public support and knew intuitively how to arouse and channel it" (Broom, 2009, p. 104). Samuel Adams and the Boston radicals are positioned as achieving a public relations triumph in helping persuade the American colonists to revolt against Britain (Cutlip, 1994).

It is not just that these specifics concern only US history and that Israel's history and practitioners need to become visible, rather than, in Holtzhausen's (2012) terms, "invisible" (p. 80). It is also the assumed universality of the United States in terms of the discipline's development that is problematic. The Israeli public relations experience, for example, is similarly rooted in a revolution: the Zionist revolution, which was an equally important force in the State of Israel. Although, like their American counterparts, the Zionists were political leaders rather than professional practitioners, they too used communication campaigns in a creative and strategic way and they too set up the principles that paved the way for the communication professionals of future generations.

The Zionist revolution

The concept of the return of the Jewish people to Zion has been present for centuries, but the term "Zionism," and the associated Zionist political movement, appeared in the late 1880s. Zionism emerged against the background of two major events in the history of European Jews. The first was *emancipation* and the constitutional abolition of discrimination on religious grounds (fully achieved by 1869), which followed the French Revolution. The new era opened previously closed doors and aroused hopes for equal status in the new democratic society. One of the results of the emancipation was the *assimilation* of some Jews into non-Jewish culture: "The German Jewish *Haskala* (enlightenment) led many Jews away from Judaism and it has come in for bitter attacks from both the orthodox and the latter-day Jewish national movement" (Laqueur, 1972, p. 17).

The second major event was the spread of modern anti-Semitism. The revolutions of 1848 were accompanied by a fresh wave of attacks against Jews all over Europe. Although the Jews were puzzled by these outbreaks of anti-Semitism, they soon realized that assimilation would not work: "The optimism of the early emancipation period had petered out by 1880 as unforeseen tensions and conflicts appeared, causing occasional pessimism and heart-searching" (Laqueur, 1972, p. 39).

The combination of the stressful physical and spiritual situation of the Jewish people in Europe, and the emergence of the idea of a modern state promising equal status to all its citizens, had shaken the traditional closed Jewish society. The Jewish press of the 1870s was the forum for vivid discussions that led leaders, such as David Gordon, Moshe Lilienblum, and Pertz Smolenskin from the *Haskala* movement, to the Zionist conclusion: the quest to change the unbearable situation of the Jewish people by means of a national liberation movement: "Zionism was an attempt to suggest a 'cultural,' even secular infrastructure to Judaism" (Elam, 1984, p. 17) [ATH]. The key word was "nationalism" because, in Zionist ideology, "the definition of the Jewish people will be based on the concept of nation with no affinity to the religion" (p. 17) [ATH]:

> According to the religious Jews the Jewish nation was created by the religion and is meaningless without the religion. The Zionist movement revolutionized this idea. The religion is the creation of the Jewish people. The people are free to shape the Jewish culture. The people are sovereign. You can be a good Jew without keeping the laws of the Bible. If you fulfil the national goals set up by the national leadership, you are a better Jew than the one who keeps all the religious commands and is not working for the national goals.
>
> (p. 17) [ATH]

Elam (1984) explains the Zionist movement as a response not to anti-Semitism but rather to emancipation and the threat of assimilation. The Zionist movement's self-appointed role was "to turn the emancipation into auto-emancipation, to turn the Haskala into Hebrew Haskala. . . . This was the Zionist message: The Jew is a human being, enlightened, liberated, equal – a whole human being demanding political and cultural sovereignty" (p. 23) [ATH]. This revolutionary feature is widely recognized as an element that shaped Israeli culture for years afterwards as "a populist uprising against the Jewish 'establishment' as well as against the conditions imposed upon Jews of all ranks by their host nations" (p. 38). This uprising was built up and organized by a small group of Zionist activists who recognized the power of the media and harnessed it to influence opinions and achieve their goals.

The Zionist campaign challenges

This section analyzes the Zionist movement's aims and challenges with current professional public relations terminology. It identifies the movement's large-scale communication goals, its target audiences, and the variety of strategic tools that it used both to convey messages and to influence public opinion and decision makers. Facing an enormous challenge, Zionist campaign activists had to achieve the following objectives:

1. *To build an ideological concept and pragmatic plan that might be credible and accepted by the majority of the Jewish people.* Zionist activists started as a small minority whom most of the Jewish people perceived as a threat: the traditional Orthodox Jews were threatened by the secular proposition of Zionism; the emancipation Jews were trying to achieve equal status as Jews in their native-born societies, or to assimilate, and they could not accept the political solution of a Jewish state; and the Bundists (members of the Jewish Labour Party Bund) believed that only by the triumph of socialism would the Jewish problem be solved and equated Zionism with escapism. In fact, before the world wars most Jews worldwide opposed Zionism's revolutionary ideology and practical plans. European Jews mainly emigrated to the United States, not to Palestine.

2. *To reach a consensus between many Zionist groups.* Besides the arguments with the anti-Zionists Jews, the movement had to deal with fundamental divisions between Zionists from Eastern Europe and Western Europe, and between the European Jews and the American Jews. Bitter arguments separated Zionist groups such as "cultural Zionists," who wished for a limited Jewish spiritual centre instead of a state; "socialist Zionists," who worked for an egalitarian model; "practical Zionists," who insisted on settling in Palestine before getting any international approval; and "political Zionists," who wanted to obtain a charter first. In addition, the "Brit Shalom" group was seeking Arab–Jewish rapprochement and a bi-national state, and later "the Revisionists" insisted on military struggle and opposed the moderate compromising strategy of the Zionist movement; the "general

Zionists" wanted to develop the economy on free market principles; and the "Mizrachi religious Zionists" wanted a state built on religious law. The first president of the movement, Theodore Herzl, stated that the goal was "to preserve the unity of the movement and to eliminate factors making for dissension" (cited in Laqueur, 1972, p. 113).

3. *To persuade world public opinion to support the Zionist goals.* The diplomatic manoeuvres involved intensive lobbying work that put pressure mainly on Turkey, Germany, Britain, and the United States. The eventual result was external recognition of the Zionist idea and the inclusion of a Jewish homeland on the new map of the Middle East organized by the British following World War I. The British recognition of Zionism, which was published on November 2, 1917 as the Balfour Declaration, was a turning point in the history of political Zionism. It eventually led to a League of Nations resolution to impose a mandate for Palestine on the British government. The period of the British Mandate (1917–1947) is referred to as the Yishuv, the pre-state period. Jews lived in Mandatory Palestine as a minority next to the Arab majority as two nations claiming national independence on the same territory.

That 30-year period included World War II, the Holocaust, and the extermination of 6 million Jews. During these three decades, the Yishuv's Zionist leadership used professional diplomacy to persuade world public opinion, and its representatives in the United Nations, to recognize a Jewish state in Palestine. This mission was accomplished via a massive and global lobbying campaign. It resulted in the UN decision on November 29, 1947 to split Palestine into two states: a Jewish and an Arab one. The Arab nations did not accept the resolution and initiated a war that ended with the establishment of the State of Israel in May 1948. Israel was accepted as a member of the United Nations a year later.

4. *To raise resources for the implementation of the Zionist ideology and political plan.* Zionist activists covered the globe in an attempt to reach Jewish communities and enlist their support. Their massive fundraising effort reached out not only to wealthy but also to poor Jewish families. Families who contributed, however small their financial donations, also made symbolically important contributions and became involved and identified with the Zionist project.

5. *To mobilize the Jewish people to immigrate to Palestine and to build the nation.* This goal proved a source of frustration. The 17 million Jews, who had lived all over the world before World War II, did not immigrate as the Zionist leadership had expected. The critical mass of Jewish presence in Palestine needed for the creation of a Jewish majority was not achieved. In 1946 there were 608,200 Jews and 1,143,300 Muslims in Palestine (Hattis-Rolef, 1988, p. 71). At the end of the British Mandate period in 1947, Jews still comprised only a third of the population in Palestine.

With regard to persuasive communication used to attract Aliyah [immigration] to Israel, Shapira (1992) noted that "Zionist propaganda had a dubious reputation as far as truth was concerned" (p. 42) and intentionally "presented Palestine as a land blessed with all positive qualities" (p. 42) with "idealizing, flowery depictions ... designed to galvanize national feeling among the Jews and to play down the difficulties" (p. 42).

The Zionist effort to persuade Jewish people to immigrate to backward Palestine was assisted by sophisticated strategies: the word "immigration" was replaced by the word *Aliyah*, which means "elevation," "rising," "exaltation," and a move from a lower stage to an upper stage. Even in the new millennium, the Hebrew word for immigration, *Hagira*, is used in Israel only for the description of non-Jews who settle in Israel, or the move of people from country to country in other places in the world. A Jew immigrating to Israel is officially an *Ole*, someone who moves up, and a Jew emigrating from Israel is, unofficially, a *Yored*, someone who goes down. The Zionist discourse relating to *Aliyah* is loaded with Jewish cultural connotations that arouse positive emotions since, among other positive associations, "*Aliyah* signifies often the shift from ordinary to holy, elevation in the religious stage" (Almog, 1997, p. 43) [ATH].

The Zionist pioneers and the Israelis used the semantics of *Aliyah* to express the supremacy of life in Israel for Jews, compared with that in other countries. It also hints at the difficulties involved in any attempt to rise up, and the sacrifices expected from those who take that higher road.

6. *To create a new identity and image for the Jewish people*. The return of the Jews involved a cultural revolution consisting of the rejection of the Diaspora traits – Shlilat Hagola [Negation of the Diaspora] – and the creation of the new native Israeli-born Sabra, a normal citizen of the world, well rooted in the land. Almog (1997) describes the Sabra as "a new improved sort of a Jew [who] became a Zionist propaganda tool used by the Yishuv and the Zionist organization of the Diaspora, especially in Eastern Europe" (p. 129) [ATH].

7. *To create a new Israeli culture in the newly revived Hebrew language*. The Zionist goal of "revival of the people" was interrelated with the revival of the language. The Diaspora Jews used the languages of their native countries, or the Jewish jargon of Yiddish and Ladino. Hebrew was the holy language of the Bible and prayers. The decision to modernize the old Hebrew, to use it for secular purposes, and to spread it as the primary language in schools, literature, theatre, and the media in Palestine and the Diaspora was part of the cultural renaissance and the process of transformation of Jewish fate. It involved organized communication campaigns that became one of the most significant successes of the Zionist revolution. According to Harshav (1993, p. 84),

> Eliezer Ben Yehuda began propagandizing the idea (though still vaguely) in his first article "A Burning Question," published in the Hebrew journal *Ha-Shahar* in Vienna in 1879, and devoted his life to it ... [He] edited Hebrew newspapers ... invented over two hundred new Hebrew words, and copied ... about half a million quotations from the historical library of Hebrew texts for his great (OED-type) Hebrew dictionary, which was posthumously edited and published in seventeen volumes.

Elon (1983) describes the language venture as a risky undertaking and relates it to the Zionist tradition of renaming the Zionists with Hebrew names, which became a norm: "for many settlers, the new surnames were mythic symbols of a personal and collective rebirth" (p. 127).

The Hebrew language became a major instrument in the construction of a new national culture and was top of the agenda: "The emergence of a new Palestinian Hebrew . . . further distanced the new generation from the world of Exile and its traditions" (Zerubavel, 1995, pp. 80), and the Hebrew language "became a major vehicle in creating a new more uniform national culture that propagated Zionist ideology and pioneering values" (p. 80). Moreover, the "Hebrew school curriculum reinforced the Zionist views of Jewish history, the values of pioneering, heroism, sacrifice, and love of the country" (p. 81) and "also put major emphasis on the study of geography, nature, and agriculture as part of the return to the nation's roots in the land" (p. 81).

The creation of a new culture involved more than the revival of Hebrew. The Zionist leadership, writers, educators, and communicators collaborated in the development of a new ethos, myths, and narratives that shaped the identity and cultural reality of Israel for future generations. Nevertheless, Hebrew was the unifying force that enabled the cultural transformation.

Strategy and communication

Significant absences

As the seven massive challenges listed above – and the results – indicate, the Zionist movement's strategic communication met most of its goals. It is also important to record the fact of significant absences that also shaped future public relations. One major public neglected by the Zionist movement was the Arab population who lived in Ottoman Palestine and who were hostile to the Zionist dream:

> The official narrative for many years was that the Zionists believed that the Jews were people without land coming to a land without people. Some described how the Zionists were astonished when they found out that the country had been inhabited by Arabs. The truth is that the leaders of the Zionist movement knew very well that there were Arabs living in Palestine and that they opposed the Zionists. From the beginning the Zionists knew that their project would involve confrontation with the local population.
> (Segev, 2001, p. 35) [ATH]

Whether or not the early Zionists were aware of the Arab resistance, they acted as if the "Arab problem" did not exist. Leaders such as Herzl and Weizmann expressed ideas about improving living standards for the Arab Palestinians, while others discussed, albeit unofficially, ideas about the "transfer" of Palestinian Arabs to the neighbouring Arab countries. Some Israeli leaders still believe in this strategy today. The "Arab problem" resulted in the development of a discourse that was used to present the Jewish state to external publics, and was internalized and adopted by Jewish people around the world.

Zionist propaganda, in Shapira's (1992) description, "sought to present the Zionist enterprise to world opinion (particularly British public opinion) as a project of peace that could provide an answer to injustice done by European people to the Jewish people" (p. 122). In order to avoid "large expenditures or unpleasant consequences, such as the oppression of the local population" (p. 122), the "propaganda sketched an idealistic picture of a land being built by a unique colonizing enterprise, bringing peace, blessings, and progress to the entire region" (p. 122) because the "Zionist interest in gaining valuable time necessarily meant avoiding the issue of a Palestine Arab national movement" (p. 122).

Strategically, the Zionist leadership tried to bypass the Palestinian Arabs by communicating with leaders of the neighbouring Arab nations, who were self-interested, did not care about the Palestinian Arabs, and could not represent them. There was a belief that the solution to the Palestinian objection to Zionist settlements on their lands would come from the Arab leaders of other Arab countries and that there was no need to negotiate with Palestinians. The Zionist narrative notes the historical 1919 agreement between Chaim Weizmann, the leader of the Zionist movement, and King Faisal of Iraq as the positive point of light, but this was initiated by the British. In 1921 the Zionist Congress called for the building of a common home for Jews and Arabs but, over the years, negotiations usually involved mediators from other countries and not direct communication.

Consequences

The Zionist movement did not open a channel of communication with the Arabs, did not listen to them, and did not relate to their fears and anger about the new Jewish immigration, let alone the future plans for a Jewish state in Palestine. The Zionists did not consider that Arabs "who had been living there for centuries could possibly object to becoming a minority" (Elon, 1983, p. 157) created by the massive immigration of Jews from other countries. Laqueur (1972) notes similar "Zionist sins of omission" (p. 232) before 1914, especially in relation to the Arabs and purchasing land: "There were possibilities of influencing Arab public opinion; of explaining that the Jews were not coming to dominate the Arabs" (pp. 232–233). However, Laqueur (1972) also expresses doubts as to the efficacy of such tactics: "Whether this would have dispelled Arab fears is less certain, for they worried not so much about the Zionist presence as about their future plans" (p. 233).

The Zionist leadership always knew that the real problem would be the Arab opposition. It was just too difficult to deal with practically, and too embarrassing from the ideological and moral point of view. There was a cognitive dissonance between putting forward a moral plea for justice to the Jewish people while ignoring the concerns of Arab people, especially when the Zionist movement became dominated by the socialist Zionists who led the pre-state and State of

Israel. Ben-Gurion, eventually the first prime minister of the state, and his associates had to find some mode of mediating between their Zionist pragmatic interests to settle Jews in Palestine and their socialist rhetoric.

Shapira (1992) describes the socialist-Zionist rhetoric – "using reasoning borrowed from the socialist, class-oriented arsenal of arguments" (p. 134) – that Ben-Gurion developed, while refusing any dialogue with the Arab national movement, during a 1924 conference: "Thus, Ben Gurion explained his refusal to consider any political proposals at that point in time by asserting that the current Arab leadership was reactionary . . . [and] the potential partner for talks would ultimately be the Arab worker" (pp. 134–135). He also "recognized that the process of developing the class consciousness of the Arab worker, still backward and weak, would take considerable time and effort. He contended that Jews had a central task in helping to advance the Arab worker" (p. 135).

Media and other interventions

The Zionist executive did press resolutions on the importance of making efforts to gain the sympathy of Palestine's Arab population. But at the same time, according to some new historians, they executed a strategy aimed at breaking the new Arab national movement from within and influencing Arab public opinion by controlling the Arab media. H. Cohen (2004) describes the action plan commissioned by Chaim Weizmann in 1920 for activities among the Arab population of Palestine. Significantly, the plan was prepared by the information office of the Zionist representatives committee and it included such initiatives as:

- An agreement with the mayor of Nablus, Haidar Tukan, that in exchange for £1,000 from the Zionist movement, he would lead a pro-Zionist petition movement in the Arab villages.
- A treaty with Arab leaders on the eastern side of the Jordan provided that they would oppose the national Palestinian movement.
- A treaty with the Bedouin sheikhs in the south, to sever their relationship with the Arab Palestinian nationalists.
- Purchase of newspapers that were hostile to the Zionist movement in order to ensure a pro-Zionist editorial line. This move was based on a belief in the power of the written word, and on assumptions that Hasbara could prevent the spreading of the message of nationalism to the wider publics in Palestine.
- Organizing a friendly relationship and the opening of clubs for cooperation.
- Inciting the Arab Christians against the Arab Muslims.

This key document was written when Jews constituted 10% of the Palestine population and it served as the basic strategy for the relationship between the two peoples.

Noting that the "Arab Bureau of the Jewish Agency did maintain a fairly wide, informal network of contacts with Arabs, more often with those from neighbouring countries than from Palestine" (p. 200), Tevet's (1985) biography of Ben-Gurion described the national institution's communication with the Arab Palestinians during the 1940s as follows: "the personnel of the Bureau knew that Ben-Gurion believed peace had no chance, and their activities remained confined to the gathering of information and maneuvers to split Arab ranks" (p. 200).

Other voices

Nor did these activities end with Ben-Gurion. A propaganda system, and control over the media, remain major elements in this strategy. In 1998, for example, during the years of the Oslo peace process, Mohammed Dachlan, one of the Palestinian leaders, who was in charge of security in Gaza at that time, said to a group of Israeli ex-generals working for peace: "You Israelis are not looking for real cooperation. You are looking only for collaborators" (lead author's personal experience).

The lack of dialogue between Jews and Arabs during the Yishuv days was part of a strategic decision by Zionist leaders. It was not always innocent negligence; at times, it was an intentional policy: "The Zionist leaders simply would not consider the presence of half a million non-Jews an insurmountable obstacle, formidable enough to make them give up their cherished dreams about the return of the Jewish people to their homeland" (Laqueur, 1972, p. 218). As a result, neither understandings nor agreements that might have prevented the tragic development of the conflict were reached.

At the time, there were other voices and some "groups – the most important among them the Brit Shalom [Covenant for Peace] Organisation – composed mainly of outstanding intellectuals, men like Martin Buber . . . stressed the necessity to come to a political compromise with the Arabs" (Eisenstadt, 1985, p. 138). Buber, who is famous as a philosopher of dialogue, promoted, as part of Brit Shalom, Zionism and the idea of a bi-national Jewish–Arab state and saw reaching a consensus with the Arabs as the most important goal, even at the cost of the Jews remaining a minority in Palestine. In 1957, he wrote in an essay that "[a] genuine, and not just tactical, understanding with the surrounding people was therefore needed. It could by no means suffice to win the trust of the Arabs merely in order that they later should not oppose our desire for autonomy" (Buber, 1963, p. 254).

There is irony here. Buber's voice in dialogues over the future of Israel was not influential, and his influential work on dialogue took a long time to enter public relations theory. Pieczka's (2011) "Public Relations as Dialogic Expertise?" notes the coincidence that "the idea of symmetry in communication became popular in the 1950s, in the same decade in which the idea of dialogue began its modern career" (p. 112) and that publication of " Buber's (1958) *I and Thou* is often referred to as the starting point in the story of modern dialogue because of the profound influence of the ideas it contained" (p. 112).

Foundational features

Political Zionism and Theodor Herzl

As part of our project to track the evolution of Israeli public relations as distinct from US public relations, the following sections provide a history of leaders whose public relations activities influenced the nation, leaders formerly invisible in the public relations literature, which is dominated by US politicians. Zionist revolutionary ideas were developed while the Jewish communities in Europe experienced pogroms and aggressive attacks, stimulated, in a way, by the nationalist movements in the emerging "national states" of Poles, Hungarians, Italians, and Germans. These states were based on nationalist concepts and, unlike the United States, rejected Jews. Therefore, Zionism, which had started as an ideological and cultural movement rather than a political one, now called for the settlement of Jews in Palestine, which at that time was part of the Ottoman Empire, in order to achieve a territorial concentration of Jews.

The desire for a Jewish state became part of Zionist thought only after the appearance of Dr Theodor Herzl and the political pamphlet he published in 1896 in Vienna, *Der Judenstaat/The Jewish State*. In this pamphlet, Herzl, then a well-known journalist and playwright, asserted that the problem of anti-Semitism could be resolved only by a Jewish state – envisaged in full detail as the only solution to *the Jewish question*. Herzl, who was 36 years old when he published *The Jewish State*, was born in Budapest and raised in Vienna in an assimilated Jewish family. After receiving a doctorate in law in Vienna, he became editor of a prestigious Austrian newspaper, and in 1891 he was appointed its Paris correspondent. It was only there that he became active in the search for radical solutions to the Jewish question.

In his diaries, Herzl wrote that "infiltration" (Jewish settlement in Palestine without guaranteed autonomy) should be stopped and all efforts concentrated upon a charter for the internationally sanctioned acquisition of Palestine: "To achieve this we require diplomatic negotiations . . . and propaganda on the largest scale" (cited in Laqueur, 1972, p. 95). From that point on, Herzl organized one of the world's most impressive international campaigns. The campaign helped establish a successful political movement and set up the principles and values that guided the movement's effort to reach and influence public opinion all over the world. With his legal and journalistic skills, Herzl won recognition as a phenomenal diplomat and lobbyist:

> The foremost task was of course to create a mass basis, to build up a strong movement. . . . He knew that he would not succeed in getting a strong following among his own people unless he had some success to show in the diplomatic field. No one was likely to listen to his message unless there was real hope of obtaining a charter from the sultan. And so he hurried from one European capital to another, trying to establish connections with the mighty of this world, seeking audiences with the sultan and the German emperor, with

the Pope and King Victor Emmanuel, with Joseph Chamberlain and Lord Cromer, with Plehve and Witte – the key figures in tsarist Russia. In between, almost single-handed, he organized the first Zionist world congresses, established the central Zionist newspaper (*Die Welt*), and ran the day-to-day affairs of the growing movement. He also wrote for his newspaper, *Die Neue Freie Presse* – for this, and not the leadership of the Zionist movement, was his pass-key in the chancelleries of Europe.

(Laqueur, 1972, p. 97)

The prominent political scientist Shlomo Avineri (1981), in a rare recognition of the importance of public relations practices in politics and society, considers Herzl's achievements in public relations as his major contribution to the Zionist movement. Avineri (1981) lauded Herzl as the first "to achieve a breakthrough for Zionism in Jewish and world public opinion" (p. 89), the one who "turned the quest for a national solution to the plight of the Jewish people from an issue debated . . . in provincial Hebrew periodicals read by a handful of Jewish intellectuals . . . into a subject for world public opinion" (p. 89). Moreover, Avineri (1981) continued, Herzl was helped to make this breakthrough by "his profession and personality: he was a journalist – brilliant, sometimes superficial – hungry for publicity and adept in public relations" (p. 89) and the realization that "such a momentous and revolutionary task could not be achieved through silent labor at the edge of world politics" (p. 89) and that articles "in obscure Jewish publications would not mobilize the massive forces needed" (p. 89).

Avineri (1981) expresses mixed feelings about Herzl's activities in public relations, including Herzl's chutzpah in presenting himself as a representative of "a Jewish empire" (p. 90) while having no movement, no organization, no money and no influence. But at the same time, Avineri (1981, p. 91) respected the fact that

[a]ll this was the virtuoso performance of a master of public relations, of a person becoming aware of the new powers-that-be of the twentieth century – public opinion, mass communication, gimmicks whose main significance is the impact they leave behind, not necessarily their substance. All this explains the overdramatization of events, the insistence on talking to people at the very top (Pope, Emperor, Sultan); it explains the theatrics of so much of Herzl's appearances – the top hat, the correct coattails, the white gloves, the ceremonial opening of the first Zionist Congress . . . but foe and friends alike had to admit that since Herzl's meteoric appearance, Zionism had begun to move in another sphere; from the parochial concern of some Jewish intellectuals it became an issue of world politics.

From its inception, the Zionist movement put media, public opinion, lobbying, fundraising, and propaganda very high on its agenda. As a journalist, Herzl understood the crucial role of public opinion and decision makers, and used persuasive tools and political influence in order to achieve Zionist goals. In *The Jewish State* he paid much attention to elements of branding: he discussed the flag and symbols that would most effectively communicate the Zionist vision through emotional associations to Jewish tradition. From the communication point of view, Herzl was to the Zionist revolution what Samuel Adams was to the American Revolution. Both of them recognized the value of using symbols that were easily identifiable, carried emotive connotations, and inspired ideals in hearts as well as minds because, as Herzl asserted proudly in 1902, "You cannot make those things only with money" (cited in Gilbert, 1998, p. 28).

By using public relation techniques, Herzl not only made a breakthrough that eventually enabled the establishment of the Jewish state but in the process made public relations central to the Zionist project and Israel.

> Public opinion. This was Zionism's only weapon when it set out to wrest a homeland for the Jewish people from the clutches of world history. The Balfour Declaration of 1917, the United Nations Resolution of 1947 calling for the establishment of a Jewish state in part of Mandated Palestine, and other landmarks on the way to the Jewish state have been achieved not through Jewish economic or political power but through the ability of the Zionist movement to enlist again and again the spiritual resources of highly literate and vocal people, adept at polemics, loquacious and oriented towards public debate. These were the weapons wielded by a weak, persecuted, and small nation in its struggle against extremely uneven odds. Herzl was the first one to realize their potential and forge them into a public force. Zionism and the State of Israel rely to a large extent on them until this very day.
> (Avineri, 1981, p. 91)

Zionist communications and socialist Zionism

The stirrings of nationalism and socialism in Eastern Europe and the revolutionary climate prevalent in Russia between 1880 and 1920 inspired another sector of Zionism: the socialist Zionists. Born in Minsk in 1902, the Zionist labour movement controlled Israel's politics without intermission from the early 1930s until 1977. Elon's (1983) research found traces of the political and moral climate of Eastern Europe prior to World War I evident everywhere "in politics, social ideology, cuisine, religious behavior, and the key concepts of national identity" (p. 37).

The young generation of Jews born in the 1880s and 1890s in Russia could not stay indifferent to the revolutionary ideas and expected that the Jewish problem would be solved within the framework of the socialist revolution. These people, the generation of David Ben-Gurion, Berl Katznelson, and others, "saw in Zionism an opportunity for self-fulfilment of ideals of universal meaning. Zionism could materialize an exemplary society that would bring blessings to the world" (Elam, 1984, p. 38) [ATH].

These young Jews were the pioneers of the 1920s, the immigrants who took a personal decision to settle in Palestine and establish the social infrastructure for the Jewish state. As Elon (1983) notes, they "became farmers less for practical than for ideological reasons" and "thought little of profits" as "they were trying to live a theory" (p. 111): "The pioneers believed that nations, like trees, must be 'organically' rooted in the soil and that anti-Semitism was a result of the 'unnatural' occupational structure of the Jews in Eastern Europe" (p. 111). Elon (1983) continues by identifying a critical difference between Israel and the United States:

> Those *olim* [immigrants] who went into agricultural work were called "*chalutzim,*" literally, "vanguard," but in the current Hebrew usage charged with ecstasy such as was never associated with the closest English or American equivalent "pioneer." In America, the "pioneer" ethos stressed individuality, daring, go-gettism. In Modern Hebrew, "*chalutz*" connotes above all *service* to an abstract idea, to a political movement, and to a community.
> (p. 111; italics in the original)

This unique pioneering spirit, which was collective rather than individual, influenced the development of Israel's value system and the development of the economy. Concepts of centralized controlled markets, and, especially, the control over media and the legitimization of propaganda techniques, all became major factors in the environment of public relations practice in Israel.

Zionist leaders as lobbyists and spokespeople

Promotion of the Zionist idea was part and parcel of the daily work of all Zionists – not only in the executive of the movement, but in every town and village throughout Europe and the United States. The movement's leaders themselves acted as writers, publicists, diplomats, lobbyists, and orators. Of the key leaders who were active on the executive of the Zionist movement, after the death of Herzl in 1904, a number became important spokespeople and diplomats.

Chaim Weizmann

Chaim Weizmann, the dominant figure after Herzl, was president of the World Zionist Organization for over 20 years between 1921 and 1946, and eventually became the first president of the State of Israel (1948–1952). When he became active in the Zionist movement, he was convinced that Zionist aspirations would be best fulfilled by the British. He was a major force in paving the way for the 1917 Balfour Declaration, in which the British government pledged support for the establishment in Palestine of a national home for the Jewish people. This document marked for Zionists and sceptics "international recognition and respectability as a national movement" (Reinharz, 1993, p. 214). Among his many contributions to the implementation of the Zionist vision is his work as a persuasive communicator and lobbyist for the British Mandate of Palestine, and a promoter of the establishment of the Hebrew University and the Weizmann Institute.

Described by his biographer Reinharz (1993) as "a one-man ministry of propaganda, foreign affairs, and strategic planning" (p. 210), communication made Weizmann the major figure in the Balfour Declaration:

> Someone had to provide the necessary background for all the British statesmen and civil servants who were unfamiliar with the history of Zionism and Jewish aspirations. Someone had to read and interpret the entire political map and fuse the various disparate human and political elements. Someone constantly had to remind those who counted of the mutuality of interests between the British government and the Zionist movement. Someone had to overcome personal hesitations and even anti-Semitic arguments. Someone had to supply the correct and convincing arguments that the British were looking for and that made sense to justify to themselves, on moral and humanitarian grounds, actions they were ready to undertake on political grounds. That person was Chaim Weizmann.
>
> (pp. 209–210)

Reinharz (1993) comments that the Arabs did not have "someone with similar personal assets and qualifications" to press their case (p. 209); thus, Arabs' opposition to the Declaration did not gain the same influence on the outcome.

Reinharz's (1993) description of Weizmann's work can serve as a job description for any student interested in what lobbying consists of: "Weizmann's method was not that of petitioner. Rather, he tried to provide the British with arguments buttressing their resolve to control Palestine. Weizmann supplied strategic, historical, religious, and general humanitarian reasons" (p. 210). The British government actually used Zionism for its own interest in the Middle East but Weizmann, as statesman and lobbyist, knew how to show them how a pro-Zionist declaration would help the British aspirations.

When lobbying for the British Mandate in 1922, Weizmann used another public relations staple method by lobbying through other groups and people, and he "induced public demonstrations in the United States which attracted much attention. Weizmann naturally employed to greatest advantage the one lobbying method he had honed and perfected into a fine art during the war [World War I] years – the personal intimate interview" (p. 381). In addition, in line with good professional practice, Weizmann's correspondence with influential people reinforced the impact of the intimate meetings. Reinharz (1993) praises Weizmann as persuader and diplomat, a charming figure who could win influence in elite British circles without downplaying his Jewish identity, "a dignified spokesperson of Jewry" (p. 398).

Zeev Jabotinsky

Zeev Jabotinsky, the colourful, flamboyant, provocative leader of the opposition, was, like so many other Zionist leaders, a poet, writer, and journalist. He was born in Odessa in 1880 and became involved with Zionism following the pogroms of

1904 and 1905: "Having embraced the new creed, no one was more enthusiastic in spreading the gospel. Within a few years he became a professional Zionist, a travelling agitator, very much on demand as a speaker all over Russia" (Laqueur, 1972, p. 340).

He was a romantic and a radical who kept criticizing the Zionist leadership. In 1923, he resigned from the executive board and founded *Betar* and the Zionist Revisionist movement, which became the expression of the opposition. He was impatient towards the British as he felt that the Jewish people faced a great catastrophe, and he "preached the conquest of Palestine through the sword" (Elon, 1983, p. 157). His doctrine upheld that without a majority there would be no Jewish state and that in view of Arab opposition to Jewish immigration, there was no political solution but a Jewish state. Jabotinsky was almost the only Zionist leader who was willing to face the Arab problem, but he advocated the use of military power and/or forced resettlement of Arabs in the neighbouring countries, a solution that was not accepted by the Zionist leadership of his times. He had bitter enemies in the Zionist movement (which sometimes labelled him a Jewish fascist) and fanatical followers in the Revisionist movement.

His communication skills were exceptional. He understood the necessity of a mass movement and therefore the need to address the masses with simple attractive ideas and associated imagery: "Like Herzl, Jabotinsky sensed that the masses of East European Jewry, downtrodden and persecuted, needed a message to sustain their faith. Hence his insistence on national symbols and heraldry" (Laqueur, 1972, p. 380). Laqueur's description of the relationship between Jabotinsky and the Zionist leaders in 1934 illustrates the environment that affected public relations development in Israel years later. A revisionist signature campaign in 1934 gathered around 600,000 signatories for an appeal "drawing attention to the plight of Jews in Europe and to the demand that the gates of Palestine should be open to mass immigration" (Laqueur, 1972, p. 366), but the "Zionist executive sharply denounced the petition campaign as yet another revisionist public relations stunt, devoid of any political significance, intended to increase their popularity in the Jewish communities of Eastern Europe, and raising false hopes" (p. 366), and Jabotinsky was charged with "a flagrant breach of Zionist discipline" (p. 366).

A tale of two revolutionary legacies

Zionism led to the establishment of the State of Israel and has fought for its legitimacy for over 120 years using successful persuasive communication campaigns. The goal of influencing public opinion was high on the Zionist agenda, and the movement's leadership was blessed with quality communicators. The discourse, ethos, myths, narratives, and semantics that were developed by the early Zionists continued to be used later by public relations practitioners who served the Zionists and other institutions.

Zionism owed much to 19th-century European life and thought. It was fuelled by deep-rooted denials of human rights to Jews and long centuries of persecution. It also reflected 19th-century nationalism and saw itself as a just, enlightened, and unique experience in a land waiting to be redeemed. These factors shaped the key messages of the Zionist movement and the slogans that expressed its goals. Almog (1997, pp. 67–81) presented the major Zionist myths and the following two in particular became the framework of ideological socialization for Israelis:

1. The "Israel's Redemption" [*Geulat Israel*] myth, which related the Jewish people's return to its land as a deterministic historical outcome of the suffering in the Diaspora. It offered a messianic miracle of "revival," "rebirth," and "the shift from slavery to freedom." This myth was rooted in the Israeli collective consciousness by the national commemoration of the Holocaust.
2. The "our right for the land" [*zchutenu al haaretz*] myth, which expresses the historic justice that legitimizes the Zionist enterprise. This myth became prominent following the annexation of territories in the 1967 war. The arguments were practical and moral: anti-Semitism, Arab initiation of war and aggressiveness, the settlers' right over uninhabited land, and God's promise to the Jewish forefathers.

These ideological messages were embedded in the daily routine of political, social, and cultural life in Israel. Almog (1997) describes how the pioneering ideology infiltrated the "social blood system" till it became a total religious experience:

> [T]he depth of penetration of the Zionist messages to varied areas of the cultural experience, such as entertainment, media, sport, and art, and the strict institutional supervision, mainly hidden, over the content, turned the Zionist socialization mechanism into a multichannel one in which ideological messages were everywhere and reinforcing the worldview of the Sabra. The young Israeli lived in a sort of "ideological bubble" in which he/she was a subject to constant shower of propaganda messages.
>
> (pp. 81–82) [ATH]

Both the American and the Zionist founders used propaganda during their revolution. Yet early American communication experts can be credited with developing a different point of view in their involvement with the constitution. The essential difference is captured in this US assessment of Harold Burson's 1987 speech:

> The creation of the most important document in our nation's history, the constitution, also owes much to public relations. Federalists, who supported the constitution, fought tooth and nail with anti-federalists, who opposed it. Their battle was waged in newspaper articles, pamphlets, and other organs of persuasion in an attempt to influence public opinion. . . . Fittingly, the first of those amendments safeguarded, among other things, the practice of public relations: "Congress shall make no law respecting the establishment of religion or prohibiting the free exercise thereof; or bridging the freedom of speech, or of the press, or the rights of the people peaceably to assemble, and

to petition the government for a redress of grievances." ... In other words people were given the right to speak up for what they believed in and the freedom to try to influence the opinions of others. Thus was the practice of public relations ratified.

(Seitel, 2001, p. 27)

Israeli public relations practitioners were not so well served by their forerunners and leaders. Whereas the American founding fathers and communicators put individual freedoms at the top of their national agenda, the Zionist revolutionaries had unity and consensus at the top. Discourses, myths, and narratives developed to further the Zionist campaign continue to be maintained by later professional communicators and public relations practitioners. The next chapter describes the political and media environment in which these practitioners functioned.

5 Shaping factors
The political and media environment

In embedding the analysis of Israeli public relations in the specific changing political, economic, and media environment of Israel, this chapter follows Sriramesh and Verčič's (2009) call "to make a linkage between environmental variables and the profession" (p. 3). They specifically mention the nation's political system, its level of economic development, and its culture and media development as part of the "infrastructure" (p. 4) as key for understanding public relations in an international context. Since other "infrastructural ingredients" are addressed elsewhere in the book, this chapter's focus is on the Israeli socio-political environment, the media, and the relationship between them.

The political environment: Israeli democracy

Israel's emphasis on an ethnic national identity rather than a civil one has generated controversies since the founding of the nation. Although Israel has been called the only democracy in the Middle East, the democratic principle of separation between the state and religion has not been achieved and Israel does not have a constitution to protect civil rights. Even in the pre-state period of the 1920s, Israel's democracy was based on a multi-party system and free representative elections, but "during that time, as well as in the early years of statehood, [it] was a formal rather than a liberal democracy, the kind that emphasizes elections and majority rather than the rights of individuals and minorities" (Peri, 2004, p. 73).

The terms "democracy" and "pluralism" by themselves are not sufficient variables for evaluating the system. They may mean different things to different people. The transitions within a democratic system over time may have significant influence on the practice of public relations. Accordingly, we identify major changes that explain different roles public relations played in different periods and environments.

Statehood [Mamlachtiut] and securitism [Bithonism]

The transformation from half-state to state in 1948 changed the nature of the socio-political environment. The government took over all the functions that were performed in the Yishuv period by voluntary institutions. The government of Israel became the sovereign centralized political power with an Arab minority who were promised equal rights. Elon (1983) described the shift from centuries of statelessness to the realities of statehood as the birth of the "cult of 'the state'" (p. 293), with Ben-Gurion (Israel's prime minister from 1948 to 1963) as "its high priest" (p. 293).

For Elon (1983), the cult was best expressed in the postulate of Mamlachtiut – approximately, "stateism" (p. 293): "Mamlachtiut is a modern Hebrew coinage, and stands for a particular matter-of-fact attitude to public affairs . . . [that] calls for the state to be the chief regulator curtailing, even substituting for, the free play of semi-autonomous social and political bodies" (pp. 293–294). Mamlachtiut expresses the centrality of national unity, responsibility and obedience, and unlimited loyalty to the state and its institutions. Aspects of Mamlachtiut included the determination to "design" a new Jewish personality – the Hebrew Israeli with a new Israeli culture – and to deny the Jewish Diaspora culture. Ben-Gurion referred to Jews in the Diaspora as "human debris" (see Abadi, 1993, p. 42), and his immigrant integration policy followed the concept of the "melting pot." This was a drive for commonality that tried to erase the many cultures and different Jewish traditions brought by new immigrants. The Hebrew language became one such unifying force at the price of suppressing the original languages of the immigrants.

Mamlachtiut stateism did not allow pluralism. The educational system changed, and several different political educational movements were unified into the state system. For Ben-Gurion's government, the state was the tool to achieve the implementation of Jewish Zionist values. The government did not recognize the concept of a "service state" that should guarantee the safety, freedoms, and welfare of all its citizens.

Bithonism [Securitism]

Ben-Gurion's government also influenced the status of Israeli public opinion during the 1950s and 1960s with a concept called "Bithonism" [Securitism]. The term was actually used by radical opposition from the left's Uri Avneri, who criticized Ben-Gurion's use of violence towards the Palestinians without using opportunities to communicate and negotiate with them. "Bithonism" described the school of mind that related to every issue in term of its contribution to the state's security. It gained very wide support from Israeli public opinion, which was influenced by the government and army messages, as much as by the rhetoric and threatening activities of the neighbouring Arab countries' leaders. In assessing government communication materials on security and the conflict that were provided to the Israeli public, Bar-On (1999) concluded that "the Israeli hegemonic elite had long-reaching influence on public opinion and on designing the worldviews that were widespread among the Israeli public" (p. 102) [ATH]. In addition, the long dominance of Ben-Gurion with his "Hasbara activity, as well as the prominence of security people such as . . . Yigal Alon, and Shimon Peres, and the support they have received from the media . . . had a lot of influence and shaped much of the public opinion" (p. 102) [ATH].

Mamlachtiut and Bithonism did not consult public opinion. Politicians and military leaders acted as "arrogant power elites who believe more in 'educating' the people than in 'serving' it" (Elon, 1983, p. 296). This continued Ben-Gurion's concept of the media as expressed in his article in *The Unity* [Ha-ahdut]:

> [W]e need to conduct non-stop propaganda for organizing the communities on popular foundations and on their unity, to clarify and explain to the mass people and to the workers their political and public affairs. . . . Most of the Hebrew Yishuv in Eretz Israel is not involved in the political life and does not understand its political interests.
>
> (cited in Tzur, 2008, p. 323) [ATH]

In also continuing the Jewish experience in the Diaspora, the missionary state kept preaching "unity" rather than freedoms: "'Unity' is another Shibboleth of new nations, especially embattled ones. In Israel, the governed and their governors repeatedly evoke the overriding need for unity and promoted less the concept of pluralism. 'Factionalism' is condemned" (Elon, 1983, p. 294).

Political transformation after the wars

Describing the events that followed the Six Day War of 1967 as a "wild euphoria" (p. 3), R. Cohen (2009) summarized the results succinctly: "Israel had defeated the armies of Egypt, Syria, and Jordan, conquering the Sinai Desert, the Golan Heights, the West Bank of the Jordan River, and East Jerusalem" (p. 3). Israel had gained control over Arab territories that were three times bigger than its size before the war. The new reality opened bitter discussions about Israel's control over the occupied territories and the Arab population living in it as well as about the future of the Israeli–Arab conflict. The national religious camp started a movement of settling in the territories obtained in 1967 and became more prominent on the political scene.

Major change came following the military failure in the 1973 Yom Kippur War. The Labor Party was criticized and lost public trust. In 1977, for the first time since the establishment of the state, a right-wing coalition won the elections and formed a government, ending almost 30 years of Mapai (a left-wing forerunner of the Labor Party) and Labor dominance. The new government's ideology supported the idea of Israel's control over the occupied territories, showed more respect to the religious sectors, and promoted a liberal economy. In spite of its activist agenda, this government signed a peace agreement and returned the occupied Sinai land to Egypt.

Peri (2004) identified key changes in Israel's socio-political environment following these shift to the right and the erosion of the political centre. He analyzed "Israeli democracy's legitimacy crisis" (p. 52) as consisting of two processes. The first was the reduction in the level of its state power as part of a global trend identified by Habermas (1976) in *Legitimation Crisis*, in which the government lost its exclusive dominance over the public sphere. The second was the "colonial situation," which "increased the size and influence of significant groups in the population who lack deep democratic convictions" (p. 55), so that the "internal division over the future of the occupied territories . . . [was] also a cultural battle over what writers call the soul of Israeli society and sociologists define as its collective identity" (p. 55).

As part of the political revolution, Peri (2004) noted the decline of the "party state" and how the defeat of the Labor Party signified "the collapse of the old party structure, based on one dominant party and its replacement by a new competitive, bipolar structure, also described as polarized pluralism" (p. 60). The most significant change was the introduction of internal primaries for the parties' candidates to the Knesset in 1992–1993. Until that time, candidates were nominated by internal party committees and did not depend much on public opinion. The new parties' primaries did not improve the democratic system and failed to give equal opportunities or produce the best lists of candidates, but it did elevate the status of public opinion in Israel and helped establish the need to communicate and consult with constituents.

Media control and the process of change: the press

As Sriramesh and Verčič (2003b) observe, "there is near unanimity among authors of public relations literature that the media and public relations have a symbiotic, sometimes contentious, relationship" (p. 11). Media relations is the major professional tool for obtaining publicity and managing an organization's reputation and public image. It includes proactive initiatives, such as distributing news releases, coordinating media stories, organizing news events, and facilitating journalists' and bloggers' coverage of the organization, as well as reactive activities, such as responding to media queries about the organization. Issues management and crisis management have become specialist areas of public relations in helping organizations to be prepared and to manage media relations under the pressure of crisis situations. In this area too, practitioners provide a significant portion of the news content of mass media and there is a co-dependency between journalists and practitioners. These relationships are shaped by the social and media environment.

Historically, the Jewish press became a central factor in the life of the Diaspora Jewish community from the mid-17th century and later in Europe and the United States. For Kouts (1998a), the Jewish newspapers put Jewish solidarity ahead of other factors, "waged international campaigns in support of Jewish causes" (p. 100), and stimulated "the physical attachment and solidarity among the world's Jews" (p. 100). The Jewish Diaspora press managed the Jewish public discourse in a transnational sphere where Jews could not share the same territory and had contradictory commitments both to the Jewish people and to the country that hosted them. The press, which equates to Raupp's (2004) third level of the public sphere (namely, the "largest public" arena, with the synagogue equating to her second level or arena, i.e. "public meetings . . . [and] such forms as the traditional speech given in the market place or at modern political rallies" (p. 311)), contributed to the Jewish community's public sphere. The press, however, was committed, from its inception, to support the survival of the Jewish people more than to the free flow of information and the truth.

Freedom of expression and the free flow of information are vital for the development of public relations. By evaluating the media system and its interrelationship with the political system, we draw conclusions about the role of public relations in society. When media are owned and censored by the government, the role of communicators is limited and focuses on the delivery of the government's propaganda. But private ownership does not automatically mean freedom of the press. Private owners have their own interests and might use their media to promote them. Freedom of information is a political issue concerned with the legal protection of the communicators, but it involves a country's culture, its public discourse, its media ownership, and its people's expectations of media.

According to Caspi (2006), the founders of the new state understood that in order to achieve international legitimization, they "had to compromise between the authoritative traditions of the Yishuv and the new democratic norms" (p. 246), and "they faced the contradiction between their wish to shape the media institution with maximum rights for freedom of information and freedom of expression and the practical need of government that had to go on supervizing and controlling the media" (p. 246) [ATH].

The four stages of the Israeli media: Acts one and two

Caspi (2006) identified four stages, or "acts," in the Israeli media plot. These were influenced by changes in other national institutions and the communication technology: the pre-state Yishuv period; the "transition period" (1948–1967); the "controlled pluralism" period (1967 to the mid-1980s); and the "open sky" period from the mid-1980s onwards (pp. 241–281) [ATH].

In the *first act*, during the pre-state Yishuv period, the press was owned by political parties and was "the mouthpiece in a double struggle: within the Yishuv [the Jewish settlers] and [as a link] with the external environment, mainly the British Mandate" (p. 248) [ATH]. It included more opinion articles than newsworthy information, discussed Zionist issues, and promoted the use of the Hebrew language.

Caspi (2006) explains the value context of this period as typical of any community in a situation of struggle for existence in which the media is enlisted by its own will for the national cause. "Publicity was considered an essential tool for mobilization, for distribution of values and opinions, and for activating the masses" (p. 252) [ATH]. All kinds of informal arrangement between politicians and the media, including acts of self-censorship by editors, assured effective control over press content, and the media did not confront the political establishment.

Radio can be a key tool for nation building. Radio listeners feel more connected to the collective through their participation in shared broadcasts, and "Israel lacked a tradition of national rituals" (Sofer, 2011, p. 162) [ATH]. In response, the Yishuv leaders used radio to help build the Hebrew nation and to consolidate its culture even under the censorship of the British Mandate. Underground Jewish broadcasts started in 1945 as part of the struggle against the British and were linked to the political leadership.

In the *second act*, which according to Caspi (2006) covered the first two decades of the state, the press continued to function as an effective tool for political influence, and public broadcasts continued to provide "information and Hasbara" (p. 254) [ATH]. The challenges of nation building, the security situation, and the traditional public discourse legitimized government intervention, ownership, and control over media channels. The mass immigration presented another challenge for the leadership, and the media were considered an effective tool for educating the new migrants and for conveying to them the new state's "basic values and cultural symbols" (p. 255) [ATH].

In 1948 the broadcasting facilities were nationalized by the new state and became part of the Division of Press, Hasbara, Broadcasts, and Films within the Ministry of the Interior. Later, they moved to the Prime Minister's Office. Zvi Zinder, director of Kol Israel [Israel Voice, the one radio station] from 1955 to 1960, stated that the "people who implemented the government intervention policy and gave the dictates and instructions were Teddy Kollek, the Director of the Prime Minister's Office, and Yitzhak Navon, David Ben-Gurion's secretary" (cited in Caspi & Limor, 1998, p. 97) [ATH]. Zinder, in a characteristic blurring of professional roles, became the first president of the Israeli Public Relations Association in 1964.

The radio provided a daily routine to the growing migrant society of the new State of Israel. The Israeli political leadership used the radio as a political tool and controlled its content, following the British example in adopting the public broadcasting model rather than the commercial model. The exclusivity of the single channel enabled wide reach to almost all the population with messages that served the dominant party. Access to other parties was limited.

Mann (2011) researched the Knesset's records and letters of listeners to the radio channel Kol Israel during the 1950s. He discovered many complaints about the fact that "the radio was the estate of Ben-Gurion and Mapai, and other voices had no chance to have a say." Listeners complained about the overload of official speeches and ministers who spoke to the microphone to explain their policies but were not available for interviews.

The four stages of the Israeli media: Acts three and four

Towards the end of this second stage, a new concept started to influence the role of the media: the concept of "social responsibility," according to which the political leadership could rely on the media to behave responsibly during periods of crisis without limiting it by legal power. A slow transition towards media that were less dependent on politicians started with self-regulation by the journalists' associations and their codes of ethics.

Caspi's (2006) *third act* of the Israeli media started with the dramatic event of the 1967 war, which resulted with Israel's annexation of Palestinian lands on the West Bank of the Jordan River and in the Gaza Strip. But the more significant event was the Yom Kippur War of 1973, which was considered by Israelis as a "debacle." The media were blamed for hiding essential information from the public and not carrying out their job. The soul-searching following this failure empowered journalists to take a more confrontational stance towards the political and military leadership. However, according to Caspi (2006), the journalists "rebuilt the special arrangements with politicians not long after" (p. 263) [ATH].

The broadcasting media went through a very slow change process. It was not until 1965 that the Knesset established a public Broadcasting Authority inspired by the structure of the BBC, and not until 1969 did the government finally allow the first television channel. Ben-Gurion and his government objected to the introduction of television broadcasts for many years because they considered them "anti-educational," "low culture," and because they were afraid of imported international content. Sofer (2011) commented that it would be a natural expectation for "young Israel to adopt eagerly television as a nation-building tool and for the sake of a modernization process for its population" (p. 225) [ATH] but notes that it did not happen and argues that the "debate around television demonstrates the vulnerability of the new Hebrew culture. It proves its tendency towards self-isolation and its fear from imported cultural content to the young Israeli sphere" (p. 225).

Eventually, the decision to allow television broadcasts resulted from the aftermath of the 1967 war, with the sudden inclusion of the Arab population under Israel's responsibility. The government took a political decision and allowed television broadcasts as part of the "hasbara or propaganda towards the Palestinians in the occupied territories and the Arab countries" (Sofer, 2011, p. 225).

Television became a central factor in the Israeli public sphere, with very high viewer exposure and daily political involvement in the content. Nomination to management and editorial roles depended, and still depends in the case of the first public channel, on journalists' cooperation and compliance with the system. For 24 years (1969–1993),the Israelis were exposed to only one, government-controlled, television channel. Not surprisingly, the introduction of commercials to Israeli broadcasts was also a matter of controversy as the government feared messages it would not be able to control.

Eventually, commercials were broadcast on Israeli radio (not the popular army radio station) in 1960, but on Israeli television not until the 1990s. The press owners commissioned research that was led by Dr Judy Elizur (1976). The resulting report concluded that commercials would increase the level of consumption: "In 1976 there are still many Israeli families who don't have a private car, Hoover, kitchen mixer, or air-conditioner. They would become 'first-time' shoppers and not just shift preferences the way an American consumer uses commercials" (Elizur, 1976, p. 6) [ATH]. It went on to recommend against commercials because such shopping would mean an "increase in the standard of living" (p. 6) and contradict "the current national policy" (p. 6) [ATH]. The new era of commercial television broadcasts was enabled eventually in 1993 following the establishment of a Second Authority for Radio and Television which is supervized by the state controller.

In 1977 a right-wing government was elected for the first time, and the political control over the government broadcasting authority was renewed and intensified, even though this government promoted liberalization of the market.

The *fourth act* in the development of the Israeli media is referred to by Caspi (2006) as the "open skies" period and is characterized by "the intense reorganization of broadcasting channels, the deepening of seeming pluralism in the print media, and the strengthening of media corporations and cross-ownership" (p. 264) [ATH]. The private press developed from small informative newspapers in the pre-state and first decade era into entertainment corporations managing many economic projects from the 1980s onwards. Most of the party papers closed down in the 1980s and new local, privately owned newspapers appeared on the media scene.

Pressure to open more broadcasting channels was growing from the mid-1980s following demands from private investors and advertisers, who needed more outlets for their marketing efforts. At the beginning of the 1990s, two new television channels, regional radio stations, and about 40 cable television channels were added to the limited communication services provided to the Israeli consumer earlier. The decision makers believed in neo-liberal principles and enabled a shift from "service orientation, to which the founders of the state were committed, to economic orientation: Media was perceived as a market sector, in which investors seek maximum revenues and not services to consumers" (Caspi, 2006, p. 269) [ATH]. The broadcasting services became open to competition between multiple channels.

The competitive market environment, including the competition between more media channels, provided the infrastructure for the growth in public relations and communication services. As we will demonstrate in later chapters, national institutions and commercial companies needed advice and professional guidance in their communication with stakeholders via the complex media environment, and this need was filled by professional public relations practitioners.

The significant shift to a multi-channel competitive and commercial media environment happened only at the end of the 1980s, and mainly during the 1990s, when a second television channel and cable television broke the monopoly of the Broadcasting Authority. The print media became major partners in the new commercial channels, resulting in monopoly and cross-ownership issues that have challenged the democratic nature of Israeli broadcasting media ever since.

Minority reports and Israeli journalists

Since the establishment of the state, according to Sofer (2011) – who cites supporting evidence from studies of minority media, covert media, and media consumption by national minorities – only two newspapers in Arabic serving the Palestinian citizens of Israel have been published in Israel. These newspapers were published by the Jewish establishment, the government, or the Histadrut. This practice follows the familiar communication policy of influencing the minority to accept the rule of the majority. Only in the 1980s did Arab political parties start to publish political, and later religious and commercial, newspapers. Avraham's (2001) research, summarized from Sofer (2011, pp. 104–107), found that most of the Hebrew newspapers devoted only marginal space to coverage of the Arab citizens of Israel and presented them in a negative way, except *Haaretz*, which consistently called for integration of the Arab minority and gave voice to the Arab protest against discrimination.

In 1948 two-thirds of Israeli journalists were employed by party newspapers but most of the party papers closed in the 1980s (Meyers, 2005, cited in Sofer, 2011, p. 74). Israeli media scholars describe the commitment of Israeli journalists to the Zionist ideology and leaders as a major characteristic of their professional values, mainly in the first two decades of the state. Critics explain the deviation of Israeli journalists from the democratic concept of journalism and their bias towards the Zionist narrative as a result of the nation-building challenges (see Sofer, 2011). In the first two decades of the state, most Israeli journalists did not see their role as that of guardians of the public's rights and did not give voice to criticism of the Israeli political and military establishment.

Following the "debacle" of the Yom Kippur War, Peri (2004) describes a rather different relationship whereby the media were allowed a broader scope for criticism but accepted, willingly, many restrictions, known as the "collateral model" (p. 85), in which

> the main idea is the compatibility of goals between the politicians and media professionals. The media do not act primarily as antagonists of politics, as a watchdog, or fourth estate. . . . They still maintain a reverent approach to political institutions, reveal more commitment to the interests of the national leadership than to those of the general public, and are prepared to respond to its demands and allow it to set their media frames.
>
> (p. 85)

Vaadat Haorhim [the Editors' Committee] also illustrates the role of the journalists in Israel's society and their self-censorship. The initiative for the establishment of this unique Israeli entity came from the newspapers' editors themselves during the British Mandate. They were seeking guidance from the political leadership and agreed to avoid publicizing information provided for them in closed meetings. This deal prevented the publication of important data and information about military operations, immigration numbers, and other sensitive issues. The editors willingly accepted the political and military censorship and cultivated a harmonious relationship with the political system. Gradually the deal came to include not only the government ministries but also other institutions, such as the Jewish Agency and the Hebrew University, and the committee was manipulated not just to conceal information but also "to create a convenient public climate for future political decisions, via editorial articles and commentary. The success of the political system in using the committee for this purpose turns the editors into, actually, Masbirim [Hasbara professionals] on behalf [of the authorities]" (Caspi & Limor, 1992, p. 180) [ATH].

A third model of relationship between journalists and the political system emerged during the 1990s as part of the transformation. It was also influenced by an international trend in the profession of journalism. Peri (2004) describes the change into "mediapolitik" or "media-centered politics" (p. 297) as characterized by the centrality of the media in policy making and by competitive, rather than adversarial relationships between journalists and politicians. In the competitive model, journalists challenge politicians and undermine their authority. The media acquire status equal to that of politicians in the new media-centred politics, and journalists change their professional self-image. They understand their role in democracy as independent from that of the establishment and so able to attack it.

The new media politics involves public relations practitioners as essential players. In addition to journalists and politicians, Peri (2004) identifies a third influential group in the political system as "the media experts and the specialists in persuasive communication. These are the experts in marketing and voter research techniques, message development, advertising, image building, speechwriters, pollsters, and particularly political strategists and consultants whose expertise lies in media manipulation" (p. 103).

The professionalization of political marketing was influenced by American experts who were employed by Israeli political candidates at the end of the century. Press conferences replaced the traditional election rallies; candidate campaign tours were designed for the media, not for the public. In the 1999 campaigns, Peri (2004) observed "for the first time the full range of political professions" (p. 131), where, as well as "the political advisers, there were copywriters, public relations experts, publicity experts for both television and newspapers, specialists in timing and positioning of advertisements, spin doctors, sound-bite writers, experts in various kinds of polls and focus groups, and other professionals in political marketing" (p. 131).

The Israeli political and media scenery has changed, and as long as "the pendulum of professional awareness has swung away from the advocacy model and is still moving toward the market model, journalists are still intoxicated by a false sense of freedom" (Peri, 2004, p. 314). At the beginning of the 21st century, the Israeli media are multi-channelled, much more competitive, and less dependent on politicians than ever before. However, they do not play their role as the providers of truth and fairness in informing participants in the democratic process (Peri, 2004). Journalists are caught in the political power of mediapolitik with all its populism and negative implications.

As of 2012, the Israeli government still controls some of the broadcasting channels and tries to limit freedom of expression. However, much of the political pressure has been replaced by pressure from local media moguls who own several broadcasting channels as well as newspapers and online news services. Commercial interests have added to the pressures on journalists. Their status and incomes have been eroded dramatically – except in the case of a few "stars" – as the owners now employ fewer journalists and do not allow time and talent for investigation and research. "Cross-ownership" and the commercial interests of the media's private owners are major current challenges for democratic open communication, both internationally and in Israel. Uzi Benziman (2011), editor of the online weekly *The Seventh Eye*, has said that "journalists, editors, and broadcasters, whose upright position and internal integrity are supposed to be the heart and the lungs of professional conduct, act today with an unprecedented sense of vulnerability. . . . Their self-perception is that of someone under warning."

The media law analyst Moshe Negbi (2011) also identifies the interests of media owners as the new challenge for freedom of press in Israel. The Reporters without Borders' Freedom of the Press 2011 index ranks Israel at 61 out of 191 countries. Negbi (2011), however, believes that the indifference and alienation of most of the journalists and media channels towards the existence of freedom of the press are playing a major role in its deteriorating state. He blames Israeli journalists for not fighting against legal initiatives that harm the freedom of the press (p. 275) [ATH] and argues that the cooperation of most of the media now results less from innocence and patriotism and more from commercial interests, since any media that will criticize "the army or the Shabak [Intelligence Services] and that will publish reports on their injustice and failures might chase away the readers or viewers, and mainly the advertisers, because such criticism is irritating the audience and spoils their peace of mind" (p. 274) [ATH].

Commercial pressures are augmented by the legal action that the government – and especially the military authorities – use to limit journalists' access to sources of information. The Anat Kamm–Uri Blau affair (http://en.wikipedia.org/wiki/Anat_Kamm-Uri_Blau_affair), in which the *Haaretz* journalist Uri Blau was sentenced for publishing classified documents leaked by the former Israeli soldier Anat Kamm (who was jailed for it), demonstrates the limitations for freedom of the press. Negbi (2011) relates to this case in describing the legal state of the profession:

> In the Israel of the new millennium, when an investigative reporter is publishing, with permission from the military censorship, a report that throws suspicion on criminal activities by the military elite, the elite is able to activate the Shabak to find out the sources that provided information to the reporter and thus neutralize his or her ability to function and terrify his or her colleagues.
>
> (p. 272) [ATH]

The concern for Israel's democracy results particularly from the fact that Israeli journalists did not fight against the secret arrest and did not stand by the persecuted journalist even though the Journalists' Association's Code of Ethics includes an item about the privilege of keeping sources confidential. Only one Member of the Knesset, Dr Nachman Shai, initiated legislation to limit the military authority's ability to use secret arrests (Negbi, 2011, p. 273).

Online media

The emergence of the internet as a new communication format was not met by the same suspicious attitude that the Israeli government had towards the introduction of television, even though both media are perceived as global and contain non-Israeli cultural values. Actually, Israel was among early adopters of the internet: it was the third country in the world after the United States and the United Kingdom to receive a state code, (il), in 1985. The level of penetration of the internet into Israel is high compare to that in other countries, according to several monitors' reports.

According to *Globes* (online), an Israel business news platform, on June 24, 2010, Israelis are the second most active internet users in the world, after the Canadians. This statement is based on a comScore survey of internet usage. The average time spent online per Israeli user in May 2010 was 38.3 hours per month, compared with 40.4 hours in Canada. The United States is ranked third, followed by the United Kingdom. Average time online by Israelis is 60% greater than the worldwide average of 24 hours per user.

> "Israel is one of the most active and dynamic Internet markets in the world," said comScore SVP Mike Read. "Israelis are particularly sophisticated, tech-savvy consumers who spend considerably more time online than average, while Israel is also known for its spirit of innovation and entrepreneurship, especially in technology and digital media industries. Though relatively small in size, Israel has contributed disproportionately to the development of the current global digital landscape."
>
> (Parag, 2010)

According to Sofer (2011), the Israeli government supported the adoption of the new communication technology from its beginning and allowed academic and research institutions to open sites in the early 1990s (p. 312). The public sphere of the 1990s was much more open compared with the first two decades of the state, in which the government refused television broadcasts. Eventually, during the 24 years of one-channel TV monopoly, and even in the current multi-channel environment, television came to contribute significantly to social solidarity and national unity. If there were any fears around the internet's influence on national cohesion owing to its global openness and interactivity, they were put to one side.

According to Sofer (2011), "the internet has not undermined the local-national concepts for the sake of global values. It is obvious that the Israeli sites are embedded in the local experience, and this is on the basis not only of their content but also of their language" (p. 321) [ATH]. He concludes: "In relation to influence on the Israeli socio-political agenda, the political discourse in the internet has not yet acquired an equal position to that managed by the traditional media" (p. 340) [ATH]. In other words, the internet is seen as a complementary source of information, not the leading one.

Conclusion

In a climate in which the government controlled most media activities, and the media obediently served the government and "the establishment," the need for public relations professional services to deal with the media did not develop. As will be seen in the following chapters, professional Masbirim [Hasbara] were employed only for promotional and educational tasks, and then mostly by national institutions. These institutions needed professional communication expertise in order to enhance the consensus about Zionist goals and to educate and create a new Israeli culture. The challenge of representing organizations in confrontation with the media, which was the major motivation for the development of public relations as a profession in the United States, did not exist in Israel till the 1980s.

The transformations in the Israeli political system, economy, and media during the 1980s and 1990s opened a door of opportunity for public relations professionals, and they went through that door. The boom in Israel's public relations services (see Chapter 11) results from the socio-political and media revolution described in this chapter. In the next chapter, we track continuity and change through the vital role played by public relations practitioners serving major Zionist institutions and how some of their major campaigns shaped Israeli public opinion.

6 Early Zionist institutions and communication practitioners

During the pre-state "Organised Yishuv" period (1917–1948), propaganda became a declared goal that was high on the agenda of the first official Zionist institutions in Palestine. This chapter describes this unique environment and analyzes the work of two official departments called "Propaganda [Ta'amula] and Explanation [Hasbara]" and "Public Relations/Public Connections" [Yachsei Zibur/Kishrei Zibur], as well as looking at two other major Zionist institutions. The chapter illustrates how the weakness of the pre-state political system, and its inability to impose laws, led to a dependency on public opinion and voluntarism. Propaganda and Hasbara services were essential for achieving the goals of the newly formed national institutions. These services helped to enlist the people's support, and resources, for the cause, for the movement, and, over time, for the survival of the organizations themselves.

To understand how this situation came about, some preliminary background is necessary. The British conquest of Palestine in World War I ended 400 years of Ottoman rule. On November 2, 1917, the Zionist revolution achieved its first political objective when the British government issued the Balfour Declaration, pledging support for the establishment of a Jewish national home in Palestine. In 1922 the League of Nations granted Britain a mandate over Palestine, creating a unique socio-political system that contained two national movements ruled by a British High Commissioner. Jews constituted 11% of Palestine's population in 1922, and by the end of the Mandate, following massive immigration waves from Europe, they made up 33% of the population (Horowitz & Lissak, 1978, p. 19). Under the British Mandate, the Zionist movement, led by the World Zionist Organization (WZO) since 1897, and its Jerusalem office (established in 1903), could start fulfilling the Zionist dream.

Important institutions which functioned in a quasi-state system were established to provide services to the small Yishuv and generated their legitimacy and authority from being recognized by the British rulers. Horowitz and Lissak (1978) explain that these quasi-state organizations lacked the sovereign authority to impose taxes, to build industry, and to recruit soldiers to fight against the Nazis. As a result, the "national institutions" had to persuade members of the Jewish community to volunteer for all the basic functions necessary for the survival and the development of the community. The Yishuv period, therefore, is characterized by a high level of persuasive communication and enlisted voluntarism. Accordingly, but for different reasons, and in different ways, public relations, in the sense of persuasive communication and "agitation propaganda" (Ellul, 1965, p. vi), featured as strongly as it had in the earlier Zionist movement.

This chapter looks specifically at the communication efforts of two major Zionist institutions that served the "ideological consensus" (Horowitz & Lissak, 1978, p. 14): the Jewish National Fund (JNF) [Keren Kayemet le'Israel] and the Jewish Agency (JA) [Hasochnut Hayehudit le'Eretz Israel]. The Jewish Agency was the unofficial "government" of the Yishuv, but chronologically the Jewish National Fund preceded the JA and was more active on the Hasbara front. Thus, we pay more attention to it.

The Jewish National Fund [Keren Kayemet le'Israel] and propaganda

The Jewish National Fund (JNF) was founded in 1901 by the World Zionist Organization for the purpose of purchasing land in Eretz Israel and developing it for Jewish settlements. Bar-Gal (1999) researched the work of the Propaganda, Press, and Youth Department of the JNF between 1924 and 1947 and published a book documenting and analyzing the work and influence of this department on Israel's culture. Bar-Gal's (1999) research reveals that the department also became the leader of the Zionist education and propaganda effort, and the creator of Israeli national holidays, unifying symbols, and myths that shaped "the collective memory and influenced the Hebrew culture in the most broad meaning of the word" (p. 11) [ATH].

Bar-Gal (1999) describes how the JNF's employees immigrated from Europe and were influenced by concepts and ideas that were popular there between the two world wars. For them, the term "propaganda" had positive connotations and they used it to describe the effort to persuade Jewish people to financially support the purchase of national land:

> The leaders of the JNF in general, and of its propaganda department in particular, did not distinguish between the terms "education," "propaganda," and "public relations," and this was due to the social concepts of those days – the time of the great ideologies . . . education and propaganda were perceived as two sides of the same coin . . . education and propaganda came to serve the same goals: to justify the existence and survival of the JNF in its socio-political environment.
>
> (Bar-Gal, 1999, p. 257) [ATH]

For the JNF propaganda personnel, the goal justified the means. Via their involvement in the education system, they persuaded the Zionist public that what was good for the JNF was good for the people: "They enveloped the Jewish children with images, involved them in weekly and annual ceremonies, and thus empowered the myths that were created at this time" (Bar-Gal, 1999, p. 13) [ATH].

Another source from which their propaganda might have drawn was the British Mandate itself. L'Etang (2004) traces the roots of British public relations and refers to the role of the Empire Marketing Board (EMB), which was established in 1926 to implement imperial preference through market research, supply chain management, and publicity (p. 35). The EMB's secretary, Sir Stephen Tallents, outlined its objectives as follows: "to support the British economy through the promotion of culture, technology, and science and an enhanced sense of national identity and core values" (cited in L'Etang, 2004, p. 37). It embraced documentary film as an important persuasive tool. Though Palestine was neither a part of the British Empire nor a colony, the British Mandate influenced the Yishuv. The Israeli legal system is still based on the British Mandate laws. In their contact with British officials, the JA, and the JNF propagandists, seem likely to have been inspired by the communication tactics, including the documentary films, used by the British.

The idea of using the new technology of visual propaganda in the film industry might have been inspired by other European countries, especially Germany. Bar-Gal (1999) notices possible links and influences:

> During the 1920s till the mid-1930s there was a symbiotic connection between the propaganda department in Jerusalem headed by Julius Berger and the centre of the JNF in Berlin headed by Adolf Folk. As we know, many propaganda innovations were created in those years in Berlin, from a theoretical point of view (mass persuasion) as well as from a technical point of view, such as print, photography, film and more. We cannot rule out the possibility of the influence of this exposure on the professional practitioners who were doing the propaganda work of the JNF.
>
> (p. 33) [ATH]

More specific influences were identified in Tryster's (1995) book *Israel before Israel: Silent Cinema in the Holy Land*, in which he describes discussions in the propaganda department headed by Julius Berger in 1924. Tryster (1995) tells of the department's two propaganda aims – "direct fundraising and general pro-Zionist influence" (p. 85) – and how they considered addressing "the aims separately by making two films: a 'soft' propaganda vehicle in the guise of documentary, and a feature film. Both Soviet films and those of the German right-wing parties were cited as models" (p. 85).

Signs of German influence can be found in the Hasbara bureau's correspondence in the Central Zionist Archives in Jerusalem. In response to an anonymous letter criticizing excessive JNF and Foundation Fund propaganda and advertising, Leo Harman, head of the Propaganda Department of the Foundation Fund, wrote in 1943:

> We have to admit that the Nazi propaganda reaffirmed an old principle, that propaganda can be effective only when it repeats [emphasis in the original] itself again and again. From this point of view we may say that the Foundation

Fund and the other institutions have not done enough propaganda till now. What we are saying and stressing is not very conspicuous, people can ignore it easily ... on the other hand it is true that there is exaggeration in the use of slogans and numbers. In the quality of our propaganda we need to remember that we pay a lot for disproportion.

(CZA, serial Alef, S23, file 199) [ATH] [NB. This and all subsequent Central Zionist Archives (CZA) documents were translated from Hebrew by lead author]

US influences and the propaganda department

The growing Jewish public relations industry in the United States was also influential. The Zionist institution offices there were in constant contact with the Israeli practitioners. The American Jewish institutions used in-house public relations services and professional Jewish PR agencies for fundraising and campaigns. They assisted European Jewry, they managed campaigns against the anti-Semitism of Henry Ford and the Ku Klux Klan in the 1920s, they organized social welfare services and assisted synagogues, they fought Nazism, and they assisted the establishment of the State of Israel: "All called between 1917–1948 for the unprecedented mobilization of Jewish public opinion as well as the winning of support from the general population" (Postal, 1997).

Nevertheless, American conceptions and their focus were distinctly different. They did not use the term "propaganda" or Hasbara. They concentrated on "bringing to the American public the nature of prejudice, the evils of anti-Semitism and bigotry, and the importance of understanding among men of all races and ethnic groups" (Postal, 1997). The agenda of nation building, which shaped efforts to influence public opinion in Eretz Israel, was not the same agenda for the American Jews. Techniques of public relations did cross the ocean but they did not bring the associated democratic tendencies with them, or, if they did, they failed to take root.

In September 1922 the headquarters of the JNF was moved from Europe to Jerusalem, and Menachem Ussishkin became the chairman of the board of directors. On September 18, 1924, the board decided to reorganize the JNF into four divisions: Land, Finance, Manpower, and Propaganda and Press. Julius Berger, who was responsible for the office of the Zionist newspaper *Die Welt*, was appointed head of the Propaganda Department, with Natan Bistritzki, M. Haezrachi, and F. Lain as assistants. In 1926, a Youth Department was established within the Propaganda Department, and Natan Bistritzki, a writer who immigrated to Palestine from Ukraine in 1920, became its director. Two years later, in 1928, Julius Berger resigned and was replaced by Natan Bistritzki and later by A. M. Epstein and M. Haezrachi, who ran the department during the 1930s.

Although he could have taken credit for a major role in the development of the propaganda department, Bistritzki's (1980) posthumously published personal memoir hardly mentions his JNF work. However, he does describe his JNF role as "innovating an educational activity for the sake of the redemption of the national land while keeping the routine propaganda work that was practiced and accepted in the institution till then" (p. 127). His memoir emphasizes excitedly, and in a very flowery and self-admiring style, his experiences as a travelling Zionist propagandist in Europe before 1920, as well as his writing, which was recognized by Zionist writers and scholars.

From its inception, the JNF was intended to be a national financial fundraising instrument, a popular institution for recruiting funds and souls from the mass public. A major part of the donations to the JNF came from very small contributions. When, in 1920, the WZO founded another fundraising tool, the Foundation Fund [Keren Hayesod], the JNF entered a power struggle for its survival within the Zionist movement. Bar-Gal (1999) describes survival needs as the major motivation for the propaganda activities of the JNF, and for its alliance with the education system, because that was an area that the Foundation Fund did not reach. In his time as chairman, Menachem Ussishkin added "national education" to the mission statement of the JNF as well as the traditional redemption of the national land. This aspect developed thanks to the fact that the JNF propaganda ideas were shared by many Hebrew educators. The Yishuv educators' mission included values such as: "physical work, love for the environment and land of Israel, service to the community, voluntarism, and defending the homeland" (Bar-Gal, 1999, p. 13) [ATH]. Eventually, the cooperation between the JNF Propaganda Department and the Teachers' Association led to one of the most influential systems in the history of Israel.

Methods and tactics

The propaganda activities reached the target audiences in their private and public sphere and the JNF employed a variety of creative methods and tactics (Shahar, 1994, p. 7) [ATH]:

- Methods for fundraising included the Blue Box (a small tin charity collection box); stamps on each official document; the "Golden Book" of big donors' names; and tree donation certificates.
- Printed materials such as books, newspapers, bulletins, newsletters, fliers, annual calendars, and posters. The most important publication for the internal public that connected the JNF board with the Zionist activists around the world was called "Karnenu" (Bar-Gal, 1999, p. 106) [ATH].
- Audio-visual resources such as films, records, slides.
- Personal contacts such as lectures, emissaries to Jewish communities abroad, volunteers, committees, conventions.
- Activities in schools and youth movements such as promoting Israeli folk songs by financing writers and musicians to create them, and by distributing songbooks [shironim] with the songs, words, and melodies; creating ceremony manuals for "new" national holidays – the planting of trees ceremony in Tu Beshvat and the Bikurim ceremony in Shavuot; and organizing parties for national holidays.

Bar-Gal's (1999) book describes four major propaganda methods in detail. The first was the Blue Box. This creative tool started as an instrument for collecting small donations of coins and developed into a national Zionist symbol, becoming a centre for cultural activities in schools and in public institutions. The collection of the coins gave an excuse for the JNF representatives, volunteers, and also paid employees to enter each Jewish home and engage in a conversation about the JNF. It gave the Zionist organization an opportunity to create lists of hundreds of thousands of JNF constituents: "In 1937, there were 700,000 Blue Boxes in private Jewish homes" (Kimmerling, 1973, p. 41) [ATH]. In economic terms the income from the Blue Box did not reach more than half a per cent of the Jewish capital that was raised for the Jewish community in Palestine between 1918 and 1938 (Bar-Gal, 1999, p. 68), but its value as a propaganda instrument was enormous. It became a symbol not only of the JNF but of the Zionist movement as a whole. It formed an integral part of the education system and a major element of the Friday and holiday ceremonies in individual classrooms.

The second propaganda method used stamps. The JNF designed and printed Zionist messages on stamps, which served for fundraising. This method was a common fundraiser for different causes in other places in the world, including the United States and Russia. The JNF stamps were small posters with political and social messages designed mainly for schoolchildren in Eretz Israel and Jewish communities elsewhere. Under Natan Bistritzki, the Propaganda Department produced activity books that turned the stamp collection into a game. The books were designed with maps and landscapes from Israel. The department used aggressive marketing tactics and imposed the stamps as a tax on Hebrew industry and Zionist institutions.

A third propaganda approach was through books, games, and toys. While these were produced by the JNF, they had nothing to do with fundraising but "were a propaganda and socialization tool" (Bar-Gal, 1999, p. 14) [ATH]. The department commissioned books for youth (Hasifria Lanoar), selected the subjects, and edited, and censored, the content of these books to serve the JNF's messages. Legends of the Arab world were excluded because they did not support the Jewish claim for the land (p. 124). The fourth propaganda method used films and other audio-visual media. The visual propaganda was produced by relatively simple and inexpensive means. Slides, short films, and magic lantern shows were accompanied by lectures to bring the landscapes of Israel to Diaspora Jews. Films became major tool of communication with world Jewry: "Zionist fundraising films were distributed throughout Europe and North America, with careful instructions as to when and how to appeal for and collect funds during the presentation" (Tryster, 1995, p. 80).

At a May 1929 meeting of the JNF and the Foundation Fund representatives, it was decided to negotiate with film companies about the inclusion of news items from Eretz Israel in their news bulletins. Interestingly, these can be seen as early versions of the current video news releases (VNRs) used by contemporary public relations practitioners. A new advertising agency owned by recent immigrants from Germany, Valish & Machner, produced short films of 30–40 slides every month for the JNF. They were then used in the visual news programme in the cinema, thanks to the cooperation of the film companies. During the 1930s, however, "the public became accustomed to feature films and it became too difficult to excite them with the JNF productions and messages" (Bar-Gal, 1999, p. 171) [ATH].

Another important visual tool used by the national institutions was photography. Ruth Oren (1997) researched the propaganda content of Zionist landscape photography between 1898 and 1948. She highlighted the connection between the photographic communication and the birth of a new Israeli nationality, as it was reflected in the images of the local landscapes. Oren's (1997) research found that during this period most of the photographs in brochures, albums, posters, etc. were produced by the two central financial funds of the Zionist movement: the JNF and the Foundation Fund, and the visual messages "constituted propaganda in the meaning of a repetitive monolithic message that was distributed by a central authoritative institution that was concerned in promoting itself and its status" (pp. 15–16) [ATH].

According to Oren (1997), the JNF Press Department in 1925 included a photography archive that commissioned photographs and distributed them, with captions written by Bistritzki, to Zionist institutions and the JNF committees around the world for further circulation and publicity. The delivery was regular – every two weeks – and was called the "photography service" (Oren, 1997, p. 20). Bar-Gal (1999) described how the Propaganda Department distributed news releases that "presented the achievements of the JNF in Israel and its different projects" (p. 106), and news bulletins in seven languages every week with attached series of photographs. The press office enlisted senior writers and journalists from world Jewry to write commissioned articles and reports for the department (summarized from Bar-Gal, 1999, p. 106).

Today, this technique of using articles commissioned from journalists would be considered a manipulative and non-ethical practice tending to corrupt journalists. Under contemporary codes of professional ethics, it would be seen as an attempt to control the way journalists reported about the organization. At the time, in the context of the propaganda effort, it was accepted as a common and legitimate tool. Once again, the emphasis was that the goal was much more important than the means by which it was achieved.

The JNF in the State of Israel

With the establishment of the State of Israel, JNF activity shifted from land purchase to land improvement as well as forestation. The government also charged the JNF with the administration of "abandoned land" (i.e. land left by previous Arab owners who fled Palestine during the war). The JNF sought to ensure that those lands, and others, were owned only by Jews. This was not a job that the democratic government of Israel could openly carry out.

The JNF derives its budget from contributions from world Jewry and operates in approximately 40 countries (Tzur, 1997). The JNF's most important projects were swamp draining in Huleh Valley in 1952–1958, forest plantations, and the preparation of desert land for agriculture work (Hattis Rolef, 1988, p. 250). The government welcomed contributions from world Jewry that financed land development in Israel.

In 1949, Natan Bistritzki was still involved in JNF propaganda and education. The minutes of a meeting held on January 2, 1949 quote him as saying, "Some say Propaganda, some say Hasbara, some say Education. The truth is that WZO has to, for the sake of preparation of hearts [*hachsharat halevavat*], use all these means – Propaganda, Hasbara, Education" (CZA serial no. A S41, file 45 102/25).

Two years before that meeting, Theodor Hatalgi joined the JNF propaganda department and started a 30-year career in the service of the JNF. As a journalist and a poet, Hatalgi (2002) had a background typical of people who became public relations practitioners then. Born in Poland but partly educated in France and Germany, he was a member of the Benei Akiva and Baitar Zionist youth movements, which built his commitment to Jewish nationalist ideology. While studying political science in Warsaw, he established a Zionist activist newspaper that protested against the British White Paper.

In 1945, liberated from a Nazi camp, he had to stay in Italy for two years, waiting for a permit to immigrate to Israel. In Italy, he started his public relations career by writing articles about the assistance to refugees in Italy provided by the American Jewish Joint Distribution Committee (known simply as the Joint) for the Joint's publications department in New York. In December 1947, already in Israel, he started to work for the JNF as an editor on the JNF's internal magazine, and took charge of media relations. At the beginning of 1953 he was appointed head of the JNF's Hasbara Division, where, as he recalled in a perfectly clear style, he "focused on field trips for journalists, and for people with influence on public opinion, in Israel and internationally" (Hatalgi, 2002) and invited foreign reporters who were stationed in Israel, or were visiting the country, "as our guests to participate in a two day tour [including hotel] to see with their own eyes how the JNF is developing the land. I had assistants who translated my releases and publications into English, French, German and Yiddish" (Hatalgi, 2002).

As his account illustrates, Hatalgi's (2002) tactics focused on media relations, especially with the foreign press, although the local Israeli press seemed to pose a greater challenge: "Our major problem arose with the Israeli press questioning of the survival of the JNF after the establishment of the state." He went on to comment that journalists

> became cynical and tough to work with. Arieh Geldblum [at the time a *Haaretz* reporter and later a public relations practitioner himself] published a famous article making fun of the JNF in the U.S. Then we had a problem with the comedy *Salach Shabati* by Ephraim Kishon – a feuilleton and a movie that showed how the JNF representatives were lying to donors, offering the same forest section to different donors, and making promises they could not fulfil. It also presented as pathetic the work that JNF offered to new immigrants from Morocco in its forestry projects. Those were called "initiated works" [Avodot Yezumot], and were just an excuse to pay a salary instead of

welfare. The film gained huge success internationally. Geldblum's article and *Salach Shabati* had an influence and they hurt the JNF image.

(Hatalgi, 2002)

Despite this, Hatalgi (2002) claimed that he never tried to stop negative publicity, and his journalistic experience contrasted with previous JNF expectations: "My strategy towards negative publicity was just to intensify the positive publicity – more field trips and more stories about the good work the JNF was doing." He explained further: "The role of the JNF as the major employer of new immigrants in times of mass unemployment was usually accepted in a positive light, so we pushed this one." Hatalgi's contributions were appreciated, and he became part of the JNF dominant coalition as a member of the board.

In Hatalgi's work between 1947 and 1977, we can trace departures from the foundations laid by Natan Bistritzki in the pre-state Hasbara department. Hatalgi did not emphasize the combination of Hasbara with education as a major strategy and, strikingly, he did not expect journalists to take orders from the organization. His Hasbara services were professional in a more contemporary public relations sense: he was looking for good newsworthy materials to present the organization's case. Although he had no reservations about the ethical aspect of taking journalists on field trips and hosting them, he had respect for journalistic freedom. His press relations principles, however, did not go as far as the inclusion of a commitment to truth and honesty. Instead, his commitment to what he saw as the best interests of the JNF and the State of Israel came first. With great openness, he exposed an important cover-up story that he was responsible for in the decade following the 1967 Six Day War:

> Officially the JNF is not allowed to purchase land behind the Green Line. De facto, the JNF purchased land from Arab Palestinians in the occupied territories via a subcontractor by the name of "Himnuta." The JNF also developed that land as a subcontractor of the Israeli government. We had to be very careful with the Hasbara communications and with the JNF's friends abroad. Any exposure of the JNF's involvement in the occupied territories could destroy the financial foundations of the JNF in those countries because the donors would lose the tax exemption. In our Hasbara abroad, we did not say explicitly that the JNF was developing land in Gush Etzion, for example, but we would say, "The JNF is paving roads by government commission." Eventually the story about "Himnuta" was published but it was quite modest and did not cause much harm. The publicity did not come from us, of course.
>
> (Hatalgi, 2002)

With commendable candour, Hatalgi (2002) describes a very misleading communication for which he was responsible in serving his organization. He did not regret it and did not feel bad about it: "I totally identified with my job. It gratified me immensely. I took part in the fulfilment of Zionism."

Third- and fourth-generation practitioners and post-state challenges

One of Hatalgi's assistants, Yechiel Amitai, joined the department in the early 1950s and served first as a mobile reporter preparing recorded stories to be broadcast on Kol Israel (the radio). He reported also to the printed press, covering the many field trips with VIPs to JNF sites. When Hatalgi was appointed head of the Hasbara Department, Amitai became spokesperson and responsible for the Public Relations Department.

When interviewed, Amitai (2002) took credit for initiating the deal between government spokespeople and Itim, the press agency that was established in 1950 by the daily press to serve all the newspapers (see Caspi & Limor, 1998, p. 67). Amitai's idea was to use the Itim service in order to deliver news releases to the press in an effective way. The institutions' and ministries' spokespeople paid Itim for the service. Itim actually offered just a technical solution for distributing the government news, but, in effect, "a news item delivered via Itim was perceived by the journalists more as a news item than as a spokesperson news release" (Amitai, 2002).

This typifies the confusion of journalism with public relations and propaganda that continued across generations in Israel. Itim claimed to use a special code that identified the source of the news item when it was provided and paid for by government spokespeople, but the editors did not always have the time to pay attention to this code. The service was deemed "effective" even though it may not have been ethical. Later, a similar deal was arranged with *Israel Sun*, the news photography agency.

While working for the JNF, and later for the Ministry of Transportation, Amitai managed a parallel career as a sports reporter that lasted over two decades. The State Service governor gave him special permission to continue with his dual career as a spokesperson and a journalist. Even though his major job was in public relations, Amitai (2002) never stopped his membership in the Journalists' Association, which helped him "to develop personal relationships with journalists who covered the JNF . . . we met at the journalists' club in Beth Agron for social schmoozing."

The challenge for the JNF propaganda machine became harder after the establishment of the state. After 1948 it had to persuade the Israeli public and its donors abroad that its continued existence remained essential. Doubts about this assumption grew stronger at the end of the 1990s, with the post-Zionist movement. The political leader Yossi Beilin (1999) was one of the JNF's "enemies," who was as critical of its post-state continuation as he was of the survival of the Jewish Agency:

> Actually, on the day the State of Israel was born, the JNF should have transferred to the government the list of its lands, announced that from now on it would be considered land of the State of Israel, dissolved itself as an institution and offered the good services and wonderful employees to the state

service for the management of the land, forestry plantations, etc. But this did not happen. The JNF's existence was convenient for the Israeli government for the sake of preventing the sale of land to Arabs and, after 1967, in order to purchase land in the West Bank (under a different hat).

(p. 164) [ATH]

Benny Mushkin, head of the JNF's Hasbara Department from 1989 to 1999 and secretary of the board from 1999 to 2005, confirmed that the criticism remains a major concern. But the JNF actually always knew how to add new goals and adapt itself to new demands in a way that would make it relevant and essential. As Mushkin (2002) explained, "Our effort was aimed at proving that the JNF was essential. It is an NGO that is dealing with functions normally performed by governments but in Israel it became a tool for involving the Jewish people in the nation building process." He concluded that "the JNF Hasbara strategy in the last decade of the 20th century focuses on conservation of the environment and developing water resources."

Even though the JNF's mission statement has nothing to do with current environmental values, since the 1980s it has presented itself as a green organization. It was always engaged in tree plantations for purposes of land conservation, but since the 1980s it has invited internal and external tourists to events organized in green parks: concerts, full-moon night tours, olive harvesting, and educational experiences teaching about the environment. The water issue succeeded in attracting donations from abroad, and the "Friends of the JNF Club" was called "In the Green Lane." Mushkin (2002) admitted that "[i]t is sometimes tricky as there is a contradiction between development of the land and conservation of the environment, but as a whole, the public identifies the JNF with contributions to the green part of Israel in a positive way."

The positive image did not help JNF to protect its reputation when under attack from the left for its discriminatory policies regarding the Arab citizens of Israel and the grabbing of Arab land (under the same sub-organization, Himnuta, which Hatalgi had to cover up). In December 2011 an investigative journalist working for *Haaretz* published the content of JNF board protocols, exposing internal discussions about the JNF's deteriorating image. According to the now-published protocols, the JNF's chairman, Stenzler, expressed his satisfaction with the fact that at least the adverse publicity mainly occurred abroad: "I want to thank communications and public relations people, who worked diligently to prevent this issue from popping up in the media. . . . In the Israeli media this issue hardly struck a chord. God forbid that it would" (Blau, 2011). Eventually it did, and caused the JNF to stop some planned evacuations of Arabs from their homes and embarrassed JNF representatives and fundraisers abroad.

Benny Mushkin, like Yechiel Amitai, was also a member of the Journalists' Association. He started his career as an economic reporter for *Haboker* in 1954 and for Kol Israel radio station in 1957. He served as spokesperson of the Hebrew University in 1973 till his move to the JNF in 1989. Although as a professional he was never actively involved in Zionist politics, he was involved with the Zionist institutions as a professional spokesperson and public relations administrator. He died in 2010.

The Jewish Agency (Hasochnut Hayehudit le'Eretz Israel) under the British Mandate

In 1929 the World Zionist Organization constituted a separate entity called "the Jewish Agency for Eretz Israel." Until the establishment of the State of Israel in 1948, the Jewish Agency (JA) played the principal role in the relations between the National Home in Eretz Israel and world Jewry on the one hand, and the Mandatory (and other powers) on the other.

> The Jewish Agency dealt with issues such as promoting Jewish immigration to Palestine; spreading the Hebrew language and Hebrew culture; purchasing land for the Jewish people via the JNF; developing the agriculture and settlements of Jews based on Jewish labor; and supplying the religious needs of Jews in Palestine without hurting individual freedoms.
>
> (Hattis Rolef, 1988, p. 182)

One JNF memorandum from the JNF propaganda and press offices, which was signed in December 1938 by Bistritzki and Tchernovitch, discusses the need for the central management of media and information issues and identifies a key communication issue:

> Journalists see it [Falcor, the WZO telegraphic news agency established in 1924] as one of the telegraphic news agencies; a reliable source, responsible, connected to the official institutions of the movement, but a source which is interested above all in the information it is delivering. It cannot serve as the centre that will guide and direct the Diaspora press. Because a journalist, even a disciplined journalist that is directed by Falcor to hide or weaken a certain news item, is not sure Falcor would not deliver the information itself to its own press ... therefore it is possible to state that the Jewish Agency does not have a press office.
>
> (CZA, S23 file 236)

This 1938 memorandum explains the background and the needs, which were identified by the national institutions, for a new Hasbara bureau of the JA that was eventually established in 1939. It is also revealing on the communication tactics and concepts of the national institutions. Falcor, a telegraphic news agency that is supported financially by the JA, serves both as its press office and as an independent supplier of news items to the general media. The JA is not satisfied when not achieving full control over the publicity via its "independent" agent and deliberately created an ambiguity about the journalist/propagandist role.

The 1938 memorandum considers core questions of reliability, transparency, and trust:

Falcor is supposed to serve as the press office of the JA. Actually, this is not the situation, because the two functions contradict each other. As a telegraphic agency Falcor is committed to make sure that it is delivering fast and full information, not hiding anything about the local events and not emphasising news items that the press is not interested in. As a telegraphic agency it does not have the time to consider and check its information. On the other hand it cannot deliver news items in advance to journalists and other news agencies because it is committed to serving its clients ... it lacks neutrality.

(CZA, S23 file 236)

In pre-state Israel, and later on, the Falcor example demonstrates the lack of competition between journalism and the publicity professions. The journalists serving Falcor were at the same time propagandists, advertisers, and public relations practitioners. They served the Zionist movement as publicists and as journalists. In this specific environment the lack of competition (see Abbott, 1988) would likely have inhibited the development of journalism and public relations as independent professions.

The new JA Hasbara bureau did not take much time to develop an impressive range of activities, as can be seen by the department's report on its first month, October 1939 (CZA Serial A, S23 file 374):

- Conducted personal meeting of its heads with all the political editors.
- Circulated the editors with written materials about the mobilization, Arab activities, and income tax.
- Sent letters to party committees, local authorities, and communities. The department director initiated personal meetings with parties' centres and other public organizations.
- Distributed 150 review papers to the parties and other public organizations.
- Gave lectures to the Press Association meeting and student organizations.
- Negotiated with the radio directors about the broadcast of four regular lectures per month on issues selected and presented by the JA Hasbara executives.
- Guided Zionist emissaries going abroad and supplied them with information.
- Serviced the international news agencies (AP), newspapers (*The Times*), and the Zionist non-Hebrew press.
- Circulated a daily press review to members of the JA board.

The list of activities, which kept developing in later years, shows a clear understanding of persuasive communication techniques. It addresses different publics, makes a major attempt to communicate with opinion leaders, and uses a variety of techniques to reach out to the community with its messages.

The JA Hasbara bureau intensified its efforts after the end of World War II and during the years leading to the establishment of the state in 1948. A report written in 1948 (CZA Serial A, S41 file 44) sums up the Hasbara contribution to the political influence of the Zionist movement. It also referred to the conditions for Hasbara under the special circumstances of the period: the British censorship and restrictions over the Hebrew press, the struggle against the policies of the White Paper, curfews, and British military activities.

Thus, in Eretz Israel the oral activities of Hasbara – lectures and meetings – replaced the written Hasbara, which was restricted by the British censor. In the first lecturers' conference, the speaker was Golda Meir, then director of the JA's Political Department. Meir spoke about the importance of mobilization and enlisting to serve the community needs of that time.

Another important tool was film. The Hasbara bureau took part in decisions regarding subjects for the filmed news journals of *Carmel Film*. It also participated in designing Hebrew and English news items as well as negotiating with cinemas that showed the news journals. This tactic of financially supporting the filmed news journals in cinemas was adopted and used by Israel's government until the 1970s. It aligns with the communication strategy behind Falcor: the national organization owned media channels to ensure control over the content of news.

The activities of the bureau during the Mandate period were linked to two concepts: the first identified the good of the organization with the good of the people; and the second saw mass media as tools that the organization should use in order to optimize its effort in achieving its goals. It was clear that achieving the goals was more important than the means used to get there.

The Jewish Agency in the State of Israel

After the establishment of the State of Israel, the JA relinquished many of its functions to the newly created Israeli government. Nevertheless, it "continued to be responsible for immigration, land settlement, youth work and other activities financed by voluntary Jewish contributions from abroad" (Hadary & Ernest, 1997). According to a report about the Hasbara activities dated March 31, 1949:

> With the establishment of the state, the Ministry of Foreign Affairs took the telegraphic news agency Falcor, which was established by the Zionist board and acted for 15 years as the telegraphic service of the Zionist movement. In October 1949 the Ministry reduced the activities of Falcor into a service for Israeli embassies abroad only.
>
> (CZA serial A, S23 file 373)

The JA Hasbara department established its own telegraphic service in November 1948. It sent daily telegrams of around 200 words (effectively, short news releases) about the activities of the Zionist institutions (e.g. immigration, absorption, housing, settlements) to Paris, London, Rome, Munich, Warsaw, Budapest, Buenos Aires, and Sydney.

In the Central Zionist Archive (CZA Serial A, S41 file 44), there are reports about the activities of the Hasbara department from 1949, and during the 1950s, demonstrating intensive attempts to make sure that the JA is perceived as relevant and can still be perceived as a national institute (The salaries of the chairperson and board of the JA are linked to the salaries of the prime minister and government ministers.) These activities, and the Hasbara mission, are highlighted in the comments of the political leader Yossi Beilin (1999):

> [T]he Jewish Agency was the scaffold that built the state, and instead of removing it when the state was established, it was preferred to leave it, simply because organizations always find some justification for their existence, and also because it was difficult to separate between the two.
>
> (p. 165) [ATH]

In 1952, legislation by the Israeli government entrusted the WZO and the JA with the responsibility for "the Ingathering of the Exiles" [Kibbutz Galuyot], and the absorption of new immigrants in the new Israeli society. The Hasbara effort was shifted to communication with the Diaspora Jews, especially in the United States, where most of the Zionist activists lived. From October 1949, the JA became responsible for the Israeli broadcasting effort to the Jewish Diaspora.

Following the Six Day War of 1967, the relationship between Israel and the Diaspora Jewry became a major issue in Israel. The JA's focus became the absorption of immigrants, education, and settlement. Since then, the JA has continued to see itself as responsible for Jewish immigration and absorption, Zionist education and the image of Jews in the world.

Conclusion

This chapter has described the roots of Israeli professional public relations practice in the first Zionist institutions in Palestine. These pre-state institutions were part of an ideological volunteer movement and they functioned within a mixed-value system with strong authority but without sovereignty. Their survival depended on voluntarism, donations, and enthusiastic consensus. This is why they depended on professional communicators to influence opinions and to enlist and motivate the public to meet difficult challenges and make personal sacrifices for the sake of building a homeland for the nation. The practitioners managed intensive propaganda and Hasbara campaigns that involved the education system and created a new Israeli culture.

The establishment of the state presented new challenges for these institutions, and the major problem became the legitimization of their survival. The practitioners assumed a more reactive role in trying to defend the organization, but they still kept the same values as their predecessors in their concept of media relations. That is to say, they benefited from deliberate confusion of the roles of journalists and propagandists, and attempted to control the media to serve their organization's agenda. The strong cooperation and blurring of responsibilities between journalists and publicists would continue to be a major feature in Israeli public relations practice, as will be seen in the following chapters.

7 Emissaries, fundraising, and nation building

While propaganda was important for achieving the goals of the newly formed national institutions, so too was funding. Historically, the evolution of the Jewish Diaspora, and its traditions, made fundraising prominent, legitimate, and valued in the Jewish community. Establishing and maintaining the State of Israel also involved extensive fundraising with the Jewish Diaspora. These factors help to explain the early, and sustained, emphasis of Israeli public relations on fundraising and the respect accorded to fundraisers.

Fundraisers and the Jewish world

Israel was established to serve the cause of the Jewish people worldwide. Jews in the Diaspora who do not even plan to become citizens of Israel regard Israel as their home. If they choose to, and can prove they belong to the Jewish people, they have the legal right to become citizens upon arrival to Israel. Contributions from Diaspora Jews made the nation-building process and the establishment of the state possible. The ability to raise money from Diaspora Jews became a major expectation of top leaders of organizations in Eretz Israel.

This chapter documents the work of major fundraisers and the public relations practitioners who worked for four selected organizations: the Hebrew University, the Weizmann Institute, the Hadassah Medical Organization, and the Israel Museum. These institutions have been chosen because they were part of fulfilling the Zionist vision, they have operated from the pre-state period to the present, and they cover major areas – education, science, health and medicine, and culture – of Israeli society. In addition, these institutions were also the main employers of public relations personnel outside of the government.

Fundraising work contributed significant assets to the nation-building process, and these organizations were recognized for their Zionist and national commitment. The practitioners also developed a community of practice that helped set high professional standards in fundraising. At the same time, the fundraising effort empowered major social services to develop in a somewhat independent way. Their significant contributions gave donors the power to participate in management decision making (not always in line with the Zionist leadership's intentions). In this way, the fundraising function of public relations contributes to the national institutions as well as to the civil society organizations that participate in nation building.

Public relations history credits fundraising as part of the profession's origins. American histories often situate the 17th-century effort of Harvard University to raise money in England as a key foundational moment:

> Probably the first systematic effort on this continent to raise funds was that sponsored by Harvard College in 1641, when that infant institution sent a trio of preachers to England on a "begging mission." ... They needed a fundraising brochure, now a standard item in a fund drive. ... *New England's First Fruit*, written largely in Massachusetts but printed in London in 1643, the first of countless public relations pamphlets and brochures.
>
> (Morrison, 1935, cited in Broom, 2009, p. 104)

More ancient, systematic, and professional fundraising, however, emerged from the small Jewish community. In Chapter 3 we described the roots of the fundraising practice in Israel as part of the activities of the historic Diaspora Jewish community. As previously mentioned, Shluhei Eretz Israel [Emissaries of Eretz Israel] were sent to raise funds from the Jewish communities all over the world for the small Jewish community that had lived in Eretz Israel since the destruction of the Second Temple in 70 CE by the Roman legion under Titus. These Emissaries used public relations methods to motivate the Jewish communities to donate, and at the same time they distributed news from Israel to stir the minds and emotions of the community and increase donations. For Diaspora Jews, the donation for a *yeshiva* [religious academy] in Jerusalem or Safed became a symbol of belonging to the Jewish nation.

Fundraisers who worked for Zionist institutions in the pre-state Eretz Israel and their successors in the State of Israel after 1948 deployed similar discourses. They addressed emotional messages to Jews in the Diaspora asking for donations of money as a means of expressing connection. The social services that were developed by the Zionist movement in the pre-state era were financed by world Jewry. Many institutions in the State of Israel were established and maintained by donations from Jews abroad, and so depended a great deal on fundraising. They therefore developed professional public relations that were linked to professional public relations departments.

The Hebrew University

The establishment of a Hebrew University in Jerusalem was on the agenda of the Zionist movement from a very early stage. In 1901 a group of activists brought the idea to the Fifth Zionist Congress, and in 1913 the congress established a committee, which included Dr Chaim Weizmann and Judah Leon Magnes, to execute the project. The major challenge of the group was raising the financial support to build and maintain a high-quality university that was expected to become the university of the Jewish people.

Fundraising was the responsibility of top management and became a source of tensions and power struggles between Weizmann and Magnes, the World Zionist Organization in London, and the Hebrew University committee in Jerusalem, including its donors in the United States. In 1921, Weizmann, the founding father of the Hebrew University (HU) and president of the World Zionist Organization (1921–1930 and 1936–1946), went to the United States to mobilize support for the university in his capacity as director of the WZO university committee. He asked Albert Einstein, who won his Nobel Prize the same year, to join him "on a fund-raising tour of America to buy land in Palestine and seek aid for the Hebrew University. Einstein readily agreed, since his interest in the Hebrew University had been growing. The tour was highly successful" (Tauber, 1997). This was Einstein's first tour to the United States and it resulted in the establishment of the American Jewish Physician Committee, which was eventually responsible for the establishment of the HU Medical School.

Weizmann tried to establish a "University Fund" within the framework of the Foundation Fund [Keren Hayesod], but this failed. Weisgal's (1972) explanation was that the American Zionist leadership objected to raising money for settlements and decided to support only private enterprises, and to supervize exclusively all the contributions from America (p. 46) [ATH]. The Americans refused to let the WZO manage their contributions to the university.

This is one example of tensions that developed between the World Zionist institutions and the university over the political control, academic direction, and organization of fundraising. For Weizmann and the Zionist movement, the Hebrew University involved a political dimension: "[T]he symbol of the university proved to be a useful weapon in the Zionist political arsenal and a morale-booster for the rank and file of the movement" (Goren, 1996, p. 203). Weizmann wanted to control the Hebrew University from the WZO offices in London. This aspiration was met with strong opposition on the part of the Jerusalem committee headed by Magnes and his wealthy supporters in America. Magnes, a Reform rabbi and a Zionist leader in the United States, immigrated to Palestine in 1922 and was eventually appointed the HU's first chancellor (1925–1935) and then its president (1935–1948).

Eliyahu Honig (2003) worked for the Hebrew University, as the director of the Public Relations Department, and later as associate vice-president, for over 40 years. According to Honig (2003), the tension between Magnes and Weizmann over the fundraising work began in 1924 when Magnes received a significant donation that was intended to be used for the establishment of a HU Jewish Studies Center (see also Goren, 1996). This started an argument between the university (Magnes) and the Zionist movement (Weizmann) about who made decisions regarding the usage of donations. Magnes had better access to the American donors, who saw him as their representative in Jerusalem, and therefore he won the debate. Magnes' ability to raise money became a major factor in empowering him as a Zionist leader.

Magnes was extremely successful in raising money from individual wealthy American Jews, the Upper Manhattan Jews, who were not Zionist. For this group, the Hebrew University represented a project they could identify with and support as Jews and not as Zionists. The group wanted to have direct influence on the new university, not influence via the Zionist institutions. Magnes was a dissident in the Zionist movement: "[H]e had been unhappy about the Balfour Declaration from the outset.... He feared that the Zionists would be regarded from now on as interlopers and invaders" (Bentwitch, 1954, p. 174, cited in Laqueur, 1972, p. 251). In 1925, along with Martin Buber, Henrietta Szold, Arthur Rupin, and others, Magnes established Brit Shalom (Peace Alliance), a small group that advocated a bi-national state and a Jewish–Arab accord. Magnes' pacifist political views and his insistence on independence for the Hebrew University helped the university connect with the American donors but led to conflicts with the Zionist movement.

This rivalry between the political power of the WZO and the financial power of the overseas donors (combined with Magnes and their other allies in Jerusalem) represents a difficult question for any organization depending on fundraising: what is the donors' role in the decision-making process? This fundraising dilemma became a major force in the development of social services for the new nation and in the relationship between Diaspora and Israeli Jews.

At this stage in the development of the HU, the dilemma was handled by the leaders, and not by the professional public relations practitioners. It became a crisis that eventually led to a split: Weizmann established a competing research institute in the town of Rehovot. When, as we will see later, the HU developed a Public Relations Department, this crisis was solved in a professional way.

In 1929, as a result of the Wall Street crash, which limited his ability to secure donations, Magnes' power was restricted. But this crisis became an opportunity when Magnes and others decided to change the strategy and look for broader-based support. This was the beginning of the establishment of the Societies of Friends of the Hebrew University all around the world. Eventually the growth of grassroots support compensated for the decrease in large individual donations, and the HU booklet from 1938 listed over 100 groups of Friends of the University in 31 countries in five continents (Honig, 2003).

The Friends of the University groups eventually became the major tool for raising support for the HU. They were active from the 1930s not only with financial support but also with developing academic relations and student exchange projects. The financial support from the United States was replaced during the 1930s by significant donations from South African Zionists. Even the Friends groups in Eretz Israel, headed by the national poet Chaim Bialik, succeeded in raising money, as the Yishuv appreciated the university's service to education. HU Emissaries [Shlichim] went all over the world to maintain the bonds and to encourage the friends. An international board of governors consisting of major donors became the source of authority for the HU leadership and management. In the pre-state era the overseas Friends societies and individuals covered almost all the university's needs. Following the establishment of the state in 1948, their contribution to the general operating budget of the university was reduced to 12–14% (Honig, 2003).

Magnes was a forceful actor in helping to establish the new groups, but in 1935 he was moved from the fundraising decision-making process and became president of the university, an honorary position. This move was made by Zalman Shoken, the founder of *Haaretz* newspaper, who served as chairman of the HU's executive council, and treasurer from 1934 to 1945. According to Honig (2003), Shoken introduced a "businesslike" structure, and in 1934 he initiated the Department of Organization and Information to deal with the fundraising and development of the Friends groups. During 1934–1947, the department was directed by Kurt Blumenfeld, Alfred Berger, and Dr Malka Spigel (the first woman to head any kind of public relations department). She served as associate director and acting director for 20 years until her retirement in 1953 and was in charge of publications and day-to-day contact with Friends organizations (Honig, 2003).

After Shoken's resignation in 1947, the university invited Bernard Cherrick from Britain to take over the directorship of fundraising. Cherrick succeeded to an unprecedented level, and during his 41 years of service as director of public relations and vice-president he pioneered a professional service that combined public relations and fundraising under the same roof.

An Irish Jew, educated at the University of Manchester and the London School of Economics, Cherrick also received a *yeshiva* education and became a rabbi at London's New Synagogue. In 1939 he joined the British Army as chaplain. After the war, he served as director of the Jewish National Fund (JNF) and United Palestine appeal.

The Cherrick era brought the Hebrew University back to the mainstream of the Zionist movement. The tensions and arguments regarding fundraising ended as a result of Cherrick's personality and his fundraising success. Right from his very first year in the Hebrew University, he was asked by Weizmann to speak in Australia on behalf of the state about to be born. The agreement was that he would speak about the state but that 10% of the income from his speaking assignments would be transferred from the Foundation Fund to the Hebrew University. Following this arrangement, he gave many speeches to raise money for the new state and for the university at the same time.

Cherrick used these opportunities to enlist members of the Zionist management to the HU's board of governors and, without giving up any academic freedom, to build good relations and trust between the state leadership and the heads of the university. Instead of competition he offered cooperation. This changed the status of the university, and with Cherrick's friend Abe Harman as president and Sam Rothberg as chairperson of the board of governors, the HU gained the support of world Jewry. Eulogies delivered at Cherrick's funeral on December 23, 1988 by three HU presidents, and many professors, made a point of mentioning Cherrick's Zionist commitment. They said he had seen in the Hebrew University the key to the rebirth of the State of Israel and to the spiritual revival of the Jewish people.

Cherrick's style and his success demonstrate the importance of personal contacts and leadership in fundraising and public relations. Under Cherrick the HU's Public Relations Department expanded and was organized to support the fundraising effort with information, publications, events management, and media relations. In 1968, when he became vice-president and Eliyahu Honig became director of public relations, the department employed 70 people. The employees were organized by language desks – English, French, German, and Spanish, as well as Hebrew for the local media – and every story was translated and used by the appropriate desk. The events management department organized moving ceremonies for visiting donors and created exciting experiences for donors during the annual meeting of the board of governors.

Other NGOs in Israel adopted Cherrick's structure and principles. However, his success, in terms of financial donations and the world reputation of the Hebrew University, was exceptional. During the 1970s he joined with Harvey Silbert, a Jewish lawyer in Hollywood, who connected him with world-famous entertainment stars. This eventually became the foundation for the Frank Sinatra Building, and the donations from Barbra Streisand, Gregory Peck, Billy Crystal, and others, who kept visiting the HU every year and attracting both public interest and rich donors. Cherrick introduced a new style to the Zionist movement by replacing the Bolshevik pathos of the Zionist founders with English understatement and a sense of humour (Honig, 2003). He developed persuasion skills as a rabbi and used entertainment to deliver his message effectively. This coexisted with a pedantic insistence on precision in language, especially in the use of English in HU publications.

Benny Mushkin served under Cherrick and Honig as the HU's spokesperson from 1973 until 1989, and then moved to become director of Hasbara of the Jewish National Fund (JNF). Mushkin (2002) described the work of the HU public relations team as serving fundraising needs first. Unlike the JNF spokesperson, who worked separately from the fundraising department, the Hebrew University media relations team was concerned with communication with the Societies of Friends around the world, and news stories were produced to connect them to the Hebrew University:

> Fundraising is based on the phenomena that people give to people; personality is crucial. Cherrick used his personality but he also understood well the media and its power to connect people. The Public Relations Department of the Hebrew University developed thanks to this combination of challenges – fundraising, media relations, publications, and events management.
> (Mushkin, 2002)

Landmark inaugural ceremonies

The Hebrew University deserves to be acknowledged for the first significant inaugural ceremonies in the history of Israel: the 1918 cornerstone ceremony, the 1923 Albert Einstein lecture, and the 1925 opening ceremony, which was considered more moving and exciting than the declaration of the State of Israel in 1948.

For Chaim Weizmann, the celebratory dates of the Hebrew University represented a great opportunity to promote the Zionist political agenda. He saw them as an opportunity to manifest the existence and the development of the Zionist ideology from vision to practice, to demonstrate power, and to unite Zionists and non-Zionists in an exciting project in Eretz Israel. Goren's (1996) description of the foundation-stone ceremony in 1918 is based on Weizmann's letters and other publications:

> Before an assembly of nearly six thousand and in presence of General Edmund Allenby, the commanding general of the British forces in Palestine, French, Italian, and American representatives, leaders of Jerusalem's religious communities ... and delegations sent by the Jewish settlements and institutions, Weizmann signed the dedicatory scroll. He then cemented into place the first of fourteen stones that formed the foundation pillar of the university. ... The pageantry had all the earmarks of an affair of state. Officers wore their dress uniforms and soldiers chosen from their former battalions of the Jewish legion formed an honor guard.
>
> (p. 204)

The first academic lecture offered Zionists a rare opportunity to excite the Jewish world and amaze non-Jews as well. Albert Einstein, who became involved with the Hebrew University during its conception stage, agreed to spend a week in Palestine. In that time, on February 7, 1923, he delivered the first academic lecture to be given under the auspices of the Hebrew University when the HU "celebrated its second beginning by symbolically opening its academic doors for the first time to none other than the most celebrated scientist of the day" (Goren, 1996, p. 206).

Again there was an impressive group, which included all the civil officials of the mandatory government, members of the consular corps, Arab and Jewish notables, heads of religious institutions, and Zionist officials, in attendance in an imposing setting: "Zionist flags and the insignia of the twelve tribes draped the hall. A portrait of Herzl alongside the Union Jack and a banner inscribed with the words, 'Ora v-tora' – 'Light and Learning' – covered the wall behind the speaker's podium" (Goren, 1996, p. 207). It was effective public relations in that the "visibility given the lecture by the presence of officers of state, together with the enthusiastic crowds that greeted Einstein everywhere he toured during his week in the country, placed the university, by association, in the public eye once more" (p. 207).

But the ultimate event organized by Weizmann for the Hebrew University was the opening ceremony on April 1, 1925. This grandiose spectacle was seen by the majority of the Jewish people as a "dress rehearsal for a ceremony proclaiming the National Home" (Almagor, 2000, p. 27). The build-up of expectations for the ceremony reached the whole Jewish world. Newspaper articles called on Jews to illuminate their homes and decorate them for the opening day. Jewish committees were set up to organize festivals in theatres on the same day. Over 500 guests arrived from abroad. The National Funds exploited the enthusiasm for their own campaigns in connection with the opening day, and the "excitement among the Jewish population in Palestine knew no bounds" (p. 29).

Prior to the official opening, Magnes was reluctant and objected to a big ceremony that would provoke the Arab world. According to Goren (1996), Magnes wrote in his journal, "The falsehood of 'opening' what does not exist. ... For sake of a big impression, *making the University a propaganda instrument*" (p. 224; italics added). But eventually he invited representatives of Arab countries and Arab leaders from Palestine to the opening ceremony, and even asked one of them to deliver a speech (Almagor, 2000, p. 28):

> All the Egyptian newspapers ... gave wide coverage to the opening ceremony, quoting the reports of Reuters news agency and of their own correspondents in Jerusalem. The prominent Egyptian newspaper *Al Aharam*, published a story on the Hebrew University and the National Library in Jerusalem, with the comment that "the university is an off-shoot of the Zionist Movement." ... The newspaper praised the president of the Hebrew University, Dr. Judah Magnes, who "opened the National Library and the regular Hebrew lending library also to Arab readers," and quoted an Egyptian scholar who was very grateful that they had loaned him books and documents without receipts, even while he was preparing his argument against the Jews in the case of the Western Wall.

Meyer Weisgal, who later became Chaim Weizmann's personal political representative in the United States, conducted the celebration from America, where he served, at that time, as national secretary of the Zionist Organization of America (ZOA). His role as secretary included the editing of the ZOA publication *New Palestine* from 1921 to 1930 and he devoted a special issue, on March 27, 1925, to the opening of the Hebrew University, with congratulatory articles written by prominent political and spiritual Jewish and non-Jewish leaders. The article written by Albert Einstein (1925) was titled "The Mission of Our University" and it said, "Our educational institutions in particular must regard it as one of their noblest tasks to keep our people free from nationalistic obscurantism and aggressive intolerance" (p. 294).

Weisgal's (1971) account in his autobiography demonstrates how this public relations maverick worked. He describes how, while riding the subway back home in downtown New York, he responded to a small news item announcing that the Hebrew University was going to be opened in April 1925 in the following way:

> Flame caught me. I went back to the office and sent a hundred telegrams to all the VIPs in the world. I had no idea about the plans for the opening in Jerusalem; I knew only that the way the opening would be reported in the *New Palestine* should be no less impressive. It is not enough that the event is first class; it should be seen as such by the whole world.
>
> (pp. 55–56) [ATH]

Weisgal did not have any budget, and his employer, the American Zionist Organization, while not objecting to his pushing the venture, was not supporting it. In order to find finances he organized pre-selling committees and sold 150,000 copies before the publication was printed. He employed five people for this project. Eventually, "the 27.3.25 issue became an exemplary collectors' item in Zionist journalism.... The Zionist administration commissioned 75,000 additional copies" (Weisgal, 1971, p. 57). However, Meyer Weisgal's contributions to Israeli public relations are associated not with the Hebrew University, but rather with its rival, the Weizmann Institute, which is the subject of the next section.

The Weizmann Institute

Frustrated and disenchanted by his inability to lead the Hebrew University in his direction, Weizmann initiated a new research centre that would be up to his scientific and academic standards. In 1934 he secured a gift from the Sieff family in Britain and founded, in Rehovot, the Sieff Institute. This was renamed the Weizmann Institute in 1949. According to Honig (2003), Weizmann raised funds and promoted his institute while still serving as chairman of the Hebrew University's board of governors and leader of the HU Friends in Britain. The potential for conflicts of interest caused a lot of criticism, but

> this situation continued into the 1940s when Weizmann directly, through Meyer Weisgal, fundraised in America, utilising the Zionist organisation and other contacts and leaders for his own institute at the time that he was being called upon to help the University, of which he was still serving as chairperson.
>
> (Honig, 2003)

Such unethical fundraising practice did not harm Weizmann's public image.

Weizmann's right-hand man was Meyer Weisgal. Weisgal, who arrived in New York at the age of ten from Poland, was not an academic but rather a practitioner of "dynamic public relations" (Samuel, 1997). Weisgal first met Weizmann in 1921, during Weizmann's visit to raise funds for the WZO and for the HU. The American Zionist leadership was reluctant about the WZO and kept a separatist local orientation. They wished to keep Weizmann's visit low-profile, but Weisgal's group, which had a more global Jewish orientation, decided to organize an exciting reception:

> We prepared the event with publicity as if it was an event of world importance. I had friends in the Yiddish press and I asked them to report extensively about the upcoming visit. The atmosphere of anticipation and awakening that was created exceeded our expectations. The boat arrived on Saturday ... during the day thousands of Jews from Manhattan, Bronx and all parts of Brooklyn arrived to the port.
>
> (Weisgal, 1972, p. 46) [ATH]

During the 1930s, Weisgal developed his exceptional public relations skills promoting Zionist affairs in the United States and Canada with creative projects that included spectacular pageants, fundraising, and media relations. The most famous events he organized were a Zionist pageant, "The Romance of a People," at the 1933 Chicago Fair, and the Jewish Palestinian Pavilion at the 1939 New York World Fair (see Kirshenblatt-Gimblett, 1997). Weisgal looked for ways to mobilize support for the Zionist cause and he turned to the performing arts: music, drama, and spectacle. No dry Zionist speeches. This was a revolutionary approach, and Wechsberg (1967) cites Weisgal's own description of his successful tactics: "Before a vast audience, united by common memories and common emotions, you could bring a dream to life, through scenery and lights and music and words.... The theatre could be the most exciting medium of propaganda" (p. 61).

In 1941, Weisgal (1971) agreed to work for Weizmann. He served Weizmann from the United States for 8 years, and in 1949 moved to the Weizmann Institute in Israel as chairman of the Executive Council, then as president (1966–1969), and as chancellor till 1977. Weizmann made him responsible for the administration of the institute even though he had no understanding of the scientific work of the young Israeli "geniuses" working there. Recognizing Weisgal's exceptional skills in fundraising and public relations, Weizmann expected him to develop an international reputation for the Institute, which did become an outstanding scientific centre and a landmark achievement in Israel.

Weizmann and Weisgal emphasized the look and public image of the institute as much as its academic work. They invested in plantations of trees and high-standard laboratories, offices, and living facilities that were comparable with those in high-level institutions elsewhere in the world. They were determined not to compromise on quality and become "Levantine," although Rehovot was, at that time, almost part of a desert, and Israel was struggling for its existence with a very poor economy. Wechsberg's (1967) book explains Weisgal's contribution to the elitist image:

> Weisgal's lifelong passion has been the theatre. In America he produced pageants and plays. In Rechovot he thinks of himself as the producer of a vast, continuous show that is being performed on the stage of the Weizmann Institute. He helps to design the scenery, worries about the lighting, gets involved with the script writing and the cast of characters, helps with the staging, and then goes out to sell the show to the world.
>
> (p. 48)

The Weizmann Institute became the showcase of the new Israeli state, presenting Israel's advanced science and contributions to the developing world – a very positive image that balanced negative news items about military struggles.

Weisgal's personal fundraising approach set out principles for future fundraisers:

His cardinal rule is never to just take money from the rich people but always to give them something in return, in addition to the coveted name-plate above the entrance to a building. Weisgal is exacting in his standards of giving and receiving friendship. Once the donors have fulfilled their promises, Weisgal accepted them into his enlarged family of relatives, friends, and fellow-workers. He understands that rich people are giving money not only to get a feeling of being recognized, a sense of being rewarded for a gift. He knows that many of them feel lonely after achieving success and have a great need for warmth and affection.

(Wechsberg, 1967, p. 54)

Like Bernard Cherrick in the Hebrew University, Weisgal used personal relationships as a professional public relations tool, and made his humour and stories a means to achieve closeness and deliver a message. But unlike the sophisticated British approach of Cherrick, Weisgal's style was influenced by the earthy and juicy culture of European Yiddish.

The first official professional public relations practitioner for the Weizmann Institute was appointed in 1963. Nechemia Meyers remained director of public affairs till his retirement in 1995. During his 32 years at the Weizmann Institute he was responsible for media and publications in English. Giora Shamis was in charge of the Hebrew media for some time but he moved to become spokesperson of the Hebrew University. For Nechemia Meyers, as with pre-state Zionist practitioners, working for the institute was a mission, not a job. In an interview in his Rehovot home, Nechemia Meyers (2002) said:

I felt that the stories I published should not only praise the Weizmann Institute but also serve the state of Israel. I wanted the Israeli public to respond positively to Israel's achievements in science, to feel good about Israel through our work.

Nechemia Meyers (2002) noticed a change in the way the Weizmann Institute and its scientists related to external stakeholders over time:

In the 1960s and 1970s the scientists were not interested in the mass media; it would be humiliating to be published in a newspaper. Only scientific publications counted. They nicknamed our publicity as "scientific *Maariv*" [the name of a newspaper]. In the 1990s they understood the power of the media and supported publicity efforts. The focus of our work in the first years was the world reputation, and communication with potential donors abroad. Our job was to serve as background music for the fundraising activities managed by Weisgal. We did not pay attention to the Israeli media and the institute did not make any effort to fundraise in Israel. The focus changed later in the 1980s and 1990s: a Hebrew spokesperson joined the department and new programmes to involve the community and youth in science were developed. But the emphasis was always international.

In the 1960s, Meyers was involved in a project in cooperation with the Foreign Ministry, which organized, in a separate entity called "the Rehovot Conference," seminars for students from developing countries. This initiative gave Israel a positive image in the world by showcasing assistance to the Third World.

Influencing Israel: the Hadassah Medical Organization

The symbiotic relationships between world Jewry and Israel's institutions, in which the function of fundraising is a major component, are best demonstrated in the example of the Hadassah Medical Organization (HMO). It also demonstrates how Israeli activities are influencing the world and how the world is influencing activities in Israel. The superb professional public relations services developed by Hadassah in the United States and in Israel in support of the fundraising effort involved world Jewry in building the nation's social services while at the same time promoting Diaspora Jews' commitment to Zionism. More than in the examples from the Hebrew University and the Weizmann Institute, the Hadassah donors from abroad were the owners and managers of the services they founded in Palestine and then Israel. The money they provided gave their organizations some level of independence. The national leadership did not have total control over the institutions that were funded by donations from world Jewry.

In 2012 the Hadassah Women's Zionist Organization of America celebrated a centennial. The organization's story begins with a visit to Palestine by an American Jewish woman, an active Zionist, Henrietta Szold, in 1909. She was appalled by the poor medical services that were available there at the time and in 1912 organized a group of 40 Jewish women in New York to fund the work of an American nurse to be sent to Palestine. This was the foundation for the Hadassah Women's Zionist Organization, which now involves over 300,000 women members in the United States and tens of thousands more members in 28 countries around the world. At the inception meeting in 1929, Szold recognized that "first the organization would have to obtain the funds" (cited in Krantz, 1987, p. 30).

For 100 years, Hadassah was able to "obtain funds" and to finance in Palestine, and later in Israel, the largest medical research and treatment centre in the Middle East, educational institutions, youth programmes, land development, and other projects that involved American Jewish women in the implementation of Zionism. In 1960 the American women donated their projects in Israel to the government of Israel but they kept the Hadassah Medical Organization, the "flagship." Hadassah, which became an international organization in 1983, is still the strongest Jewish women's organization in the United States. Its members still finance the hospital in Jerusalem with small and large donations.

The good reputation of both the Hadassah Women's Zionist Organization and the Hadassah Medical Center depends on the relationship between the two. Their co-dependency means that the American headquarters rely on the good reputation of the HMO and the constant supply of stories, news releases, visitors, and publicity from Israel. This information is delivered to members in the United States and other countries via *Hadassah* magazine, newsletters, presentations, and branch meetings. The HMO's stories help strengthen Hadassah's membership, and motivate donors by providing evidence of Hadassah's contribution to the nation-building efforts of the Jewish state. Hadassah's American Jewish women are able to feel partners in the Israeli experience when they participate in Hadassah activities and are exposed to the HMO's news.

On the other hand, the medical centre in Israel relies on American donations to keep developing its excellent services, and for that purpose is involved in enhancing the American organization's reputation in Israel. Intensive collaboration between the public relations departments in America and in Israel is essential for both sides. Actually, the Israeli public relations department's daily functioning is supervized by representatives of the American organization who migrated to Israel and kept their volunteer involvement with Hadassah (lay leaders). These volunteers make sure that the publicity Hadassah receives in Israel is in line with its image in the United States (personal experience from the lead author's work as Hadassah Medical Organization spokesperson from 1979 to 1985).

The Hadassah organization used professional public relations services at a very early stage. Archives in New York contain files with copies of news releases from the 1920s, written professionally on *Hadassah News Release* letterheads, announcing Henrietta Szold's trips to Palestine and her activities in the United States and Israel. However, a professional public relations department of the Hadassah Medical Organization in Israel was established only in 1955. It was actually a pioneering idea in Israel; other hospitals or medical services that belonged to the government or to the health funds did not have this kind of service. During the 1980s, hospitals bypassed this directive, following the example of the Hebrew University, by using groups of "friends of" for fundraising, and these groups employed public relations practitioners and spokespeople who actually served the hospitals. Lucian Harris, first director of information services of the Hadassah Medical Organization in Israel (1955–1977), commented about it in a 1973 presentation as follows:

> Ours was the first Medical Public Relations Department to be set in Israel. Kupat Holim [Health Fund] have always had the most negative public image because of the poor organisation of so many of their clinics and no PR effort on their part has ever succeeded in remedying this situation. The Ministry of Health hospitals and public health services receive very intermittent publicity and are often the target of severe newspaper and political criticism. At this moment, Sha'arei Zedek [a private hospital run by the religious community since 1902] has set up a Public Relations Department which engages in promoting their fundraising here and abroad.
>
> (Harris, 1973)

Harris's report confirms the fact that none of the medical services of Israel had the advantages of Hadassah. The alliance with Americans who understood the value of professional public relations gave an advantage to Hadassah in Israel. Nevertheless, Harris felt inferior to the status given to the public relations services by the Hebrew University, the partner of Hadassah in the Medical School. In the same report, Harris (1973) commented:

> The Hebrew University, which obtains three quarters of its annual budget from the Israeli taxpayer, has for years a unified and overall Public Relations Department, staffed by professionals and secretaries divided into various sections dealing with Hebrew language and English language publicity to press, radio and TV, publications, films, photo archives, tourism, ceremonies, etc. I'm informed that for the purely press, TV and publications duties (excluding special officers for tourism and ceremonies), the Hebrew University employs at least ten senior professional officers as well as eight secretaries. By comparison with the bodies I have mentioned, we are in danger of lagging behind . . . we may find it increasingly difficult to retain the leading position which Hadassah now holds in the minds of the Israeli public.

Harris's team comprised three employees and a special external contract with Philip and Hadassah Gillon: a *Jerusalem Post* reporter and his wife who wrote stories in English for Hadassah New York. The Gillons served Hadassah as writers from 1962 till the 1990s. The contract of Hadassah with the Gillons, dated April 5, 1962, is preserved in the Hadassah Archive in New York, signed by Mrs Siegfried Kramarsky, national president, and Mrs H. Salpeter, chair of the press, radio, and television committee (Hadassah, 1962). It explains the Gillons' role as independent consultants who received directives from the press, radio, & television department of Hadassah in New York City, directly or via Mrs Annabel Yuval, chairman of the public relations department of the Hadassah council in Israel (Hadassah, 1962).

The Gillons' role was limited to writing stories and reporting to the New York office, and they never represented Hadassah in public, or pitched to journalists. However, Philip Gillon's dual contracts as a journalist on the *Jerusalem Post* and as a writer for Hadassah did not comply with journalistic ethics. Nevertheless, this arrangement went on for 30 years.

This is yet another example (see also the references to Falcor, the Jewish Agency's "news agency" and the Jewish National Fund's deal with Itim in Chapter 6) of the confusion and overlapping of roles between journalists and public relations practitioners (see Nahum Sokolow's concepts in Chapter 3) serving the Zionist cause. These examples illustrate the slowing of the process of the professional development of public relations in Israel through the sociologist Andrew Abbott's (1988) ideas on the jurisdiction of professions. In essence, as long as there is no competition between journalism and public relations about the task, there is no need for the latter as a profession. Harris's status in Hadassah did not equal Bernard Cherrick's status in the Hebrew University, nor did his public relations extend to the same scope of operation. Nevertheless, both represent the first professional public relations efforts connected with and inspired by donor organizations abroad.

Hadassah developed a system of recognition that acknowledged donors with certificates, plaques, inscriptions on the hospital walls, emotional events in honour of the donors and their families, tours, and even the Yahrzeit [Memorial Day] in Israel project: the name of the person being memorialized is inscribed in one of 13 parchment and leather memorial books on display in the hospital's synagogue, and every year on the date, the name is mentioned during the Kadish [Memorial for the Dead] prayer, which would cost the donor $750. A Hadassah catalogue for fundraisers from 1984–1985 lists hundreds of ways in which Hadassah gratefully acknowledges gifts, including "Love of Peace" walls, "Pillars of Hope," "Wall of Healing," "Wall of Tribute," "Book of the Builders," "Benefactors," and many more (Hadassah Women's Zionist Organization, 1984–1985).

The same techniques are used in the 2012 centennial celebrations, providing potential donors with many opportunities to get involved and be recognized. The creativity of Hadassah's public relations in acknowledging donors has motivated donations from both rich women and women with very modest incomes. The small donations accumulated into phenomenal sums of money that were sent to Eretz Israel not only to build and maintain high-tech hospitals, but also to build its membership organization in Jewish communities all over America and internationally.

The persuasive talent of Hadassah women is best demonstrated in the story about how they persuaded the notable Jewish artist Marc Chagall to design windows, in what became one of Israel's art treasures, for the new Hadassah Medical Center's synagogue in 1962. Dr Miriam Freund Rosenthal, Hadassah's president from 1956 to 1960, had noticed a news item about Chagall's new work for a French cathedral and wanted him to create the windows for the HMO Center then under construction in Jerusalem. She went to France and approached Chagall directly:

> We could never repay you enough for doing these windows. I cannot even ask you what your price is since all I can spend is $100,000. That has to cover everything. I know this is no fee for you . . . but you will be shaping the art history of the new country. All young Israelis are interested in art. You will be their loudspeaker.
>
> (Rosenthal, cited in Levin, 1997, p. 296)

The dedication ceremony of the Chagall windows synagogue became a national event attended by the prime minister (Ben-Gurion), the American ambassador, and 400 overseas guests. A Freedom Bell, shaped like the Liberty Bell, on which was inscribed "Proclaim Ye Healing Throughout the Land," was ceremonially rung. But some art critics, and Chagall, thought the tiny Hadassah synagogue was not an appropriate home for the magnificent windows. They wanted to move them to the Israel Museum (Levin, 1997, p. 298). The Hadassah women insisted – after all, they had paid for them – and the windows became a tourist attraction, very well used for Hadassah's public relations and fundraising purposes. Hadassah even developed a tourist department to develop and attract visitors – a unique open door strategy for a medical centre.

Hadassah's success in fundraising is related to its success in developing a reputation for being a world-class university medical institution associated with innovation, excellence, sophisticated equipment, caring, and commitment. Its international exposure is also based on its strong commitment to human service offered equally with no regard to politics, and with the inclusion of diverse staff members. Teddy Kollek, former mayor of Jerusalem, wrote, "Another vital and potentially explosive area where Hadassah has contributed so much is promoting the ideal of equality. Hadassah has, since the first day, taken in all comers, regardless of how and where they worship" (cited in Levin, 1997, p. 429).

A tradition of openness to all humankind, Arabs as well as Jews, was set by Hadassah's founder, Henrietta Szold. She was a member of Brit Shalom and, with Buber, Magnes, and the rest of this small group, insisted on negotiations with the Arabs and objected to the establishment of a state prior to reaching an accord with them. In an old press release from December 7, 1929 on a Hadassah letterhead, Hadassah New York announces the departure of Miss Henrietta Szold on the *Île de France* for London to meet with Chaim Weizmann before proceeding to Palestine. In Jerusalem she would resume her duties as director of education and health on the executive. During her time in the United States, the Hadassah New York (1929) press release announcement continues: "Miss Szold urged a closer bond between Arabs and Jews in Palestine. She recommended the teaching of the Arabic language, literature and history, and acquaintance with Arab cultures and the Moslem religion as a part of Jewish cultural equipment."

These principles were internalized in Hadassah's medical work and public relations. The 1967 war had opened Jerusalem to the Arab section, and Hadassah welcomed back Arab patients from Jerusalem and the Arab world. Harris explained that the Hadassah Public Relations Department's work changed in 1967:

> From 1961–1967, we laid the emphasis on the contribution of the Center to the health and welfare of Israel, to the consolidation of our national capital, Jerusalem, and to the enhancement of the name of Israel throughout the world, with a special reference to university and scientific circles.... Since the Six Day War of 1967, we have entered a period of immense achievements ... the vital role played by our medical center since 1967 in the treatment of thousands of Arab patients who come to us from east Jerusalem, the West Bank, and latterly (under the "open bridges" program) from as far away as Egypt, Iraq and Kuwait.... We must prepare ourselves for adequate public relations work at the Hadassah Hospital on Mount Scopus, which may provide us with as yet unimagined opportunities promoting Jewish–Arab coexistence and understanding in Jerusalem and in the Middle East.
> (Text of presentation to HMOIC 1973 Jerusalem:
> CZA Serial A341, file 28)

Not many in Hadassah, the United States, or Israel at the start of the 21st century hold to the founder's political beliefs, but Szold's humane principles are still practised in Hadassah institutions and enhance its reputation internationally. On

December 21, 2002 in the United States, the prestigious ABC television show *Nightline* broadcast a half-hour programme about Hadassah: "It is a place where the wounded from both sides are treated equally," said ABC correspondent John Donovan (2002), "a place where Israelis and Palestinian show what could be." The broadcast was aired at the peak of the second Palestinian Intifada, when Palestinian acts of resistance and Israeli attacks had become a daily routine in the region. Nevertheless, Donovan (2002) continued that this was a Jewish hospital "that from its beginnings more than a century ago, saw its mission as treating everyone, everyone regardless of anything: who they are, what God they pray to, what their politics might be," and concluded that "the philosophy here is that medicine is a neutral zone."

For more than 90 years, Hadassah focused on the same strategic message and maintained a consistently high international reputation. This joint venture of the Women's Zionist Organization abroad and medical centres in Israel enhanced each other's reputation through well-coordinated public relations. Hadassah is one of the cornerstones of professional public relations in Israel. Although not typical of other social services in Israel, it certainly brought concepts and tactics from the United States that later spread to wider Israeli professional circles.

Fundraising was a key motive in the construction of Israel's institutions and it was the motivational force in this joint project. As with the cases of the Hebrew University and the Weizmann Institute, fundraising was the reason for the development of a public relations department. The Israel Museum, established, with no connection to the Zionist movement, as the country's national museum in 1965, enjoyed the fruits of the lessons learned from these public relations pioneers.

The Israel Museum

Traditionally, plastic and visual arts were not a major component of Jewish culture. The Bible's Ten Commandments include a prohibition on the making of "any image or likeness of man or beast," meant originally for the purpose of worship. Taken literally by religious Jews, it inhibited the development of figurative art. The Haskala [Enlightenment] movement and Zionism wished to make art part of their revolution, a tool for the creation of a new Jewish culture. Max Nordau, who co-founded the World Zionist Organization with Herzl, said in the Fifth Zionist Congress in 1901 that art should serve as a propaganda tool (Mishori, 2000, p. 16) [ATH]. Martin Buber developed this idea further and saw art as a tool for creating a new, whole Jewish human being who would be prepared for the fulfilment of national goals (p. 16). Although not very high on the agenda, the establishment of a national museum in Jerusalem thus enacted another element of Zionism and nation building. It was not until 1965 that the Israel Museum opened its doors to the public, with a mission

> to collect, preserve, study and display the cultural and artistic treasures of the Jewish people throughout its long history as well as the art, ethnology, and archeology of the Land of Israel and its neighboring countries. It also aims at

encouraging original Israeli art. The building and art displays were financed by donations from Israel, America and Europe, mostly from Jews.

(Biran, 1997)

The initiator, fundraiser, and a driving force behind the museum was Teddy Kollek, who became mayor of Jerusalem from 1965 to 1993. No less important in this endeavour is Meyer Meyer, who headed the public relations department of the Israel Museum for 28 years (1964–1992). His work took Israeli fundraising and public relations a step further through enhanced creativity and strategic planning. Bernard Cherrick and Eliyahu Honig from the Hebrew University and Lucian Harris from Hadassah had been not just competitors but also friends who shared information about donors and ideas – a collaboration that probably impacted on the development of the profession as a whole.

Meyer (2002) described his fundraising techniques as a combination of fundraising on a personal level, strategic media relations, and extraordinary event management. His background included studies at the London School of Economics and the London School of Journalism in 1947 and work, as a soldier, for the Israel Defense Forces (1948–1950) in the Hasbara Department. His Hasbara experience was enhanced by seven years of work in the Ministry of Foreign Affairs (1950–1957) and then by journalistic work as political correspondent of the daily newspaper *Maariv*. He became the first spokesperson of the Israeli Prime Minister's Office and from 1952 to 1964 worked with Teddy Kollek, its director. The fundraising and planning effort for the Israel Museum was performed as a national project by Kollek while he was in the Prime Minister's Office, and Meyer was involved.

In addition to the fundraising principles that placed personal contact and donor recognition in the centre, Meyer developed event management to a high art. It started with the inauguration ceremony on May 11, 1965, which he planned and managed for 3,000 participants. The audience was amazed and felt part of history in the making (Gilbert, 1998, p. 355). Meyer credits his media relations planning for the success. He started creating anticipation for the opening event five months before the date. He supplied reporters with a constant flow of stories about the pieces of art, the donors, and the building progress. Meyer (2002) also records offering encouragement – despite reservations from the Journalists' Association – to get items into the news by rewarding specific reporters: "[W]e gave a medal to Zvi Lavi, a reporter from *Maariv*, and Natan Ribon, a reporter from *Ha'aretz*. The publicity they gave to the museum attracted half a million visitors in the first year."

The medal to journalists for good service to the organization is another instance of the strong collaboration between journalists and Hasbara people in Jerusalem. As was demonstrated in the case of Zionist institutions and Hadassah, Hasbara executives and journalists worked on the same side to promote the cause of Zionist projects.

Meyer Meyer's reputation owes much to the creative theme parties he organized for the museum's International Council members and Friends of the

Museum groups. The council, which included major donors, came from abroad to discuss management issues. Meyer wanted them to have a memorable experience, and his parties promoted donations:

> The first party in the end of the 1970s was held in the desert of Qumran where the Dead Sea scrolls, exhibited in "The Shrine of the Book" next to the museum, had been discovered by Bedouins and researched by Israeli archaeologists. The guests did not have an idea about the location. Two hundred elegant guests, some of the richest people in the world, were driven to a Bedouin tent, seated on the floor, and served basic foods of the time of the Second Temple in clay dishes. We created the atmosphere of the time with dancers and music, food, and unique location. It was such an exceptional and shocking idea but proved a huge success.
>
> (Meyer, 2002)

These kinds of theme events have become a common public relations professional service in Israel since the end of the 1980s and the economic boom. But Meyer was a pioneer. He not only created a novelty but also executed it perfectly, and continued to use it for fundraising in later years when board members expected unconventional annual dinners:

> We organized a Sultan dinner in the Hisham Palace in Jericho, a Roman dinner in the Kardo, the old Roman market in the old city of Jerusalem, and a Crusade dinner reconstructing the picture of Pieter Brueghel in the forests of Aqua Bella near Jerusalem.
>
> (Meyer, 2002)

Meyer not only raised money but also acquired a lot of works of art, especially donations of Judaica items. Like Cherrick and Weisgal, Meyer Meyer (2002) used personal solicitations and developed friendships with donors:

> You have to love them and pamper them, not to "milk" them. We have established Friends of the Museum associations all over the world and supplied them with information about what has been done and what can be done. We excited them and it worked.

Another of Meyer's contributions to the field was his pioneering academic course in public relations in the Communication Department of the Hebrew University in the 1970s. For 12 years he conducted a public relations workshop for communication graduate students. He did not use any textbook and just shared his experiences and the lessons from his own career.

Conclusion

The unique connection with world Jewry, and the heritage of Shluhei Eretz Israel [the Emissaries], enabled public relations practitioners to contribute to nation building. Fundraising was a major drive for public relations development, it accorded fundraisers status, and it brought professional values from abroad to Israeli practitioners. This chapter has examined different styles of practice in four major institutions, which sometimes even solicited the same donors. We have seen that the practitioners at the service of these institutions were very highly educated and were motivated by Zionist ideology. They did not perceive themselves so much as professionals, but more as part of the Zionist effort to return the Jewish people to Israel. They felt enlisted to working within an enlisted society. The high level of collaboration with the journalists they worked with is also part of the enlisted environment in Israel and the type of institutions that they served.

Their high level of commitment is demonstrated by the lengthy service that many gave to the one organization. They were connected in a professional network and influenced each other. In their area of public relations specialization, they developed a model closer to ideas of 21st-century practice as building "mutually beneficial relationships" (Heath, 2001, p. 3), rather than earlier approaches designed more for "engineering acceptance" (p. 3). The challenges of fundraising, especially international fundraising, acted as a stimulus to professional development. In order to achieve their goals they had to create more professional public relations departments to cultivate such mutually beneficial relations (especially with the donors). The next chapter examines the role of public relations in the development of the national economy and markets, and it looks at major campaigns that were part of economic development and change.

8 Economics, market changes, and major campaigns

Duhé and Sriramesh (2009) argue that "[t]he unique interplay between political system and economic system impacts the public relations process – whether in the corporate, nonprofit, or government realm – in profound and identifiable ways" (p. 25). Their argument suggests that to understand the role of public relations in a specific society, it is important to use political economy theory from a state-centric perspective and "by first examining the interests and constraints of the state to better understand the economic phenomena occurring within it" (p. 34).

There can be few better places than Israel for demonstrating the proximity between political ideology and economic development, and the immediacy of the link between an open and competitive liberal economy and the growth of public relations services. This chapter charts the abnormal development process of Israel's economy, describes the Israeli market's major sectors, and considers the role of public relations practitioners in promoting economic and political interests. We identify the changing status of the major sectors, agriculture, industry, and commerce, which were dominant at different periods of time. Significant public relations work was involved in the issues these sectors faced and in their relationship with the government and others, as well as in their intersectoral struggles.

Background

The shift away from deep government involvement, and a protectionist and isolated economy, towards an open, competitive market happened only from the 1980s. During the first three decades of the state, Israel's economy was shaped according to the political ideology of the founders and collective nation-building efforts. The national narratives set up expectations that the individual would subject self-interest to the national challenges and sacrifice economic comfort for the collective mission. Zionist ideology led the economy in a controlled and monopolistic system. The Organization for Economic and Co-operation and Development (OECD) described the change as follows:

> Historically Israel's economy was an agrarian three-sector economy – the public sector, the Histadruth . . . and the private sector. During the 1980s a

process of macro-economic and structural reforms, including disengagement of the government from the economy and deregulation across all sectors, was begun. This was accelerated in the 1990s while at the same time Israel pursued a foreign policy designed to further integrate the country into the world markets, concluding a range of bilateral and multilateral economic agreements.

(OECD, 2002, p. 2)

Israel's economic growth was dramatic: "[B]etween 1950 and 2009, Israel's GDP rose 34-fold, and its GDP per capita increased almost six-fold in real terms. By 2009, the population reached 7.9 million, the national income was almost $203 billion, and income per capita came to $27,275, using 2008 prices and exchange rates" (Rivlin, 2011, p. 1). In May 2010, Israel was accepted as the 32nd member of the OECD, and would need to abide by OECD standards in liberalization of the market, business ethics, environmental and social responsibility, and more.

We identify the changing status of the major sectors, agriculture, industry, and commerce, which were dominant at different periods of time and the involvement of public relations in major campaigns for the three sectors: from agriculture during the first 50 years of the 20th century, through industrialization during the 1960s–1990s period, to commercialization as the dominant factor in the 1990s and the new millennium.

Period one: agriculture

The first pioneers, who migrated to Israel at the beginning of the 20th century, were motivated by the Zionist ideology that wished to create a new Hebrew Jew [Yehudi Ivri] there as opposed to the Diaspora Jew (see Almog, 1997, pp. 15–17), and turned to agriculture as a transformative tool. The connection with the land had to be created by working the land and by education (see Chapter 6's account of the propaganda and education projects of the pre-state era). Against international trends, as the developed world moved into urbanization and industrialization, the Zionist pioneers [Halutzim] tried to turn a nation of merchants into farmers. Elon (1983, p. 111) described the rationale for this process:

> Technically speaking, they were colonists. Yet by temperament, motivation, circumstance, and choice they differed sharply from other immigrants of that period who colonized Australia, Africa, Canada, or the United States. They were not in search of fertile land, gold, unlimited opportunity, or steady employment in a fast-expanding economy. Nor were they sent by chartered companies or government anxious to rid themselves of surplus populations, expand the territories under their control, or make the flag follow the trade. This was colonizing without a motherland. . . . They became farmers less for practical than for ideological reasons. . . . It might have been easier and quicker to develop trade and industry; but for ideological reasons they did not.

Working the land was glorified for many reasons: the transformation of the Jew's image from a "parasite" in the Diaspora economies into a normal productive human being; the Tolstoyan concept of acquiring "moral" ownership of a land by cultivating it; and also, the political power provided to the leaders of the Yishuv, and the new state, by the agricultural collective movements of the kibbutzim and the moshavim. Research into the kibbutz economy describes how the national institutions of the Yishuv allocated public resources in the 1930s:

> In spite of the fact that most of the Jewish market in the land of Israel was built in the days of the fourth and fifth Aliyah [1924–1939] by private money, which constituted the major imported capital, most of the resources of the settling institutions were invested in the Working Settlement Movement [Ha-Hityashvut Ha-Ovedet], i.e. the Moshavim and the Kibbutzim that belonged to Mapai and to other parties of the Labour Movement, who participated in the Zionist institutions and the Yishuv institutions.
> (Aharoni, 1991, pp. 53–55, cited in Rosolio, 1999, p. 100) [ATH]

Justman (2002) adds another reason for the leading role of agriculture: the settlements would define the borders of the country by their sheer presence. Agriculture offered a way to conquer the land (a logic, incidentally, that was adopted later, by the religious settlers' movement, following the 1967 annexation of Arab territories):

> In the past, agriculture was at the forefront of the Zionist movement, epitomizing the Jewish people's renewed physical connection to the land and defining the borders of its emerging national entity. The communal and cooperative settlements – the kibbutzim and moshavim – that comprised a bulk of the agricultural sector carried a unique message of collective solidarity, egalitarianism, and a reliance on one's own (rather than hired) labor. ... For all of these reasons, the pre-1985 agriculture sector enjoyed extensive preferential treatment, operating in a protective bubble in which water prices and quantities, the allocation of land and land rents, production quotas, and marketing channels both at home and abroad were all centrally controlled by agricultural interests.
> (p. 460)

The land and water conditions in Israel were not ideal for developing agriculture, but the government insisted on supporting it because agriculture had a major educational value for mobilization and for building the nation.

The Israeli elementary school curriculum included a special course on agriculture that gave the young children an opportunity to grow vegetables and flowers on the school's farm. In their nostalgic lexicon "Where We Were and What We Did," Dankner and Tartakover (1996) describe the entry on the "Agriculture Course" as follows:

An important part of the Zionist education. Because the settlements and agriculture were considered the splendid creation of the national project, and the connection with nature in general taken as a serious value, every elementary school had a special course in agriculture in which sons of shopkeepers who would eventually become bankers, and daughters of clerks who would eventually become clinical psychologists, were standing bent in the garden-beds planting and seeding and hoeing and raking and getting in touch with father nature and mother land and singing "who to thank for, who to bless, labor and work."

(p. 193) [ATH]

For many reasons, the political economy of the first six decades of Zionism focused on collective agriculture:

The dominant version of Zionism, at least until 1977, was the state-led one that evolved out of European, left-wing ideologies at the end of the nineteen and in the early twentieth centuries. Collective action was regarded, at least until the early 1960s, as the most effective way to realize national interests. This ideology tended to view profits as parasitic and services as unproductive.

(Rivlin, 2011, p. 22)

The high status of the agricultural sector entailed both a lower status for industry, and no legitimacy for merchants. It was not until the mid-1950s that the government started to encourage industry. Leaders of the Zionist movement identified the pioneering spirit with agriculture and romanticized it because it was the way to seize land. Industry would not go to frontier areas, where the cooperative farms of settlers were conquering the land of Israel.

Period two: industry

Eventually the Zionist leaders came to understand the importance of industry to economic development, and especially to the employment of new mass immigration, but they were unable to support it ideologically. Industry, like commerce, was considered private business founded by private investors and therefore not to be supported by public funds. Industrialists, and their organized associations, belonged to the right wing and would not support the leading Mapai party. The Zionist ideology supported only the idea of cooperative enterprises owned by the organized workers (i.e. the Histadrut and the General Federation of Labor, which were linked to the dominant Mapai and other parties of the left). The Histadrut, established in the 1920s, which became "one of the most powerful bodies in the Yishuv and later in Israel, was not only a trade union but also an employer and provider of welfare services" (Rivlin, 2011, p. 14).

Industry changed its status from "a step-daughter" (Beilin, 1987, p. 10) [ATH] of agriculture into a legitimate sector, with Pinchas Sapir as Minister of Commerce and Industry in 1955, and then as Minister of Finance from 1963 to 1974. Sapir supported investments in new development towns and encouraged industries, mainly the food and textile industries, that were able to employ great numbers of unskilled new immigrants:

> In the second half of the 1950s, when it appeared that industrialisation should get priority to provide employment for immigrants and to stimulate economic growth, resources were shifted from agriculture to investment in industry. ... There was active encouragement for the growth of major financial and industrial empires which now rival the Histadrut enterprises in resources and entrepreneurial talent, providing competition and enhancing central government control.
>
> (Shimshoni, 1982, p. 283)

The Sapir days were known for a system of dependency on government bureaucracy, and especially on Sapir himself, who held the control over investment resources. Sapir's central control was enhanced by the "Sapir fund" of donations that he personally raised from Israeli industry and foreign donors and channelled to institutions and municipalities, reinforcing his interdependency with them (Shimshoni, 1982, p. 246).

In his retrospective evaluation of Zionist economic policy, Beilin's (1987) possible assessment is that the "marginalizing of the industry in the first quarter of the century was an expensive mistake that lasted in this form or another till 1955" (p. 239) [ATH] and concludes that the "assumption that it would be possible to supply work to all the citizens in agriculture at a time when the entire western world had turned to industry, was a naïve mistake" (p. 239).

Industry and commerce

Eventually the growth of industry was welcomed and integrated into the nation building ethos. Then, following the 1967 war (and the annexation of the Arab territories), Israel's sources of ammunition abroad declared an embargo. The Israeli government decided to develop its own military industry, which laid the foundation for the highly developed technological industry of Israel in the 1980s and 1990s. The demand for more and better products increased, and industrialists became heroes.

However, this was not the fate of the commercial sector and the merchants. In a celebration organized by the Chamber of Commerce in 1989, the prime minister, Yitzhak Shamir, expressed public regret about the way the organized Yishuv had treated the merchants:

> To be a merchant in those days meant to continue the Diaspora style ... with the feeling of a shameful smile Israelis today may recall how great people among us called Jewish merchants "human dust," while praising the working people, as if only warts on the hands are signs and identity cards for working men.
>
> (cited in Bettelheim, 1990, p. 11) [ATH]

The association of commerce with the image of the Diaspora Jews had a very strong emotional impact on Israelis. Neither industrialists nor merchants were glorified in the discourse of the first six decades of Zionism. Belonging to the business sector that worked for profit, they were not part of the people who were working to settle the country, and therefore industrialists and merchants could join together in a struggle for recognition. When, finally, industry was elevated to a higher status on the Zionist agenda, while commerce still stayed behind, the animosity between manufacturers and merchants grew into competitive rivalry. This problematic status of manufacturers and merchants was reflected in the activities and communication of their organized associations and the relationships between them.

The establishment of the Histadrut in 1920 stimulated an effort by the small sector of employers, including industrialists, merchants, and builders, to become organized to deal with labour disputes. Later on, in 1925, the industrialists separated from the merchants and builders and created the Association of Industry Owners in Eretz Israel. From that time, this association managed public relations campaigns to pressure government decisions regarding taxation and economic policy, while also making an effort to improve the image of industrialists and prove their value to the new Israeli society.

Arie Shenkar, who served as president of the industrialists between 1930 and 1960, was a charismatic centralist leader. However, according to Beilin (1987) he avoided political activity in principle and therefore the association did not influence the national agenda (p. 204). Shenkar was followed by second-generation industrialists who created coalitions with the cooperative sector of the Histadrut and the government, and turned industry into a major force in both the Israeli market and the political decision-making process.

Period three: commercialization and the trade associations of industry

Chambers of Commerce were active from the early 1920s, when they were supported by the British Mandate authorities. There were independent chambers in Tel Aviv, Jerusalem, Haifa, and other Jewish and Arab towns. The Tel Aviv Chamber was the dominant and representative group. Eliezer Hofein served as its second president from 1922 to 1943 and led its struggles with the authorities, including the Tozeret haAretz campaign (see the description later in this chapter), which was at the centre of the controversy between the manufacturers and the merchants.

During the 1920s there were fewer than 800 shops in Tel Aviv, and most of them were small businesses. The Yishuv's economy during the Mandate depended on capital from abroad and suffered from instability. In 1932, when new waves of immigration from Germany brought private capital and a high level of education, industry and commerce enjoyed a real period of development.

According to Bettelheim (1990), the British government was in charge of managing a fair and responsible market and tried to enable the development of both the Arab and the Jewish economies, without satisfying either side. The competition with British firms, which, with the help of the Mandate government, took the place of local importers, added more reasons for complaints.

Both the Industrialists' Association and the Chambers of Commerce had to fight for common interests against the British Mandate government and the national institutions in the pre-state era. Both used public relations techniques. Both felt unrecognized and discriminated against in the allocation of resources and as regards taxation and status. They had common interests and were able to cooperate during the 1930s in their lobbying and communication efforts. Yet the relationship deteriorated in the 1940s. Arguments developed over the issues of Tozeret haAretz, the marketing of local-made products, and the importing of competing products. The cooperation turned into bitter controversy that lasted until the end of the 20th century.

Zvi Amit (2002), who served as general director of the Israel Chambers of Commerce from 1976 to 1997, explains:

> The Israeli economy was built upside down. Everywhere else, merchants were respected as innovators, discoverers of new continents. In developed economies, commerce is the biggest employer; services and commerce are expressions of progress. But in Israel, commerce and services were considered parasites and had to pay more taxes and deal with lots of restrictions. The assumption was that local industry would create jobs and prevent the spending of foreign currency. In fact, the government policy of protection prevented competition, increased the prices of products, and was responsible for the lag in the standard of living. Patriotism and promotion of local products exists everywhere but it does not lead to antagonism between the manufacturers and merchants to the level of a total boycott on imports.

The manufacturers demanded protection. Their public argument was employment. Competition with imported products would shut down Israeli plants and would push many employees out of the workforce. The merchants wanted liberalization of imports and free competition. Their argument was that a healthy market should be regulated by laws of supply and demand. Competition with world markets would benefit the consumer and raise the standard of living.

The merchants had, in addition, a hidden agenda: they wanted to be recognized and included in the political decision-making process regarding economic policy. Until the 1980s, those decisions were made by the "sacred triangle" of the Ministry of Finance, the General Federation of Labor, and the Association of Industrialists. Dan Gillerman was appointed in 1985 as president of the national Chamber of Commerce. He used public controversy about liberalization of the market to lever the status of the merchants to a level that would include them as partners in the economic leadership of the country. He was assisted greatly by the work of Zvi Amit, the chambers' general director, who since 1976 had raised the profile of the chambers internally and externally. He had integrated the local groups into a national Chamber of Commerce, developed internal newsletters and magazines, used the chamber logo to identify businesses of members, created club activities, and increased membership from 800 in 1976 to 3,300 in 1997 (Amit, 2002).

The Industrialists' Association did not like these developments. It had a long-term relationship with the government ministries and did not need a new partner, especially not one that supported Ministry of Finance initiatives regarding import liberalization. The industrialists recommended a slower, gradual move towards the abolition of the barriers of customs, standardization approvals, and purchase taxes. In 1993, according to David Eshkol (2002), who was retained as public relations consultant to the Industrialists' Association,

> Dov Lautman, the president of the industrialists, could not stand Dan Gillerman, who was suddenly interviewed in the media following the monthly index announcements. He saw himself as the representative of the whole business sector in relation to the Finance Ministry and the Histadrut. He was personally offended by Gillerman's opposition and the attention the media gave him.

The 1985 Economic Stabilization Program, led by Shimon Peres as Minister of Finance, brought about a dramatic change in Israel's economic development:

> Government intervention in the markets of production factors and finance was significantly reduced, and deregulation has made the markets more competitive. The structure of main industry groups has become more intensive in trade and services at the expense of all other industries, including manufacturing. The nature of manufacturing, too, has changed profoundly; the share of human-capital-intensive civilian high-tech industries has been growing steadily and that of defense and traditional industries has been diminishing.
> ... The stabilization program marked a turning point in the economic approach of the two large political parties: from an economy in which the government is deeply involved, directly and indirectly, in almost all areas of economic activity, to an economy increasingly based on market forces.
> (Ben-Bassat, 2002, p. 1)

The Stabilization Program included a change in Israel's international trade policy. A series of agreements with the European Community, which were signed during the 1965–1975 period, were fully applied by 1989; the agreement with the United States was signed in 1985 and fully implemented in 1995.

The problem was with imports from "third countries," those with which Israel had no trade agreements. The cheap products from Third World countries bypassed the barriers via the agreement with the Europeans and Americans. This became the issue of dispute between the manufacturers and merchants during the 1990s. Eventually, by the end of the millennium, Israel moved into almost total exposure to foreign trade (Ben-Bassat, 2002, p. 28). The profound change in economic policy involved intensive public relations campaigns led by representatives of the industrialists on the one hand and by representatives of the merchants on the other.

Public relations campaigns

The realities of the Israeli market involved the national leadership of political and economic organizations attempting to mobilize public opinion about issues and interests. This subsection overviews major campaigns to explain changes in the public agenda regarding the national economy and also to show how public relations tools influenced that agenda.

Avoda Ivrit [Hebrew Labour]

The campaign for Avoda Ivrit [Hebrew Labour] during the Yishuv period was a key nation-building campaign by the Jewish Agency, the Histadrut, and other national institutions. It implemented major Zionist principles and illustrates self-contradicting Zionist values:

> Hebrew labour was . . . the true infrastructure for integrative nationalism: The cult of labour was a tool for conquering the land and means for metamorphosis of the Jewish person, an obvious expression of the moral revolution and a condition for the big national revolution.
> (Sternhell, 1995, p. 199) [ATH]

However, behind the Zionist slogans lay bitter competition with cheap Arab labour over scarce employment in the farms and the port.

The Avoda Ivrit campaign created a deep cognitive dissonance for the socialist Zionists, who saw themselves as part of the working-class socialist solidarity movement at the same time as they were advocating discrimination against the Arab employees. The rational for "Jewish Labour" was that "native labour must not be 'exploited' in the reconstruction of the country by Jews" (Elon, 1983, p. 170). "Hebrew Labour" became a slogan that raised controversy and criticism. It involved violent demonstrations and strikes. It started in 1929 on the farms with a demand from the Jewish farmers to employ Jews. Shapira (1973) evaluated this campaign as a failure but a propaganda victory: "In the public mind it stayed as a memory of a beautiful, heroic, and just campaign for Hebrew Labour" (p. 229) [ATH]. In 1934 the campaign moved to the towns and demanded the employment of Jews in the port and building industry. The tool used by the Histadrut might be considered as a predecessor for Mao Zedong's People's Guards decades later:

> [T]he "mobile guard" appeared. This consisted of a large group of workers who moved from one Arab workplace to another, and tried to convince the Jewish employer to employ Jews instead of Arabs. Where persuasion did not work, guards were stationed. In Haifa they stood next to the workplaces with signs explaining that in that place Arabs were employed. More than once the

members of the guard fought with the Arab employees, or, as the discourse of that period called it, "taking them off" the work. Often the employer had to call the [British] police.

(Shapira, 1973, p. 229) [ATH]

According to Elon (1983), the results left an impression of "cultural arrogance . . . upon Israel's national character" (p. 170) rather than the "'colonial vocation'" (p. 170) common to settlers in other parts of the world: "By avoiding the typical pattern of colonial settlers elsewhere, the policy of Avoda Ivrit bred in their hearts a deeply felt, and totally sincere, sense of moral superiority over other colonialists" (p. 170). Berl Katzenelson, one of the prominent leaders of the labour movement and the founder of its newspaper *Davar*, managed the campaign against the "Radical Left," whose members were protecting the rights of the Arabs to work. Sternhell (1995) cites Katzenelson's explanation of how that negated the struggle of the Jewish worker in the name of equality and proletarian solidarity, since the

> equality in question, says Katzenelson, is only a fake equality, because the Arab market is closed for the Jewish worker and so is the Governmental [British] sector that decides a labour fee which Jews can't accept. The whip of "equality" is just a means for hitting Hebrew Labour.
>
> (pp. 199–200) [ATH]

For the post-Zionist movement, which was active in Israel in the late 1990s, the Avoda Ivrit campaign exposed the hypocrisy of the Zionist founders. Kimmerling's (2001) book about the Ashkenazi hegemony, which, drawing on the American term WASP, he calls "Achusaliut" (an acronym for Ashkenazi, Secular, Veteran, Socialists and Nationalist), argues that the Zionist socialism was no more than rhetoric that covered up political interests: "The proletarian struggle was managed from the beginning against low-paid skilled Arab workers who were employed by the settlers and the city bourgeois" (p. 21) [ATH]. Using "the slogan 'Hebrew Labour' they were asked to replace the Arabs by Jewish workers and guards, who were better paid and were less skilled, but had that nationalist and socialist consciousness" (p. 21) [ATH].

The Hebrew press served as a tool of the Histadrut and the Jewish Agency leadership by backing the campaign and using such words as "foreign labour" and "cheap labour" (Shapira, 1973, p. 230) (ATH). In an internal debate of the Mapai party in 1934, some members argued that this campaign was unethical, especially when there was work for everybody. In this meeting, Moshe Shertok, then head of the Jewish Agency's Political Department, demanded that the guards' activities be limited and advocated caution in the publicity given to this activity in the press. Those opposing him "argued that it would be impossible to promote Hebrew Labour without agitating public opinion and creating a certain public atmosphere. Reducing the campaign and 'lowering its profile' meant giving up its most effective tool" (pp. 230–231) [ATH].

Significantly, in terms of public relations, the leaders of the Histadrut and the Jewish Agency could decide the tone and content of the press coverage. They did not have to worry about press questioning or criticism of the campaign, as it served what the Yishuv's leadership defined as the national interest.

Tozeret haAretz [Local Hebrew produce]

The campaign to promote local Jewish products, Tozeret haAretz, was inspired by the same ideology and needs. This time it was competition with cheap products and a demand for the protection of Jewish products. It became a major message in a long-term campaign managed by the Zionist pre-state institutions and later the Israeli government and civil society. The campaign, which started in 1925 in a youth movement (see Almog, 1997, p. 446), was continued in 1935 by the president of the Association for Industry Owners, Arie Shenkar, who established the Center for Tozeret ha-Aretz (Felber, 1996, p. 13) [ATH]. This centre was a coalition of the Zionist national institutions leaders, the Histadrut, the Vaad Leumi [National Committee], the Association of Industry Owners, and local organizations. As Beilin (1987) observes:

> The campaign for Tozeret haAretz, like the campaign for Avoda Ivrit, mixed several interests. Both were expressions of a national-Zionist struggle; both were managed against simple economic interests: Arab labour was cheaper, and sometimes more efficient, than Jewish labour, and Jewish products were more expensive and sometimes of worse quality compared to the imports. Just as the labour movement fought its campaign for Avoda Ivrit, for securing jobs for organized labour in the Histadrut framework, so did the industry owners in their campaign for Tozeret haAretz. They wanted to make sure their products would be preferred over imports.
>
> (p. 197) [ATH]

The Center for Tozeret haAretz organized "battalions" that pressured merchants and builders to sign commitments to use only Jewish products. It published advertisements calling on people to avoid the purchase of imported merchandise and organized vigilante guards near shops that sold imported products. It used posters with slogans that later became part and parcel of Israeli nostalgic culture. The Zionist Archives of the Jewish Agency in Jerusalem (retrieved December 4, 2002) and the Judaica library in Harvard University (retrieved August 9, 2002) keep a collection of posters from different periods calling on people to fulfil a Zionist commitment and to "Buy Blue-White" (the colours of the Israeli flag).

A commemorative book produced by the Chamber of Commerce in 1990 contains a series of documents from the 1930s and 1940s that describe the violence of the campaigners against merchants and importers. A letter of complaint sent to the Jewish Agency by the president of the Chamber of Commerce in December 1946 describes

[t]he wild, anarchic behaviour of people who call themselves "the people's guard." ... In January 1947 the Chamber of Commerce received a letter from an "industrial supply company" that complained against leaflets carrying overt threats to importers. Among others, the leaflets published names of importers and the products that they imported. In addition to the fact that this attitude smells of Fascism, and the merchants reject it totally, we think that this is a harmful tactic with regard to the economic future of our country.
(cited in Bettelheim, 1990, p. 75) [ATH]

The campaign became a real war which involved a bomb that destroyed a warehouse full of building materials, setting fire to shops, and beating importers (see Bettelheim, 1990, pp. 75–78) [ATH].

From 1935 the Tozeret haAretz campaign used press publicity in a similar way to the earlier promotion of Avoda Ivrit and addressed the "moral and the national interest to secure its place among the consumers" (Shapira, 1973, p. 231) [ATH], and that was "also the reason for the ideological partnership between the Association of Industry Owners and the labour movement: both demanded that the economic interest of the individual be subject to the national interest" (pp. 231–232). The campaign was also based on a consumer boycott and the creation of what Abba Hushi in *Davar* in 1935 called "an appropriate public opinion and public atmosphere that will intimidate and terrify those considering buying non-Hebrew products" (cited in Shapira, 1973, p. 232) [ATH]. The Tozeret haAretz campaign used guards, press publicity, and denunciation of uncooperative consumers by mobilizing public opinion against them.

Beyond publicity, the campaign for Tozeret haAretz followed the Keren Kayemet le-Israel model (see Chapter 6) by using the education system to deliver the message. Almog (1997) describes it as part of the socialization process of the Sabra, whereby "Buy Tozeret haAretz" (p. 324) reflected the importance of the value of self-sufficiency and Spartanism in the pioneering and the Sabra culture, where the "call to buy products made in Eretz Israel [by the local Jewish manufacturers] got wide publicity in the kindergartens and schools" (p. 324) [ATH], and one textbook even said: "Dear children! Your parents are spending a lot of money every year for your clothes and shoes. You should know that they can buy all this from Tozeret haAretz (i.e., from what is being produced in Eretz Israel)" (p. 324).

The campaigns led by national institutions during the Yishuv era were continued after the establishment of the state and had a long life. Both Avoda Ivrit and Tozeret haAretz demanded a sacrifice and a high price from the public. Beilin (1987) noted the "similarity between the demand of the Labor movement from the farmers to employ only Jewish workers and the demand of the industrialists to buy only Jewish products Tozeret haAretz" (p. 217) [ATH] because when "the workers fought for their employment, they fought for a national interest" (p. 217), and when "the industrialists fought for selling their products and for their livelihood, they were fighting for a national cause" (p. 217).

The exclusionary nature of the messages that urged the Jewish settlers to employ Jews rather than Arabs, to buy only local products made by Jews, to speak

Hebrew, and to connect to the land resulted in a high level of unity and helped mobilize people to focus on the collective, almost sacred, goal of building the nation.

The associations' communication

From their beginnings in the 1920s, both the Association of Industry Owners and the Chambers of Commerce acted like pressure groups and used communication and public relations tools, albeit without professional services. Beilin (1987) quotes a report of the Association of Industry Owners' first convention in 1926, which complains that

> [i]nstead of concentrating all our energy in constructive building, instead of expanding our plants and creating new infrastructure for new plants, we had to campaign all the time: we had to explain, clarify, fight against right and left, provoke and be on guard for our interests, which were always discriminated against.
> (Zionist Archives, S8/2243, cited in Beilin, 1987, p. 196) [ATH]

In 1937 the Association of Industry Owners started to produce its own monthly magazine, *The Industry* [Hata'asia], which has been published ever since. In 1941 it launched an industrial exhibition "as part of the effort to persuade the British and allies to order products produced in the land of Israel. This exhibition became an annual event for many years" (Beilin, 1987, p. 200).

The Tel Aviv Chamber of Commerce documents reveal a similar communication effort from 1924 and include correspondence with editors and evidence that the chamber provided its meeting decisions to all the daily newspapers. The chamber had a special section in the professional monthly *Commerce and Industry*. In 1947 it issued a monthly that provided information about the development of the Hebrew market:

> From its first day, the Chamber kept informing journalists about its struggles and invited journalists to its general meetings. Later on, the secretary "discovered" the magic of "background conversations" with journalists, to promote the interests of the Chamber, or to block procedures of the British government that contradicted the interests of the merchants. . . . The establishment of the state, the struggle for the status of the commerce in Israel, the controversy with the government about the role of the merchants, and the severed relationship with the Industrialists Association – all these increased the need for publicity and public relations for the Chamber of Commerce. . . . A memo from 1952 reports about a programme to hold frequent press conferences, periodical cocktail parties for diplomats, ministers, and officials, and to manage a consistent public relations activity.
> (Bettelheim, 1990, pp. 162–165) [ATH]

Economics, market changes, and major campaigns 117

During the same period the American National Association of Manufacturers (NAM) similarly justified corporate public relations as part of its campaign for public recognition and for opposing government policies. Marchand (1998) described the NAM's discussions at its 1935 convention, which called on businesses to "sell the American way of life" (p. 203) to the American people, and to educate the public towards what business was really doing for the economy. The need to hire the expert storytellers of the public relations firms and advertising agencies became evident: "While launching a counterattack against the New Deal, major corporations institutionalized the public relations function within their managerial structures" (pp. 202–203).

The Israeli manufacturers and merchants managed their campaigns without the help of professional public relations firms until the 1960s. At that time, public relations firms started to function in Tel Aviv, but they were few, small, and did not represent many clients (see Chapter 11). The Israeli business sector did not enjoy the public legitimacy of the American sector, and the public relations profession was not recognized as an essential part of it.

Later controversy

Tozeret haAretz became the centre of the controversy between the Industrialists' Association (a new name for the Association of Industry Owners that reflected a new policy: the inclusion of industry managers who were not industry owners) and the Chamber of Commerce years later, in the 1980s and mainly in the 1990s. This public controversy stimulated professional public relations efforts by both organizations over a number of years. The issues were basically the same as in the pre-state era: open market versus closed market; liberated economy versus protectionist economy; and integration in the international markets versus the isolated economy.

The controversy of the 1980s and 1990s involved the work of several public relations practitioners: Eli Laniado, spokesperson and head of Communication and Industrial Education of the Industrialists' Association from 1983 to 2001; David Eshkol, owner of Logos Public Relations, a consultant for the industrialists' campaign, from 1993 to 1997; Zvi Amit, general director of the Chamber of Commerce from 1976 to 1997; and Orly Frumer, Bosmat Mardor, and Linda Shimon, who served as spokespersons for the Chamber of Commerce in different periods. Though Zvi Amit was not a public relations practitioner, his experience in journalism empowered his leadership of the Chamber of Commerce campaign. He designed the messages and decided the strategy. The spokespersons served in the media relations role (Amit, 2002).

According to Eli Laniado (2002), the industrialists made a very big effort to present the merchants as anti-Zionist and greedy. The industrialists' messages to the media described the merchants' intentions as being to flood Israel with junk products. There was also a personal campaign against Dan Gillerman, who, while supporting the liberalization initiatives of the Ministry of Finance, used very tough language against the industrialists. According to Laniado (2002), "We sent letters to Israel's economic attachés in the world advising them not to meet with Gillerman because he was not representing Israel's interests. It was an emotional campaign." Eshkol (2002) even revealed moves to destroy Gillerman's credibility in a tactic that would be considered unethical today: "A third office [Shabtai Raviv, a PR consultant] issued press releases that described the Chamber of Commerce as the enemy of Israel's economy. It used a lot of data about the size of imports to the country."

The leaders of the industrialists, Dov Lautman and Eli Horowitz, took part in street demonstrations against the Ministers of Finance Moshe Nissim and Yitzhak Modai in front of the ministry's office. Modai responded with anger and published a message to the manufacturers advising them to give up their membership in the association. The other strategic message of the industrialists' spokespeople focused on the historical contribution of industry to the development of Israel's economy. Eli Laniado (2002), a former journalist in Israeli television and communication adviser to Israel's embassy in Cairo, described the effort to "upgrade" the image of the industrialists:

> We initiated research about the history of industry in Israel and decided to celebrate "100 years of industry," connecting 1987 to the year the first manufacturer, Stein, immigrated to Israel. We produced a "story" about his life and used it in ceremonies, exhibitions, and parties. It became a central national theme in Israel's 40th anniversary events, and a special stamp was produced in honour of Israel's industrialists. Our celebrations were organised by a public committee headed by Israel's president, and the major event was held in the national official Jerusalem Convention Center Binyanei-Hauma. We commissioned a book, written by Shabtai Raviv, called *Industry and Action*, which was printed in a very fancy format as a special gift to decision makers. Most importantly, it became a subject in the syllabus of the "Industry Education Project."

The Industry Education project was another tool to improve the image of the Industrialists' Association, which was criticized at that time in Yossi Beilin's (1987) book. The Industrialists' Association established an "educational centre" with interactive presentations that attracted thousands of students and soldiers, who took courses lasting a day or a whole year. Laniado (2002) eventually moved to head this project as his exclusive responsibility and said it gave the association a great opportunity for networking with government officials from the Ministry of Education, the army, and other influential connections.

The industrialists' impressive professional effort was met by a no less intensive campaign on the part of the Chamber of Commerce. The campaign leader, Zvi Amit (2002), who was a former financial and economic reporter for *Yediot Ahronot* and a very skilful writer of slogans and headlines, explains his media tactics:

> We differentiated ourselves from the industrialists and we designed aggressive headlines such as "Mafia interest rate" instead of just "high interest rate."

I used a lot of surveys and price comparison tables to provide the media with useful illustrations for our arguments. Price comparisons gave us double-spread coverage space in the newspaper. We supplied a lot of information to the media and it made a big impact. Journalists appreciated our materials. Dan Gillerman was a very good spokesperson for the organisation – he was eloquent and cool on television and the message came across well.

The Chamber of Commerce adopted some of the industrialists' techniques as well. In 1989 it organized an official event to mark a hundred years for Israeli commerce with the state president, prime minister, and ministers; used a documentary film it had produced; and commissioned a book called *The Merchants* from *Maariv* newspaper reporter Avi Bettelheim (1990).

The campaigns of industrialists against merchants continued until 1998. In the end the globalization process won. Many of the leaders of the industrialists became involved in imports themselves and could no longer appear as protecting local employment. Dan Proper, the president of the Industrialists' Association in the second half of the 1990s, introduced Nestlé International to his food company, Osem. Dov Lautman, former president, moved textile plants to foreign countries where labour was cheaper than in Israel. Globalization blurred the distinction between manufacturers and merchants, and, as Zvi Amit (2002) comments, "Finally the Israeli politicians accepted the idea that there was no point in producing something that can be produced cheaper somewhere else. We had better produce what we excel in and import what is possible to import cheaper."

And on the other side, Eli Laniado (2002) admitted defeat on the part of the industrialists by acknowledging that their campaign did not win over the public since the "moment people were exposed to a variety of prices they were not ready to pay for Zionism from their own pockets ... [and] buy 'Blue-White'," although in 2002 "the Minister of Industry and Commerce, Dalia Itzik, still used the slogan and came up with a project to promote Tozeret haAretz ... it would not work. The markets are full and the importers are celebrating." In the new millennium, commerce and services are the largest group in the business sector. Their production increased by 124% in the period from 1985 to 1998 and they create more new jobs and contribute more to employment in the country than others. Justman (2002) observes that a "socialist tradition that emphasized agriculture and manufacturing as core economic activities and viewed services as their derivative was also reflected in the meager statistical data on the service sector" (p. 471), and this was only "rectified in some measure" (p. 471) over the past few years.

During the 1990s the liberalization and the improvement in Israel's political situation, thanks to the peace process, attracted direct foreign investments. Israel's technological skills attracted international partnerships in high-tech companies and opened it to the most advanced global industries. The share of the public sector – the government and the Histadrut – in manufacturing declined with slow privatization. However, the welfare state principles of solidarity and care for the deprived have been eradicated as a result of privatization of social services. In 2011–2012 the widening economic gap, which is one of the highest in the developed world, was the major topic of the Israeli version of the international Occupy Movement protesting against economic and social inequality.

It is also relevant to note that while the business culture in Israel is very competitive and innovative in some ways, it is still influenced by past values, especially with regard to information. The democratic value of transparency has been far from completely absorbed, and the idea that the public has a right to know cannot be taken for granted. Israel is ranked 36 out of 183 countries on the Transparency International Index 2011, down from a ranking of 30 two years earlier. Nevertheless, Israel transformed itself into a modern technologically advanced economy that became integrated into global markets. Dan Senor and Saul Singer's (2009) *Start-Up Nation: The Story of Israel's Economic Miracle* publicizes the large number of innovative and entrepreneurial start-up companies in Israel: "In addition to boasting the highest density of start-ups in the world (a total of 3,850 start-ups, one for every 1,844 Israelis), more Israeli companies are listed on the NASDAQ exchange than all companies from the entire European continent" (p. 11).

Rivlin (2011) also praises the economic transformation: "[T]here is no other country in the world that has been at war for all of its history, and to have reached income per capita level approaching $30,000 is therefore a considerable achievement" (p. 243). As a postscript to both analyses, as Senor and Singer (2009) concede, "Another commonly cited factor in Israel's success is the country's military and defense industries, which has produced successful spin-off companies" (Senor & Singer, 2009, p. 17). Nevertheless, the strategic role played by high-tech industries and foreign investments – including some from Diaspora Jews and Israelis – contributed to the rapid expansion. It also created the appropriate environment for the development of public relations.

Conclusion

The use of public relations in the service of nation-building efforts committed to Zionist ideology and policies, and the associated involvement of public relations in the education system, is evident. This happened even though until the 1960s it was conducted by leaders with no professional training in public relations. The fuller professional services emerged with the growth of a competitive economy and with the opening of the Israeli market to the global economy.

This chapter and the preceding ones discussed the changes in the environment and events, and how they influenced the Israeli public sphere and discourse. The next chapter will describe public relations practice and practitioners who represented the Israeli government. They link the unique Israeli political, social, cultural, and economic development described so far with the professionalization process of public relations.

9 Speaking on behalf of government (1)

Government practitioners and Hasbara

In the formation of a national public relations profession, the role of government varies in different countries. In her account of Britain, L'Etang (2004) emphasizes the "large role played by local and central government and the relatively small contribution of the private sector" (p. ix), and isolates such official activities as a significant feature of British developments. Early in the 20th century, government officials in Britain identified a need to improve their communication with the local populace. Their responses included forming the Institute of Public Administration in 1922 and establishing the journal *Public Administration* in 1923 (Pieczka & L'Etang, 2001, p. 230).

From 1917 to 1948, Britain also governed Palestine under a mandate from the League of Nations and laid down infrastructure for the future State of Israel. The heritage of the British Mandate included the Israeli legal system, administrative institutions, and such communication channels as the Government Press Office, the radio station, and censorship. The Israeli government made public relations part of its newly established agencies and became an important employer of practitioners. As part of the newly forming government bureaucracy, practitioners, or Hasbara officials, helped in the shaping of the new Israel state.

In line with their predecessors, these Israeli leaders preferred the goal of creating unity over democratic consensus building. In order to achieve unity, and to educate a nation willing to fight and make significant sacrifices, the leadership used persuasive communication, education, and public relations campaigns under the government's own auspices. This chapter looks at government practitioners' work in the context of the newly formed state.

The model of public relations used by the government practitioners was akin to the old-style engineering of acceptance rather than the more recent building of "mutually beneficial relationships" (Heath, 2001, p. 3). Israeli culture was created, in part, through an intentional strategic communication programme. This was run by national institutions such as the JNF and the Jewish Agency (see Chapter 6), and by government organs, first by the Prime Minister's Office and later, mainly, by the Ministry of Education and the Israel Defense Forces (IDF).

The key developments in the change from the pre-state Yishuv era to the established State of Israel created new realities for inhabitants of Israel and public relations practitioners alike. On November 29, 1947, the decision of the United

Nations General Assembly to partition Palestine into an Arab and a Jewish state ended 30 years of the British Mandate. On May 14, 1948, the State of Israel was declared. The next day, the British left Palestine and the five surrounding Arab countries started a war against Israel. It took a year and a half until armistice agreements were signed and the state, then numbering around 600,000 Jews, started to establish its political, social, and cultural structures. Zameret and Yablonka (1997) accurately describe the first ten years, from 1948 to 1958, as "the shaping decade of the State of Israel" (p. 7) [ATH]. These years demanded sacrifices from Israelis. Challenges faced by the poor and tiny new state included security, the need to absorb mass immigration from many different countries, an austerity regime in a struggling, isolated economy, and the need to create a new Israeli identity for the new citizens.

Ben-Gurion and the first decades of independence

David Ben-Gurion was Israel's prime minister from 1948 to 1953 and Defense Minister from 1955 to 1963, and had a formative influence on Israel's emergent character though his two central principles: "Statehood" [Mamlachtiut; the primacy of the state]; and "Bithonism" [the use of force, activist defense, and foreign policy]. Ben-Gurion's plans emphasized the reshaping of the Jewish people in some detail:

> There is a need for Zionist control over the public. There is a need for a channel that would deliver the message of Zionism to every man and woman ... there is a need to plan state alternatives to the pioneering youth movements that would educate in the spirit of Labor Eretz Israel ... there is a need to design and style the holidays.
> (Ben Gurion Archives, Ben Gurion diaries, March 3, 1947, cited in Zameret, 1993, p. 57) [ATH]

Ben-Gurion's strategy – to educate the people "from above" by the state, and not by the volunteer pioneering frameworks developed during the Yishuv period – was part of his systematic attempt to create a New Hebrew person in Israel who would be the opposite of the Diaspora Jew.

Arye Carmon, the founder and president of the Israeli Institute for Democracy, criticized Ben-Gurion's concept of statehood as an obstacle to Israel's democratic system. Since Israel's society was immersed in fundamental conflicts and, at that time, needed to sustain pluralism, Carmon (1994) saw Ben-Gurion as rejecting "the tradition of political tolerance that existed in the Yishuv [pre-state period] in conditions of ideological pluralism" (p. 49) and concluded that because of Ben-Gurion's total commitment to statehood, "the public discourse about the goal of Israel ... , which could have enriched the developing ethos of Jewish sovereignty, was cut off at an early stage (pp. 49–50) [ATH].

Carmon's (1994) insight into Israel's defining values helps explain how Israel's public relations evolved differently from public relations in other countries.

This is particularly evident in nations with a stronger tradition of open public debate and consultation, such as the Netherlands. In the Netherlands, van Ruler (2004) traces the roots of Dutch public relations "as a history of the battle between information and emancipation on the one hand, and education and persuasion on the other hand," with the paternalist and authoritarian "'Dutch uncle' . . . dogma of 'knowing what is best'" being opposed by the "dialogue, negotiation and consensus-building . . . which for centuries has relied on the practice of consultation and the involvement of as many people as possible in decision-making" (pp. 264–265).

The Government Press Office

During the Independence War of 1947–1948, the Yishuv's Hasbara effort moved from the Jewish Agency in besieged Jerusalem to the army information services in Tel Aviv. Dr Moshe Pearlman, an author and journalist from London, and a graduate of the London School of Economics, was "in charge of the army press liaison unit and served as the army chief spokesperson" (Editorial Staff Encyclopedia Judaica, 1997). According to Mike Arnon (2002), who served as the spokesperson of the Ministry of Foreign Affairs until 1951, many foreign journalists were posted in Tel Aviv during the war and the army did not know how to deal with them. Moshe Pearlman and Abe Harman, who later became president of the Hebrew University, took charge and organized a press office in the Hotel Ritz in Tel Aviv. They framed the narrative that would continue to be used for generations to come. It told the story of a successful struggle by one small army of persecuted people against the many armies of aggressive Arab nations.

Once the British moved out, the new temporary government took control of the radio broadcast services and the Government Press Office (GPO) of the British Mandate. From June 1949, according to the first Government Annual Report 1949/1950, all the information services of different units were concentrated in the Prime Minister's Office. They included the Government Press Office, which communicated with Israeli media, the Foreign Press Office (those two were united in 1951), and the Broadcasting Service, which included the former British Kol Yerushalim and the underground Jewish broadcasting service Kol Israel, which had functioned since 1945 (GAR, 1949/1950, p. 23) [ATH].

The new government, following the practice of the Jewish National Fund and the Jewish Agency, used the same terms – Hasbara, propaganda, and public relations – to describe the same kinds of activities [ATH]. Within the Prime Minister's Office the information services managed a variety of functions described in detail in the government's annual reports. The 1953 report, for example, describes the work of the different departments. This included media relations (139 foreign reporters were working in Israel in 1953), brochures, and a wall newspaper with photos [marot Israel], and pre-prepared radio programmes. The Hasbara department was involved in organizing tours for new immigrants and citizens for them to view government accomplishments (GAR, 1953, p. 19) [ATH].

Media controls

The relationship with foreign media involved the use of the censorship laws inherited from the British Mandate. In April 1961 the Government Press Office (GPO), headed by David Landor, was responsible for over 100 foreign reporters in Jerusalem for the Adolf Eichmann trial. Gabi Shtrasman's (1961) *Maariv* article covered the arrangements made by the GPO, using about 50 people from the GPO office, to assist the foreign press:

> Prior to receiving an information file and a permit the foreign reporter needs to sign a form written "in English, French, and German," which explains the censorship regulations. It says there that the censor has no control over the news from the Eichmann trial but that the reporter should know that the censor's pencil would still control the rest of the news.
>
> (p. 4) [ATH]

Caspi and Limor (1998) criticize the Government Press Office's authority to issue "Press ID" permits as a practice that "allows the political establishment to participate, even though in an indirect way, in the definition of journalism as a profession in Israel" (p. 25) [ATH]. This permit-issuing process carried over from the Mandate days. For Caspi and Limor (1992), the retention of that authority is not just as a testimony to the political establishment keeping "hold of the communication media, but also to the weaknesses of the communication media establishment in defining journalism as a profession and its weakness in self-establishing its external symbols, such as permits to those practicing communication" (p. 25) [ATH].

Significantly, the Government Press Office still uses its legal power in an effort to control the media in the 21st century. Dan Seaman, head of the GPO from 2000 to 2010, drew repeated and harsh criticisms from journalists for allegedly refusing to grant or renew press credentials for political or personal reasons (Izkovitch, 2010). Seaman was also accused of discriminatory treatment against Arab journalists and of blocking foreign media access to major event locations (e.g. the Gaza Strip during the 2008–2009 military operation).

In 2011 the Government Press Office moved from the Prime Minister's Office to the Public Diplomacy and Diaspora Affairs Ministry, which is also in charge of the Masbirim Israel campaign (see Chapter 1). The new head of the GPO, Oran Helman, declared a commitment to a "Brand Israel" project. As part of that, Helman tried to present Israel as a democracy and highly developed country. However, in his one year as head of the GPO he initiated the extension of granting press ID cards to bloggers and warned journalists against considering joining the international flotilla that tried to break Israel's siege on Gaza (Levin, 2011).

The GPO's letter to international media warned that joining the flotilla would result in a ten-year ban on entering Israel. The Foreign Journalists' Association protest and legal action argued that the GPO tactics prevented foreign press from covering events in Israel and opposed freedom of expression. Inside Israel, Lory's

(2002) article in *Haaretz* similarly criticized the way the GPO tried to stop foreign reporters and photographers from reporting stories from Israel that did not favour the government line through a "punishment policy" (p. 26) that created a negative reputation for Israel.

The information services

The Government Press Office was part of the information and Hasbara services, which the government kept renaming and moving between ministries. From 1966 to 1977, Israel Galili, a Member of the Knesset, was a minister without portfolio responsible for the information services. In 1968, following the new broadcasting authority law of 1965, and the first broadcasts of the new Israeli television service in 1968, Galili was appointed head of the Broadcasting Authority [Rashut Hashidur]. From 1967 to 1969 he served as Minister of Information. He appointed Dani Rosolio, a teacher and political activist, as head of the Hasbara services.

Rosolio (2002) describes Galili's concept of Hasbara as "definitely indoctrination," and saw Galili as interested in coordination between all the Hasbara offices (internal as well as external). Galili had established a forum that included Moshe Ben-Horin from the Ministry of Foreign Affairs, Lieutenant Colonel Efrat from the Israel Defense Forces spokesperson's office, and Shlomo Gazit, representative of the Ministry of Defense. These people met every week and discussed practical activities.

Galili's influential position in the government, especially during Golda Meir's time as prime minister, meant that the forum also had a lot of power that it used against undesirable publicity:

> A day before the 1969 Independence Day, 14 soldiers were killed in the Suez Canal and their bodies were brought to Israel in an airplane at the evening of the celebrations. Galili forbade the broadcast of this information till the end of the celebrations on the next day, in order not to spoil the public mood. On another occasion he stopped the broadcast of information about the successful Israeli Air Force operation that took down a Russian airplane. Though the information was published abroad, he delayed and prevented publication in Israel. The whole idea of critical journalism, which started to develop in the 1970s, was new and shocking to the political system. Meir Nitzan, mayor of Rishon Lesion, was interviewed on TV denying a rat plague in town while the background visual showed footage of rats running behind his back. Nitzan appeared in Galili's office knocking on his table with anger, and Galili called the reporters to advise and guide them about their reporting limitations.
>
> (Rosolio, 2002)

In addition to the activities of the coordinating committees, Galili was advised in private by the public relations consultant David Eshkol (2002). Eshkol, who was a political activist and a former reporter, kept a rare, and revealing, document from those days. Entitled "Coordinated Communication Program for the State of

Israel," it was submitted by the New York public relations firm Ruder & Finn in October 1967 after the June 1967 victory of the Six Day War. To present Israel as a responsible nation, the report suggested various tactics, including publicizing government policy on such key issues as direct negotiations with the Arab countries, and Israeli initiatives to solve the Arab refugee problem.

According to both Eshkol (2002) and Rosolio (2002), Galili was terrified by the idea that the opposition leader, Menachem Begin, would find out about a public relations programme which included a suggestion that Israel should be taking responsibility for the Palestinian refugees issue, so he ordered it to be hidden. Eshkol (2002) noted that, years later, someone in the office was looking for the programme, a 100-page professional document, and eventually it was found on the chair of one of the secretaries, who used it to elevate her seat. As Eshkol (2002) commented, "There was no respect for the idea of public relations at the time." Eventually the Ruder & Finn agency was employed, and its representative in Israel, Harriet Mushli, dealt with tours for foreign journalists in Israel, publicity, and conferences (Arnon, 2002).

Hasbara challenges

Complaints about what was perceived as the information and Hasbara services inability to counteract Palestinian propaganda and the growing criticism of Israel's military operations resulted in a special government committee. Headed by Elad Peled, the committee investigated all the Hasbara services provided by different ministries and the Israel Defense Forces. The committee, like many later committees, recommended centralization of the Hasbara efforts, major messages, research on the state of Israel's image abroad, and tactical tools. The idea that to gain international trust and legitimacy Israel might need to initiate non-military dialogues and compromise to end the conflict with the Palestinians was not covered by this, or later, Hasbara investigation committees.

Instead, Israelis seem to have high expectations from public relations about the way their case is put to the world. These persist despite suggestions that the government rather than the communicators might be at fault, as in Keller's (2012) ironic blog on the disproportionate use of force against the 2009 flotilla seeking to send humanitarian aid to Palestinians besieged in Gaza:

> The State Controller has concluded that the Hasbara system of the State of Israel collapsed and did not function and did not perform its task (i.e. to explain and to convince the whole world that the activities of the State of Israel, and its army, and its marine force, and the commando unit of this marine force were justified). It seems that it would be too much to expect, even from the State Controller, to think about the shuddering possibility that some activities even the best professional propagandists, and the most eloquent Masbirim [Explainers], and the fastest word-jugglers would not be able to explain and justify. Not even when repeating hundred and thousand times the same old well-loved expressions, "small country surrounded by

Speaking on behalf of government (1) 127

enemies," and "the only democracy in the Middle East," and "the Axis of Evil," and "total war against global terrorism." It is especially difficult to explain to the world why Israel has kept the occupying rule over the lives of millions of Palestinians for more than two-thirds of the time of its existence, and why it keeps building and extending non-stop settlements in the territories it concurred, and extends this occupation to the centre of the Mediterranean Sea, in international water tens of kilometres away from its shore.

The Israeli government's concept of the media as "a tool for preserving the political power and a channel for delivering ideological messages" (Caspi & Limor, 1998, p. 97) explains the environment in which public relations practitioners, spokespeople, and propagandists employed by the government worked. The government also set up the expectations they were supposed to meet. The government agenda deployed propaganda, Hasbara, and public relations to shape the nation according to its ideology.

The Ministry of Education

Chapter 6 described how the pre-state propaganda department of the Jewish National Fund [JNF-KKL] enlisted the Teachers' Association as an executor of Hasbara campaigns. These relationships continued after the establishment of the state. Government agencies, under the Prime Minister's Office, cooperated with the Ministry of Education in campaigns designed to promote the new Israeli culture and national identity.

Ben-Gurion's strategy was implemented rigorously by Professor Ben-Zion Dinur, Minister of Education from 1951 to 1955. Dinur also believed in the total responsibility and sovereignty of the state to direct educational values and to control educational content:

> In 1952 Dinur established "a Committee for Civil Education and Israeli Lifestyle" . . . at its first meeting, 7.4.1952, it decided to provide the public with a common model for celebrating Independence Day. It was agreed to call the public to organize family and neighbourhood dinners, and it was emphasized that 2–3 minutes of silence should be held that evening in memory of the "holy victims of the Independence War." It was decided to issue to the general public, very widely distributed, a brochure that would include a text and songs appropriate for the celebration . . . later in 1952 Dinur proposed new models for celebrating the Shabbat dinner. . . . In May 1954 he initiated a huge national campaign of "language instruction."
>
> (State archive, 3794/gimel/5551, cited in Zameret, 1999, pp. 52–56) [ATH]

The initiative of the Ministry of Education in creating new holidays and celebrations as part of nation building continues the JNF's pre-state work (e.g. Tu Be'shvat, Shavuot ceremony, the Kabalt Shabbat with the Blue Box). Zerubavel

(1995) refers to it as attempting to create "collective memory and the invention of national traditions" (p. xix). She analyzes how the narratives and myths of Tel-Chai, Masada, and Bar-Kokba were developed by the Zionist institutions and the Ministry of Education in order to reinforce social solidarity and self-sacrifice for the national cause.

This explains the legal status of national holidays in Israel: in 1949, the government decided that Independence Day would become a holiday and the prime minister would have the authority to give instructions regarding the celebrations and flag postings. The 1951 Government Annual Report describes what had been done by the Hasbara department in the Prime Minister's Office to celebrate the 1949 Independence Day. In addition to leaflets distributed to each household reporting the state's progress, the department "produced an album with photos and diagrams, 'Israel 1949'. . . . All the celebrations were filmed. With the assistance of the department, the Writers' Association produced a special newspaper for Independence Day" (GAR, 1950/1951 [Yod Bet], p. 22) [ATH].

In April 1951 the first Knesset decided on an annual commemoration day for the Holocaust, Yom Hashoa (GAR, 1950/1951 [Yod Beth], p. 6) [ATH]. The responsibility for shaping the cultural content of the Israeli holidays and national celebrations became one of the major Hasbara roles. The list of the events organized included:

- the project and event of Lighting of 12 Beacons [Hadlakat Hamasuot] by 12 people representing a different theme every year on Independence Day;
- the Israel Prize award ceremony;
- Holocaust Day (with Yad Vashem);
- state commemoration days for Herzl, Weizmann, Ben-Gurion, Jabotinsky, and Rabin;
- Adar 11th day: the commemoration of Trumpeldor and the Tel Chai myth of sacrifice and other events that reinforce the government's unifying narratives.

The Israeli government in the 21st century still takes responsibility for the content of national ceremonies and organizes them through its own organ, Merkaz haHasbara, along with collaboration from the Hasbara services and the education system. Indeed, as Kimmerling (2005) notes, the school system had been mobilized from the start in support of building the nation and "sought to create the 'New Jew,' a productive pioneer who would conquer labor" (i.e. take jobs from Arab workers), settle the land (taken from the Arabs), and "guard" (*shimira*) the community (against the Arabs)" (p. 211).

Merkaz haHasbara

Merkaz haHasbara is a unique Israeli government institution in charge of

> strengthening the identification of the citizens with the state – its democratic regime, its national goals and struggles; increasing the willingness of citizens

to participate, in practice, in solving the state's problems and in designing its political, social, economic, and cultural image; increasing the knowledge, understanding, and rapprochement between groups; deepening the connection between Jews in Israel and the Jewish people in the Diaspora.

(Shatz & Ariel, 1998, p. 760)

It was established under the title Minhal haHasbara in 1954 within the Prime Minister's Office, and Zalman Aran was the minister in charge of it, as well as of the Government Press Office, and the government's radio station, Kol Israel. Over a number of years, the Hasbara Center kept moving between government offices, and in 2009 it was moved to the Ministry of Public Diplomacy and Diaspora. During the 1970s the Hasbara entity employed more than 100 people. In 2002, this number was reduced to 40 employees working on the event management of national ceremonies, publications production, and organizing tours in the country.

As Doron Shochat (2002), director of Merkaz haHasbara from 1996 to 2003, commented, the institution "was established to create consensus, a sort of political education bureau." He notes that there is "no such effort to shape the citizen's life anywhere else in the world." He sees the nearest US equivalent as "the USIA [United States Information Agency], which is promoting American-style democracy as an attempt to influence external publics overseas," with the crucial distinction that the United States has "no similar effort directed towards internal publics." Finally, he observes that

> Independence Day in the US is organised by volunteer organisations, not by the government. The fact that Israel was built to serve as home for the Jewish people, and its strong ideological background, made the difference. The state is still under construction. It does not even have defined and agreed borders. It still absorbs mass immigration with no democratic culture. The Hasbara effort was about finding elements that would connect the people to the state, and this work has not yet been completed.
>
> (Shochat, 2002)

Shochat (2002) expressed ambivalence about the role of Merkaz haHasbara. While he identified it as a traditional propaganda tool, he tried to change its mission into a professional centre, a supplier of public relations services, such as event management and publications, to government and non-government organizations. He wanted to get away from the concept of propaganda and position it more as an information centre.

Ten years prior to assuming this role, Shochat (2002) established the Citizenship Education for Democracy in the Ministry of Education to develop tolerance and acceptance of "others" and cultural differences in schools. In Merkaz haHasbara, he had to deal with adult education from a different perspective: "I had difficulties dealing with this system. The Merkaz should be a centre that promotes good citizenship and not government advocacy" (Shochat, 2002). He did keep using the tools developed earlier by the Merkaz: organized tours for new immigrants, government employees, local authority employees, about 100,000 people per year who enjoyed guided tours to see a new highway, historic sites, and border settlements: "Subsidised trips are a good Hasbara tool . . . the Israeli government is unique in organising these tours, consistently since the early days of the state" (Shochat, 2002).

Shochat's views of the role of Merkaz haHasbara are not shared by the practitioners who performed this effort earlier. Dov Ben-Meir (2002) expressed no reservations concerning the Hasbara advocacy work. He started his career in the "Oral Hasbara" [Hasbara Beal Peh] unit in 1954 and recalled how the unit worked:

> We organised "Hasbara stages" [Bamot Hasbara], reaching out mostly to new immigrants all over the country. Ministers and government officials were sent to speak to the public on Friday evenings and Saturday mornings. During the 1950s we used a van equipped with a slide projector and film screen and we reached every immigrant camp with the government messages. It was a free event, which was the only entertainment in "town" at the time, and attracted an audience. The presenters used texts that we prepared for them and they read them in between slides. About 300–400 lecturers were prepared by the unit to speak about the state issues. They were aided by special guides produced by the Hasbara publications department. Other publications, such as "Facts and Figures" and "How to Celebrate Independence Day," were distributed to thousands of people, mostly professionals and opinion leaders.

The Hasbara activities at this early stage of the state already included most of Merkaz's functions: responsibility for national ceremonies such as the tenth anniversary exhibition and celebrations in 1958; organization of subsidized tours; educational projects such as the "Citizenship Study Groups" [Chugim l'Ezrachut] to teach the general public about the democratic institutions; Bamot Hasbarah, and publications. Ben-Meir (2002) admits that his work in media relations was easy and said that on Saturday mornings he "would walk into the radio station of Kol Israel, which was controlled by the Prime Minister's Office, and just dictate the news to the reader, reporting about the lectures given by ministers and government officials on Friday evening."

Yakov Shatz, who headed Merkaz haHasbara for 18 years (from 1978 to 1996), was neither a political activist nor a professional bureaucrat. His 38 years in the Hasbara services did not clash with any of his values, as he agreed with Merkaz haHasbarah's mission as he defined it: explain the government policies; teach good citizenship; design and give content to the national holidays; and serve government ministries and local authorities with social campaigns. He also felt very strongly about commemorating the Holocaust as an important unifying message for all Israelis.

Shatz abolished the "Hasbara Stages" [Bamot Hasbara] that were organized in the 1950s by Dov Ben-Meir. He said that since Israelis had started watching television, in 1968, there had been no interest in political meetings organized by the Merkaz. On the other hand, he supported a new Merkaz project for targeting Israelis abroad as spokespeople for Israel. During the years 1967–1969, following the Six Day War, the Merkaz produced brochures called "Know How to Respond" [Da Ma Shetashiv] and distributed them at the airport to Israelis going abroad (a forerunner of the 2010 Masbirim Israel campaign described in Chapter 1). Prominent editors and journalists were commissioned to write these brochures.

Merkaz haHasbara's "propaganda of integration" (Ellul, 1965, p. 74) approach is best understood by comparing its work across time. Comparing 1978, following the peace agreement with Egypt, with 1993, following the Oslo Agreement with the Palestinians, Shatz (2002) observed a much bigger effort to promote peace in the earlier period:

> Then [in 1978] peace was made by the Likud government headed by Menachem Begin and the consensus about it was bigger. We published the agreement text, organised conferences, and cooperated with academic institutions in projects that supported the peace agreement. Nothing of this kind happened in 1993. The Oslo Agreements were much more controversial. PM Yitzhak Rabin's Secretary of Government, Eitan Haber, organised the peace events from the Prime Minister's Office without involving Merkaz haHasbara. There was no effort to promote the content of the Oslo Agreement and to reach out and involve the public in the peace process.

The comparison between these two peace agreements represents a change in the climate of Israeli public opinion. The consensus achieved in the late 1970s was partly due to the work of Merkaz haHasbara and the general readiness of the Israeli public to support, eventually, the government's decisions. In the 1990s, as described in Chapter 5, the public sphere became more open to controversy, the media were much more critical, and the opposition to the peace initiative was vocal and violent. The 1993 peace initiative concluded by Prime Minister Yitzhak Rabin, the Oslo Agreement, was a much more difficult challenge and his government hardly used any Hasbara campaigning. Eitan Haber, Rabin's chief of staff and media adviser, even rejected help offered by Alain Modoux, UNESCO's director of communication, to promote dialogue and implement the Oslo peace agreement (personal communication with the lead author in 1994). Rabin's government failed to "sell" the idea of a peace agreement to the Israelis, and this may have been one of the reasons for its failure.

Ideological spokespeople: the Ministry of Labor

A major issue in public relations professionalism has to do with the question of loyalty and commitment to the employer and the public. Should government spokespeople be totally loyal to the political minister and serve as political advisers, or should they function as civil servants for the society as a whole? Webb and Salmon (2005, p. 878) comment on the US experience:

At the federal level, government communicators are both political appointees and career civil service employees. Political appointees at the federal level generally stay in their position for approximately 18 months and are often perceived as "political hacks" or dilettantes by the career staff. Career staff, on the other hand, are often perceived as intransient bureaucrats by the political staff. These relationships effectively form the first barrier to the creation and implementation of effective public relations strategies.

In the Israeli government public relations experience, tensions between the political and civil service employees are extensive. The development of these tensions forms part of the unique political, social, and cultural environment, and the changes it has gone through over time: from an ideological political orientation to a more professional civil service orientation.

No government practitioner exemplifies the idea of the "ideological spokesperson" model better than Zalman Hen (1915–1995), a political activist committed to Ben-Gurion's Mapai party. In Hen's 38 years as spokesperson he served his political ideals and principles without making any distinction between the party and the ministry. He simply worked for what he believed was just. Two people were interviewed about him: Vicky Gineo (2003), who worked with Hen in the Ministry of Labor; and Netiva Ben-Yehuda (2002), who was Hen's assistant from 1967 (and the daughter of the father of modern Hebrew, Eliezer Ben-Yehuda). Both described Hen's personality as enthusiastic, warm, poetic, human, and loaded with socialist-Zionist ideology.

In the pre-state years, Hen, who migrated to Israel from Latvia as a child, worked as a spokesperson of Mapai. Hen's famous production from those days was the song "Shuru Habitu Uru" (Look and See the Glory of This Day), which he composed on the spot for the inauguration event of a new kibbutz on December 20, 1936. Avraham Harzfeld, a Mapai leader, adopted this song and used it to open every event. The song became the hymn of Mapai. Hen's later books were devoted to the glorification of the Zionist ideal as a model for a just and equal society.

In 1950, when she was appointed as Minister of Labor, Golda Meir, later prime minister (1969–1974) and Mapai leader, invited Hen to work as spokesperson of the ministry. At that time there was no distinction between spokesperson of the ministry and spokesperson of the minister: one person did it all, including party work:

> Zalman Hen was involved not only in delivering the messages but also in the legislation process itself. He was instrumental in the first social legislation, the establishment of the National Security system, the employment services, public works initiatives, equal pay for equal work laws, the status of women in the workplace laws – he cared about justice and worked with all the Mapai ministers very closely to influence the new laws. Israel Katz was the first Minister of Labor who was not appointed by Mapai and he brought a new spokesperson to work with him as a minister. This was a novelty. Hen stayed spokesperson of the ministry, not the minister, till Katz was replaced by

Abu-Hazera, who did not want Hen as ministry spokesperson. In 1974 he was appointed spokesperson for the employment services in the Ministry of Labor and performed this job for another 14 years even though he reached his retirement age.

(Gineo, 2003)

The political affiliation of spokespeople in government ministries was an issue that reflected the changing concepts and the professional self-image of spokespeople in general. Ministers used to take it for granted that the ministry spokesperson would, following Zalman Hen's example, be involved with their political work, would promote them in the party, and would identify with their political interests. Later this assumption changed. Ministers, on their appointment, brought to the office a political personal spokesperson (a trust job) while the ministry spokesperson stayed and served ministers from opposing parties (e.g. Yehiel Amitai, Ministry of Transportation). But in the early stages there was collaboration between politicians, journalists, and spokespeople from the same party. Gineo (2003) spoke about Zalman Hen's media relations, where journalists visited him in his office, "staying there for hours discussing party issues. Arye Tzimuki, a reporter for the Mapai daily *Davar* was a regular and when one of the ministers, Yoseftal, once criticized Hen, Tzimuki wrote an article defending him."

Netiva Ben-Yehuda was appointed in 1967 to assist Hen with foreign reporters. The minister at that time, Yigal Alon, was an active leader of Ahdut ha-Avoda, which was a different socialist-Zionist party, but he backed Hen and Netiva and trusted them. Hen functioned more as a spokesperson for the minister, following Alon's activities, while Netiva was more focused on ministry affairs.

In the 1970s, Netiva became a nostalgia guru in Israel, commemorating the mythology of the Palmach (the pre-state military combatant unit in which she served as a soldier). She is considered the "mother" of slang Hebrew. In the Ministry of Labor she introduced a new style, "a more '*dugri*' style," as she described it in a telephone interview (Ben-Yehuda, 2002). Katriel (1986) describes Netiva Ben-Yehuda as an arch-Sabra (Israeli-born) and uses her own definition of the *dugri* style: "*Dugri* means speaking straight to the point ... a label for an honest person who speaks straight to the point" (p. 10). *Dugri* is at the opposite pole from Zionist pathos.

Ben-Yehuda described the new style she introduced to the Ministry of Labor with the example of the radio programme she produced called "In Production Rhythm" [*Bemiktzav Yotzer*]. This daily broadcast was devoted to *dugri* conversations with listeners about employment issues. Until her retirement in 1980, Ben-Yehuda edited the materials on behalf of the Ministry of Labor and was responsible for the connection between the radio and the ministry. This daily programme was perceived by listeners as a regular radio production but was actually financed by the Ministry of Labor.

At the end of the 1990s a similar programme, *Shalosh Arba la Avoda*, was financed by the Histadrut (lead author's experience as public relations consultant for the Histadrut, 1993–1995). Those radio programmes illustrate yet another incident of the unethical confusion of journalism, public relations, and advertising. These programmes were used by government practitioners as unseen power, promoting messages that endorsed the government policies for nation building or the Histadrut agenda. As the next chapter will show, beginning with the Ministry of Transportation and the General Bureau of Statistics, the level of this enlistment varied across time and across different areas of government.

10 Speaking on behalf of government (2)

Other civil servants and military spokespeople

Away from the more direct propaganda and public relations of Hasbara departments, other government practitioners were influenced by nation building and its politics. This chapter considers a range of institutional civil servants and spokespersons from the less ideologically intense arenas of transportation and statistics to the high-intensity environment of military spokespersons. The chapter suggests that compared with government public relations in Britain or the United States, Israeli government public relations seems much more involved with politics and has a less publicly oriented civil service system.

The Ministry of Transportation and General Bureau of Statistics

In the 1970s, mostly in offices of economic affairs, a professional, non-ideological approach to the role of government spokesperson developed. Yehiel Amitai offers a good example for the new concept, which was very different from that of Zalman Hen. Amitai's 25 years in the Ministry of Transportation followed 16 years as assistant spokesperson and spokesperson of the Jewish National Fund with Theodore Hatalgi. Describing his career in a published farewell interview, he said it represents a "non-party affiliation identity" (Ben-Ari, 1993) [ATH]. In an interview, Amitai (2002) explained that his appointment was "the result of a tender by the state service commissioner and it gave me the power to work as a professional, and not a political communicator." From that position, he said,

> I explained to the ministers I served that I would not follow them to party functions and would not distribute press releases that serve political interests. I kept politics out of my work and only my wife knew my political views

and concluded that that was how he "survived 11 ministers."

The State Service regulations gave the minister the privilege of appointing a few "trust jobs," but that of spokesperson was not included among them. Many ministers, notably Ariel Sharon, when he was appointed Minister of Agriculture, complained about this arrangement and wanted the spokesperson to be a personal appointment. In 1999 the State Service Commissioner appointed a committee including Yechiel Amitai as chairman, Nisim Ben-Shitrit from the Ministry of Foreign Affairs, and Eti Eshed, spokesperson of the Ministry of Justice, to examine the function of spokespeople, Hasbara, and public relations in government offices. The committee interviewed 12 spokespeople who were in charge of Hasbara and public relations in different ministries and described their responsibilities as concerning mostly media relations and sometimes publications. The committee found out that in some ministries the minister employed a special "communication adviser" who had a personal contract and was not part of the state service. The committee recommended that

> [t]he spokesperson be considered a civil servant, appointed by a tender and not involved in political work for the minister. The spokesperson should report to the ministry's general director and be a member in the senior management of the office. The spokesperson should not report to the communication adviser who works for the minister and vice versa, and would not serve the minister's personal political interests.
> (Letter signed by the members of the committee delivered to Mr Yaakov Bar-Ner, the state service commissioner deputy, August 1999)

The 1999 committee's report was, according to Amitai (2002), the first document to clarify the role of the government spokesperson and it created the first official separation from the minister's personal political agenda. Until that point, the government spokesperson role was not defined as a civil servant job and no minister cared about it. In the highly politicized environment of Israel the ambiguity served the personal interests of leaders of the new nation.

Amitai became the "legendary spokesperson," because of the success he achieved not only in media relations but with many more activities in the office, especially with campaigns for road safety. He was promoted to vice general director in charge of Hasbara, external relations, and international relations. Nevertheless, in his résumé he presents himself first of all as "a journalist, 45 years in the profession" and describes his work as sports reporter for *Yediot Aharonot* and Kol Israel in Jerusalem (Amitai, 2002). His media relations work was based on intense personal relations with journalists, building credibility and seeking "creative" control over content and, while not lying to journalists, he "did not tell them the whole truth either. When I saw misleading information that came out of the office I avoided requests for responsive interviews. I suggested admitting mistakes committed by the ministry and journalists loved it" (Amitai, 2002).

Amitai (2002) credits himself for the way he used the minister's responses to formal questions from Members of the Knesset: "I prepared the response in advance in print and distributed it to the Knesset reporters immediately after the minister had read it in the Knesset. The reporters loved it and used it as is, with their own byline." He also notes how, later, "other ministers copied this technique" and how also, at press conferences, he prepared the queries for journalists and the responses of the minister" so that responses "to queries are the ministry policy and ... had to be designed by me" (Amitai, 2002).

The close relationships between spokespeople and journalists were described in detail by David Neumann, who served the Central Bureau of Statistics as spokesperson, and later was also in charge of international relations, for 41 years altogether (1957–1966 and 1968–2000). Neumann was responsible for issuing very sensitive information such as the monthly index and data about government ministry activities. He never had an incident with leaked information. The bureau was headed independently by professional statisticians and keeping the credibility of the data was paramount. With no political involvement expected, he could develop the professional dissemination of information in a conservative way. Neumann (2002) emphasized cooperation with journalists:

> There were no clear boundaries between journalists and the spokespeople. Journalists were not attacking or criticising much. The newspapers were smaller and there was no space for a lot of information, therefore the news releases had to be very concise. But spokespeople and journalists had much more information and they exchanged it in personal face-to-face communication, especially in Jerusalem, the centre of government work. Every day at 6 p.m. there was an informal meeting of economic reporters and economic spokespeople in the press club. We did not have printed materials; we just dictated to the journalists our stories. It went on this way till the mid-1960s. The spokespeople came from journalism and there was great friendship and collaboration in those meetings. The face-to-face communication was very effective for both sides and there was respect for each other's role.

The spokesperson as civil servant

Amitai's (2002) professional concept demands high status for the spokesperson in the ministry hierarchy: "[A] spokesperson should consult and be involved in the policy making process to prevent fires" and "No one in the ministry was permitted to speak to journalists without my permission." He was inspired in his visits to the United States by the status and important function given to spokespeople there, and explained the idea to ministers upon his return.

It is interesting to compare this with the British democratic system and public administration ideals: "In addressing the theme of relationships between public servants and the public, Finer suggested that an essential aspect of the role of the public servant is an 'obligation to stand as the representative of the vast, unrepresented, anonymous public'" (Finer, 1931, p. 9, cited in L'Etang, 2004, p. 24). L'Etang (2004) comments that "neutrality and the public interest were important in terms of responsibility as public relations sought professional status" (p. 25). Amitai's (2002) concept was diametrically different: "My mission was to glorify, praise, and present the minister to the public in the best light," as he saw himself as paid by the ministry, not by the public, although he does add that when he saw the ministry was doing something wrong, he "would go to the minister and bring to him the public's point of view."

An extreme example of a spokesperson who used the power of his minister and his ministry to control information was that of Israel Cohen, spokesperson of the Ministry of Education in the 1970s and 1980s. This was particularly the case while he was working for Zevulun Hammer, the Minister of Education. Hammer was a religious activist and had a Jewish education agenda but he wanted very much to create an image of a national leader, not a representative of a sector. Israel Cohen used unrestricted communication tools to achieve this goal for his master.

The Ministry of Education controlled educational television and the Broadcasting Authority, including Kol Israel radio and the (by then) influential TV 1 station. Cohen used this power over journalists in those media in a way that was criticized as unfair and anti-democratic. Spokespeople had power over journalists and could intimidate them or promise them promotions while abusing their government authority. Some journalists went so far as to suggest new rules of ethics to prevent government spokespeople, especially in the Ministry of Education, from using government authority in their relationship with the media. It was claimed that the tactics used by some government spokespeople against media and journalists who were critical of ministers included outright boycotts, information bans, and loss of advertising income.

As criticism grew in the 1990s, political spokesperson jobs became totally identified with cover-ups and lies. These were mocked by the media. Shai Bazak, the communications adviser to Prime Minister Bibi Netanyahu, epitomized this kind of practice. Journalists used to interview him just to expose the contradictions in his own reports and used his efforts to cover up dubious practices in order to track those practices, because when a "casual news item has just been published and immediately a denial by Bazak is flashing in front of it" then if "someone will research the subject, he would discover, probably, that most of the Israelis know about the failures in the PM's work not from the hostile news items about him but from the immediate denials from his advisers" (Barnea, 1999, p. 442) [ATH].

An example of a different approach is described as an exception in the case of the spokesperson for Prime Minister Ehud Barak (1999–2001), Gadi Baltianski. A former spokesperson of the Israeli embassy in Washington and a journalist, Baltianski eventually resigned when his communications policy was not accepted by his minister. An article, one of many that were published deploring Baltianski's resignation, praises him as "a combination of integrity, fairness, intelligence, and also some unseen cunning" (Shavit, 2001, p. 36) [ATH]. Such superlatives are rarely given by journalists to public relations practitioners. Baltianski resigned because the prime minister preferred the advice he received from advertising consultants over his own:

> In an election campaign you work with TV commercials, gimmicks and slogans. But in the long run, this system would not be effective. Following the election campaign you need to work with people who have media skills.

The reason is simple: a small headline in the newspaper is much more effective than a big advertisement.

(cited in Shavit, 2001, p. 36) [ATH]

In the 2001 Camp David negotiations, Baltianski felt that he could not identify with the system and asked to resign. Shavit (2001) explained that although Baltianski was perceived as a credible source, he was still part of what was described by communication analyst Dr Daniel Dor (2001) as "communication manipulation" (p. 25). Barak conducted that manipulation in order to convince the Israeli public that the Palestinians were "not a partner ready for peace negotiations" and to put the blame for the failure of the 2001 Camp David talks on them. Dor (2001) argues that the Israeli press accepts the official spokespersons' version of events too easily and "limits the range of relevant facts to those that are provided by Barak's people. This is not how a newspaper is supposed to function; this is how a public relations office functions" (p. 25). In deciding to quit when he felt his professional integrity was in jeopardy and when his personal beliefs did not align with the prime minister's action, Baltianski acted as an ethical professional.

Government spokeswomen

Women started joining the government service in the role of spokespersons only in the late 1970s, and Deborah Ganani was considered the pioneer as spokesperson for the Ministry of Health. But by 1990, women constituted 50% of the government staff responsible for communication and public relations, with most working under the title of spokesperson (Avisar, 1990, p. 10) [ATH].

Interestingly, in an interview in *Maariv* newspaper, nine government spokeswomen discussed their work and focused not on gender issues but on the same issue that was high on the agenda of their male colleagues: political versus professional status (Avisar, 1990). The week before the interview, the Israeli government had been dissolved and the spokeswomen were concerned about the change of guard in the ministries because even if they are not "identified politically with the minister [they] have a stamp on themselves as if they are affiliated with the minister. . . . 'No one can promise that the minister who will arrive tomorrow will wish to go on working with us'" (Avisar, 1990, p. 10) [ATH].

According to Eti Eshed, then spokesperson of the Ministry of Justice, who got her job by responding to a newspaper advertisement, "The work of a spokesperson is built first on the trust between the spokesperson and the minister" (cited in Avisar, 1990, p. 10). Sari Zimerman, then spokesperson of the Ministry of the Environment, agreed with the "painful fact" that "a spokeswoman could give her soul to her work and avoid the political issues, but when the minister is changed, suddenly all kinds of people would identify her politically with the outgoing minister and she would find herself replaced" (cited in Avisar, p. 10) [ATH].

Clearly, it does not seem that Israeli government spokeswomen had any feminist agenda to promote. As distinct from US counterparts, they had no "female-centered definitions of public relations" (Hon et al., 1992, p. 434; see also Aldoory,

2005; Grunig et al., 2001). These authors assume that feminine qualities such as consensus building and listening will lead the profession from one-way male-defined values to two-way female-defined values. In the Israeli case, this process did not seem to happen. Women competed with men in the government service on common ground and wished to be perceived as doing the job regardless of gender. Indeed, all expressed a

> high level of satisfaction with their job and none wanted to change it, mostly because of the intense challenge and the interesting issues they were involved in, in spite of the very long endless hours and the collision with family commitments.
>
> (Avisar, 1990, p. 10) [ATH]

Eti Eshed (2003), who spent 12 years as spokesperson for the Ministry of Justice, comments about the ethical norms of government spokespeople and how they manipulate information: "We select the information that we submit to the media and we present it from an angle that favours our needs. The services we give are similar to the services of a lawyer: whoever can afford it enjoys it."

The Knesset: a different spokeswoman style

Israel's parliament, the Knesset, did not have a spokesperson till 1977. Even then it was not a Knesset initiative but rather a case of a young woman, Sara Yitzhaki, creating the job. She worked as the Knesset ombudsman's secretary, and when he retired she asked the Knesset chairperson at that time, Yitzhak Shamir, if she could replace him. Then she added media relations and many more projects with the objective of informing the public about the Knesset's activities. As she freely admits, no one had asked her to do it:

> Shamir's [Israel's prime minister 1983–1992] background was in the underground movements and he could not care less about publicity and the media. Publicity was not that essential at the time for members of the Knesset – they were nominated by the party committees, not by the party members. When the primaries system was established by the two major parties, Labor in 1992 and Likud in 1993, it all changed and I could not control any more the direct contact of each member of Knesset with the media. They became publicity junkies.
>
> (Yitzhaki, 2002)

In her 22 years of service as spokesperson of the Knesset, Sara Yitzhaki developed a routine of exposing the Knesset's work to the public with an eye on democratic education. The Central Election Committee was a major project she worked on to increase the general public's understanding of the election system and to promote voter participation. She had to fight for budgets for photographers and even for simultaneous translation for foreign reporters covering the visit by the president of Egypt, Anwar Sadat, to the Knesset in 1977 and worked to avoid "any party connection. I dealt only with the image of the Knesset as a democratic institution. I had no influence on the way the Knesset functioned but I was involved in the way it was perceived by the Israeli public" (Yitzhaki, 2002).

Communicating on behalf of the security and military authorities

Security and military organizations play a unique role as instruments of nation building. In some nations they use their power to seize the civil leadership following a revolution and the creation of the new nation. By their nature, military organizations are more committed to citizens' rights to security than to civil liberties and the democratic values of "freedom of speech" and the "right to know." Thus, public relations practitioners who serve the military actually represent a public organization, funded by the government, which has the right to keep information about its activities secret. Often, transparency is not possible for reasons of state security.

According to Perlmuter (1969), "the military as an instrument of nation building in [pre-state] Palestine was a concomitant aspect in the creation of a pioneer settlement social and political system" (p. 127). Once the state was established in 1948, the military was depoliticized and assigned the civil roles of education and social integration of the mass of immigrants. The Israeli security system's [Maarechet Habitachon] Hasbara effort is a subject large enough and important enough for a separate book. Nevertheless, while lacking the access to produce a more comprehensive work, we try to shed light on specific characteristics and particular professional challenges experienced by the security system spokespeople. To do this, we present key accessible examples for different concepts and approaches to military Hasbara.

Israeli military Hasbara

Security is a major issue within Israeli society, and the security forces are both involved, and influential, in all aspects of life. According to Kimmerling (2001), "Military and national security considerations constitute a considerable part of the central organising principles of the Israeli collectivity" (p. 215). Wars and military operations against neighbouring Arab countries and the Palestinians living in Gaza and the West Bank have been part of the Israeli way of life since the first Zionist settlement in the region.

The Israel Defense Forces (IDF) is one of the strongest military forces in the world today. Military service is mandatory for non-Arab Israelis, and reserve service of up to one month a year lasts until the age of 43. Thus, almost all Israelis, apart from groups exempted on the grounds of religion or disability, know the army from within. According to public opinion polls, Israeli Jews' level of trust in the IDF, and in its spokespeople, is higher than in any other public institution

(Lebel, 2005, p. 19) [ATH]. Consequently, criticism about IDF deficiencies, or claims that it has acted illegally or inhumanely, are very hard for Israelis to accept.

The military struggle in the pre-state era was organized by different political parties in different units. Political agitation was part of the training of the young soldiers, and the role of the *politruk* (a Russian word meaning political commissar) was not ignored. With the establishment of the state, Ben-Gurion centralized all the political military units into one army under the state, and developed the concept of "Bithonism," which, "according to its critics, expresses the use of the security issue by the governing establishment in a manipulative way and the tendency to solve all the state problems by the use of military power" (Bar-On, 1999, p. 63) [ATH].

In a well-known 1951 speech, Ben-Gurion said that the IDF's challenge was not only to defend the Israeli people but also to be a force for pioneering, educating, nation building, and redeeming of the desert: "The IDF should be the creator for the nation's pioneers and the cultural tool for the merger of exiles, their unification and their cultural elevation" (GAR, 1951 [yod Alef], p. 21 [chaf vav]) [ATH]. The army was very involved in the education system and also in Hasbara work. According to Doron Shochat, director of Merkaz haHasbara from 1996 to 2003, the army organized all the national events of Independence Day [Yom Haatzmaut] till 1997. Merkaz HaHasbara was the more public face of the event.

The Government Annual Report of 1949/1950 describes the organization of the new Ministry of Defense and mentions 11 divisions, including a Public Relations Division (GAR, 1949/1950, p. 59) [ATH]. The mission of this army division was

> a. connecting the Defense Ministry and the army with the civil population and the Jewish people; b. systematic propaganda, with the help of public committees, for keeping the defence preparedness of the country even in times of peace. The division is responsible for Hasbara, publications, information, connections with the media and the institutions, and any connection with the public.
>
> (GAR, 1949/1950, p. 67) [ATH]

Ben-Gurion asked Yitzhak Ziv-Av, a civilian, and an editor of the daily *Haboker*, to head the Hasbara department, which was named Public Relations. Ben-Gurion and the Minister of Education, Ben-Zion Dinur, expected the IDF not only to protect the citizens of Israel but also to educate them, especially the new immigrants, and to motivate them for service in the IDF (Zameret, 1999, p. 53). The IDF Education Corps, which included a Hasbara service, was responsible for educating the soldiers and equipping them with Zionist values. An IDF programme to prepare high school students for their mandatory military service, in collaboration with the Ministry of Education, has been practised since the early days of the state and still continues (see Shalev, 2005, p. 7).

The internal orientation of the security system's Hasbara in the first two decades of the state shifted later. It moved into an external effort to present Israel's defence policy to audiences abroad, especially following the 1967 war and the annexation of Arab territories. This activity was not always in the public domain but it was a focus for criticism. Between August 2001 and January 2002 the State Controller's Office conducted an investigation into the deployment of all the state Hasbara organs on issues of security and foreign affairs. The report relates to the Prime Minister's Office, the Ministry of Foreign Affairs, the Ministry of Defense, the IDF, the Ministry for Internal Security, and the Israeli police. The Controller repeated a complaint that was heard for many years:

> The severe deficiencies from which the state Hasbara suffered for decades, which were characterized by the lack of a clear and complete Hasbara concept for security and foreign affairs issues at the national level, is continuing and even increasing in the face of a situation of military conflict.
> (Israel State Controller Annual Report, 2002, 53 Aleph, p. 9) [ATH]

The report mentions the lack of cooperation between the many different units, the lack of systematic learning processes, the lack of information about important events before they happen, the lack of unified messages, the lack of one source of information for foreign correspondents, the lack of appropriate care of Jewish organizations and pro-Israel organizations, and the lack of initiation of communication and Hasbara events (Israel State Controller Annual Report, 2002, 53 Aleph, p. 15) [ATH].

A major issue not mentioned in the Controller's report of 2002 was the political involvement of the security system spokespeople. In 1991, Shlomo Gazit, a retired general who was the commander of IDF intelligence and a researcher in the Yafe Strategic Research Center, wrote:

> Since 1967, when the IDF spokesperson stopped serving both the security system and the IDF, non-political spokespeople of the IDF in military uniform had to serve in a role that was totally political and sometimes present very sensitive issues in the Israeli sphere.... Three years ago I served in a committee appointed by the Chief of Staff to check the IDF system of spokespeople and Hasbara. In our report we wrote: the success of the IDF spokesperson in the announcement and Hasbara activities would be achieved by *strict disengagement of the IDF from the public political debate* [emphasis in original] and by making sure that each announcement issued by the spokesperson would be 100% credible.
> (Gazit, 1991, p. 7)

Gazit wrote this article following a public controversy over the suggestion to appoint Dani Nave, who was involved politically, as IDF spokesperson to replace Nachman Shai. Shai succeeded in serving the IDF without any political association, and his professionalism was mentioned in the controller report as an exception.

The Controller related to the national Hasbara work that was organized by the IDF during the Gulf War (January–March 1991), when the IDF spokesperson functioned as the assistant to the chief of staff. It is worth studying this case, particularly because, unusually, there is insider documentation available. The IDF spokesperson during the Gulf War, Nachman Shai, himself provided a rare documented account. Shai was a prominent Israeli communicator who served as a senior reporter on Israeli television, press secretary for the Israeli delegation in New York, press adviser of the Israeli embassy in Washington and spokesperson of the Israeli Ministry of Defense, commander of the IDF radio station Galei Zahal, and the first director-general of the Second Broadcasting Authority.

In July 1998, Shai wrote a Discussion Paper, "The Spokesperson – in the Crossfire: A Decade of Israeli Defense Crises from an Official Spokesperson's Perspective," for the Joan Shorenstein Center at Harvard University's John F. Kennedy School of Government. In his introduction to this paper, Professor Thomas E. Patterson (1998, p. 1) observes:

> Nachman Shai builds a strong case for the proposition that "truth" rather than "spin" is the basis for effective public information efforts, even in that most trying of situations – a nation at war.... [Shai] concludes that the only "bulletproof vest" available to the military spokesperson is truthfulness... during the Gulf War he had the task of explaining wartime events to the Israeli press and public, and it was his voice that people heard over the radio as they huddled in bomb shelters during Iraqi missiles attacks. One writer said: "Nachman Shai, not Yitzhak Shamir, was the hero of the Gulf War. He was the one that conducted a personal dialogue with the public." A nation-wide poll indicated that 67 percent of Israelis regard him as "completely trustworthy" while 26 percent found him "mostly trustworthy."

The discovery of truth as the best weapon resulted from a crisis in Shai's credibility. Shortly after the Gulf War, it was alleged that thousands of defective gas masks had been distributed to the public. During the war, Shai had assured Israelis that the gas masks were completely safe, and some journalists accused him of covering up for his superiors. This is what the public expected anyway, after previous experiences with IDF spokespeople and false information during the Yom Kippur War, the Lebanon invasion, and the Intifada. Such was the reputation of the IDF.

Shai's (1998) paper proposes that the truthfulness of the messages is not just about the spokesperson's integrity but about the integrity of the whole system. He emphasized the importance of the flow of information within the system so that the spokesperson would be consulted and informed. He wrote that as spokesperson in the dramatic events of the Lebanon War 1982, the "Bus #300" scandal in 1984, the Intifada in 1987, and the Gulf War of 1991, he always felt that his job as spokesperson was to "protect" the organization, and the ministers he represented, from damaging their credibility. His paper actually advocates a move from a "press agentry/publicity" model of communication into the "public information" model. Nevertheless, it still clearly conceives of the role of the spokesperson as one-way rather than dialogic.

Open–closed strategies used by recent IDF spokespeople

Toledano's (2010) chapter considers attempts to increase IDF transparency over a decade. New technology, which has increased citizens' access to information in real time, and cultural and legal liberalization, have enforced a policy of relative openness to the public and transparency about military institutions (Lebel, 2005, p. 20) [ATH]. Ruth Yaron was appointed as the IDF spokesperson and occupied the post from 2002 to 2005. The hope was that she would improve the IDF's image in the eyes of the world. The expectations arose because she had considerable experience in dealing with the media and because she was from outside the military (having come from the Ministry of Foreign Affairs and serving in the Israel embassy in Washington).

Her mission proved to be a challenge because the IDF structure did not allow as much change and openness to the media as she intended. However, in an interview with the lead author in 2009, Yaron claimed that she did succeed in opening the military to some degree although it was 2003 before the IDF consulted with the spokesperson in the planning stages of military operations. At that point the then chief of staff, Bugi Yaalon, decided in principle to include representatives of the Spokespersons' Unit in planning meetings at all levels of command and, when possible, to open activities to embedded journalists. Yaron set the values of relevance, credibility, and legitimacy as guidelines for the unit's work.

Yaron was the first woman to be appointed to the role of IDF spokesperson. She was replaced by another woman, Miri Regev, who put openness, publicity, military media relations, and military political involvement on the Israeli public agenda as major controversial issues. Regev, who served as the IDF spokesperson from 2005 to 2007, conducted the IDF and Israeli police evacuation of the Gaza Strip settlements in 2005 as a media event. She timed operations to suit the TV news timetable and embedded journalists in units, following examples from the US military's communication strategy in Iraq. A year later, during the Israel–Hezbollah war in Lebanon, Regev was unable to follow this policy when the IDF operation went wrong and officers were afraid to embed media with troops. A government investigation committee criticized Regev's openness strategy, and the media blamed her for being part of an effort to create an opportunity for an "image of victory" for the IDF at the cost of soldiers' lives. Toledano (2010) argues that Regev was consistently more committed to controlling the media than to making the IDF transparent.

During the Israeli attack on Gaza in 2008–2009, the then IDF spokesperson, Avi Benayahu (2007–2011), reversed the openness strategy. He mandated total closure and denial of access to media so that Israeli and international journalists had to rely entirely on the IDF spokesperson's announcements and visuals. Following this operation, and the 2010 Israeli raid on the Turkish boat that participated in the flotilla to break the siege on Gaza (and resulted in the death of nine activists), Israeli officers and officials were accused of war crimes, and an international committee investigated the IDF operations. There was the usual narrative putting the blame on the Palestinians or the demonstrators, but criticism

– some internal, but most of it international – followed. It was not met by any persuasive communication from the military spokesperson.

Israelis did not seem to care. Avinoam Brug, the director of an Israeli public opinion research company, explained the lack of interest as emerging from crisis situations such as war and continued that "individuals are looking for a sense of mastery of their lives. The openness of 2006 gave them a feeling of chaos which they resented, whereas Benayahu in 2008/9 gave the feeling that things were under control. The Israeli public liked it" (cited in Toledano, 2010, p. 595). However, the cost of the closure policy in international public opinion was devastating:

> Neither IDF spokesperson attempted dialogue or allowed competing voices to be heard. Both used their privileged power to restrict the public discourse: Regev's openness was severely limited and, as much as Benayahu, she tried to cover up mistakes and malpractice and to silence alternative voices.... Neither spokesperson was interested in allowing an argument for advancing peace, or allowing criticism of possible human rights abuse, although, over time, these may serve the public interest better. The citizens' right to know is a fundamental value for ethical public relations. However, in certain situations, such as war, the public might not want to know the truth and prefer to surrender freedom of speech for the sake of such emotional needs as fear reduction and national pride.
>
> (Toledano, 2010, pp. 595–596)

Conclusion

Contemporary Israeli public relations has clear roots in the extensive endeavours of Zionist institutions to enlist support, to gather resources, and to educate a new nation. Expectations to support the official line from what were called "spokespersons" of government entities commonly went beyond the roles expected from government public relations as civil servants in countries such as Britain and the United States. For example, Webb and Salmon (2005) identified the origins of US government public relations in the establishment of the first federal press bureau in 1905 by the Forest Service and argued that

> [i]t was, perhaps, the creation of this office that led the U.S. Congress to pass an amendment regulating the use of public relations experts in the 1913 Appropriations Act for the U.S. Department of Agriculture.... The amendment stated that appropriated funds could not be used to pay a publicity expert, unless specifically appropriated for that purpose ... this little-known codicil continues to govern the use of public relations in the federal government today.
>
> (p. 877)

Webb and Salmon (2005) also observe that "[t]oday the U.S. government has one of the largest public relations operations in the world, with the U.S. Office of

Personnel Management reporting nearly 15,000 public relations jobs" (p. 878). Compared to these descriptions of British and American government public relations, Israeli government public relations seems much more involved with politics and much less organized within a civil service system and ethic of public service. The Israeli focus started to shift from an ideological to a professional public relations function in government offices only in the late 1970s, and in many cases spokespeople for Israeli government still do not separate political service and civil service.

The survey and analysis of key Israeli government spokespeople in Chapters 9 and 10 indicate the following as being characteristic of the Israeli experience:

- The nation-building effort of the first decades of the state used services called propaganda, Hasbara, and public relations to do the same work (i.e. to use persuasive communication for the sake of the state). It was only in the 1950s that the term "propaganda "[Taamula] started to be omitted. The term "Hasbara" is still commonly used in Israeli government practice, where it refers to both internal and external communication.
- The government's formal civil servant senior communicator in charge of mainly media relations is called *spokesperson*, whereas an external consultant is usually called a *communication adviser*. The spokesperson is usually the official representative of the ministry, and the post is a non-political job, while the communication adviser serves the minister with political communication and joins the staff only for the restricted time of the specific minister's service. Government spokespeople need to struggle to protect their professional status as civil servants, and only recently has their non-political role been defined by the state service commissioner.
- The boundaries between journalism, public relations (spokespeople), politics, and education are blurred. What takes place is a joint effort by the different functions based on strong consensus about the goals: the implementation of the Zionist vision and nation building.
- The government uses political communicators for education and indoctrination projects, and party politics is a dominant issue in government public relations work. The government, by using its own Hasbara organs and media, controls a lot of the messages and the public discourse. Censorship is a major tool in this kind of Hasbara.
- The use of ideological spokespeople decreased in the 1970s when practitioners acquired experience and felt more confident and professional, and less dependent for their employment on the political leadership of the government service.

In Israel's enlisted society, the leaders usually required work closer to propaganda than public relations from their spokespeople, and the media were expected to be, and often were, very cooperative with the government establishment. L'Etang (2004) identified the origins of British public relations in local government as civil service (p. 21). In Israel, partly because of the nation-building process, government spokespeople were the prominent public relations practitioners at the pioneering stage. Local authorities only adopted the service later. Caspi and Limor (1992) provide further explanation for this phenomenon:

> For many years, the dominant concept in the political establishment and the communication establishment was that Israel is a centralized and homogeneous society, and it did not have geographically independent local entities. Even the declared policy, in the first years following the establishment of the state, empowered the concept of centralization. This was expressed, among other things, in the structure of the Israeli communication: a centralized whole state structure that relates to the whole society as one unit.
>
> (pp. 68–69) [ATH]

The difference between the Israeli and the British origins of the profession helps explain the different concepts. Practitioners in Britain were, from the start, aware of their commitment to the public and not only to the employer, and, for them, "[a]chieving better understanding between the populace and local government began to be seen as intrinsically important to the job of administration and to the improvement of democracy" (L'Etang, 2004, p. 25). This concept is just emerging in Israel. The question of the nature of a practitioner's commitment – to an ideology, to the employer, or to the public – is a major criterion in the effort to identify the emergence of professional public relations. The next chapters will present the contribution public relations in private consultancies made to nation building and how it was shaped by the specific circumstances of Israel's challenging environment.

11 The emergence of private consultants

The emergence of private public relations firms is an important indicator of the stage reached in the professionalization process. This chapter examines the belated establishment of these firms, and how they functioned in Israel, to provide insight into the evolution of public relations as a profession in general. More specifically, it describes how the nation-building challenges and limited competition inhibited the need for professional services and how the liberalization and openness of the Israeli market from the 1980s onwards enabled its development.

The chapter moves beyond describing public relations practitioners who were employed by major national institutions, the Israeli government, or by not-for-profit organizations. It looks at public relations firms, agencies, and consultancies (i.e. businesses providing strategic and/or tactical services to a range of clients). The practitioners who work in this environment form a different group and cannot be identified exclusively by one organization. They are often retained by an outsourcing contract and their role might be managerial, technical, or both (see Dozier, 1984).

In the United States:

> Beginning in the 1980s, many "public relations agencies" changed their titles to "public relations firms." The change reflects an increased emphasis on counseling and strategic planning services, viewed as more professional than the communication tactics produced by press agents and publicity agencies.
> (Cutlip et al., 1999, p. 80)

Along similar lines, Wilcox et al. (2003) quote Harold Burson's (of Burson-Marsteller) description of the transition to counselling: "In the beginning, top management used to say to us, 'Here's the message, deliver it.' Then it became, 'What should we say?' Now, in smart organisations, it's 'What should we do?'" (p. 114).

Analyzing the evolution of public relations firms is significant for understanding the evolution of professionalization. That is to say, following Abbott's (1988) cultural logic of professions, the formation of a viable public relations business demonstrates that a field of expertise had been defined to the extent of being able to be paid as such by businesses, just as they pay for the professional services of accountants and lawyers. Or, in L'Etang's (2004) words (in identifying the importance to the field of the growth of consultancy), consultancy "signified a clear identity for the practice [of public relations] and symbolized professionalism in terms of a structure that mimicked established professions . . . [and] made public relations available to a greater range of organisations because [distinct and identifiable] services were available on a project basis" (p. 123) without the need for employing specialist in-house staff.

Cutlip's (1994) history describes the 1900–1919 period in the United States as "[t]he seedbed years of counseling" (p. 1) and attributes this development to the country's expansive growth:

> The fundamental force setting the stage for the emergence of the first public relations agencies in the early 1900s in the United States was the wild, frenzied, and bold development of industry, railroads, and utilities in America's post-Civil War era. In the 25 breathtaking years from 1875 to 1900 America doubled its population and jammed its people into cities, developed mass production, enthroned the machine, spanned the nation with rail and wire communications, developed the mass media of newspaper and magazines, and replaced the plantation barons with the titans of finance and princes of industry and the versatile frontiersman with the factory hand. . . . Contemporary public relations emerged out of the melee of the opposing forces in this period of the nation's rapid growth and emergence from isolation into an imperial power.
>
> (p. 1)

The first public relations agency was the Publicity Bureau, which started in Boston in the mid-1900s, and Bernays opened the eighth public relations agency in New York in 1919 (Cutlip, 1994, p. 2). Most of the work done by the pioneering consultancies is usually classed under public information, the second phase of the four-phase model describing public relations work (see Chapter 1). The first agencies replaced the concept of "the public be damned" that characterized the first phase of press-agentry with the idea that "the public be informed" (Grunig & Hunt, 1984, p. 33). This was sometimes expressed as an early – if not confirmed by practice – commitment to transparency, as in Ivy Lee's famous differentiation of public relations from advertising: "This is not a secret bureau. All our work is done in the open. We aim to supply news. This is not an advertising agency" (cited in Hiebert, 1960, p. 35).

A different development direction for public relations agencies, firms, and consultancies emerged in Europe. As late as 1948 in Britain, for example, consultants did not count "as a separate category of practitioners . . . because so few existed (L'Etang, 2004, p. 103), and out of "the 101 organisations listed as founder organisations . . . only 4 were operating as consultancies (p. 103). L'Etang (2004) finds the beginnings of public relations consultancy in the post-World War II era in Britain in advertising agencies that "financed the growth of some public relations consultancies (p. 105).

The evidence given by the Israeli practitioners makes it clear that public relations in Israel also differs from that in the United States in both development and timeline, with public relations in the private sector emerging at the first stage from advertising agencies, and at the second stage from journalism. The process lagged decades behind the United States and Europe, and followed changes in the specific Israeli political and economic context rather than foreign models. The Israeli evidence also reveals bitter competition between public relations and advertising that indicates demarcation disputes, or struggles over what Abbott (1988) terms jurisdiction, whereby "professions compete by taking over each other's tasks" (p. 33). This emerges from the testimonies of two veteran advertising people who also practised public relations.

Advertising and public relations agencies: Eliyahu Tal and Shimon Lineal

In 2002, for his 90th birthday, Eliyahu Tal (2002b) produced a brochure called "A Tribute to a Lone Wolf." In it he describes himself, in the third person, as a lone wolf in Israel's Hasbara campaign, and as the "Godfather of Israel Advertising." According to this brochure, "to old-timers in Israel, Eliyahu Tal and his agency 'Tal-Arieli' [a leading agency in partnership with Amnon Arieli from 1948 to 1965] are regarded as the major factor in shaping the backward, conservative trade of local advertising into a thriving, vibrant industry" (p. 16). Tal also published the first book in Hebrew on advertising, *What Is Advertising?* [ATH], was a chairperson of the Israel Advertising Association (founded 1934) in the mid-1960s, and directed an advertising school set up by the Advertisers' Association of Israel (itself only founded in 1961).

Tal (2002a) had clear feelings about the early role of public relations in Israel:

> In the first era of advertising in Israel, the client expected the advertiser to provide public relations as part of the advertising campaign package, for free. As an advertiser, I had to organise press conferences and deal with free publicity for the advertising messages. For me this was a headache, a burden that I did not want. Public relations services did not include any commission money from the media (whereas for advertising the commission was up to 25%, of which 10% was paid back to the client). Public relations at that time could not support itself financially as it was offered by the advertising agencies for free.

In spite of his resentment, Tal organized some creative public relations events, including a midnight street party to inaugurate the first ATM service in Tel Aviv in 1969. Featuring the Hakameri Theatre actors Hanna Maron and Bomba Tzur, the event was covered by the *Financial Times* and the *Wall Street Journal*. Tal also organized "an award for excellent service" project for the appliances company Ampha that recognized the good work of people (e.g. a veteran newspaper distributor and a midwife). This project supplied stories that attracted a lot of media attention while connecting Ampha's image to the concept of "good service." In current public relations terminology, this project would be called something like "community relations" or "corporate social responsibility."

Eliyahu Tal began his advertising career as the advertising manager of Shemen Oil and Soap Mills of Haifa in 1935. He was involved in the early industrialist campaign to promote local products (Tozeret haAretz), which became a major issue for the Zionist institutions and the Jewish Agency (see Chapter 8). Later, according to his story, he mobilized the Yishuv to enlist for service in the British Army in World War II by distributing leaflets that raised fears about German parachutists (Tal, 2002a).

Shimon Lineal, Tal's assistant in Shemen's advertising and sales promotion department, demonstrated a stronger public relations involvement by an advertising practitioner. Lineal (2002) started working as an apprentice in Shemen in 1936 when he was 13 years old, and in his 16 years of work there he had an opportunity to experience all aspects of advertising, marketing, and public relations. In 1944 he organized the 20th anniversary celebrations of Shemen, which included a party for 300 Jewish and Arab VIPs, along with the British governor. For this occasion he published a book about Shemen, telling its story as a Zionist project and as a centre for Jewish cultural activities (including a Hebrew teacher for the employees). Shemen produced many of the Yishuv-era products, which were exported to 68 countries. The establishment of an industrial plant in this neglected corner of Asia is described in Shemen's 20th anniversary book as an act of heroic pioneering of people with burning vision and ancient belief, an act of Genesis.

At the age of 19, Lineal was responsible for Shemen's advertising, packaging, marketing, design, and all media relations. It is not surprising, therefore, that his professional identity developed in both advertising and public relations. Indeed, eventually he joined the professional associations of both professions. In a brochure produced by the Public Relations Association for its annual meeting in 1965, Shimon Lineal is mentioned in its list of members, and as head of the advertising agency Bing-Lineal, which he founded in 1952 in Haifa. Lineal's (1965) presentation at this meeting describes competitive relationships between advertising agencies and the few public relations firms that started to establish themselves in the Israeli market in the 1960s with people deciding to practise public relations, who started out declaring, "'we will not deal with advertisements, we will not mix advertising with public relations, we will practise public relations in the most pure and clean way'" (p. 10) [ATH] but "after a while – six months or a year – all those public relations firms became agencies for advertising and public relations" (p. 10) [ATH].

Lineal's (1965) presentation also identified an ethical problem arising when the media expect income from advertising in return for publishing newsworthy information delivered by public relations. In a later interview, Lineal (2002) said that eventually advertising agencies stopped offering public relations services because such services caused them too much aggravation with clients: "In advertising, you have control over what is published and when. In public relations you have no control and clients became frustrated and angry at us" [ATH].

Public relations firms were not welcomed to the small market controlled by the few advertising agencies, which offered a full range of services, including free public relations. According to David Eshkol (2002), Lineal's comments in the 1965 annual meeting of the Israeli Public Relations Association actually related to the "head to head" competition they had over three clients in the 1960s: the Israel Electricity Corporation, Shemen, and the Haifa Theatre, all of which were based in Haifa. Lineal resented the paid-for public relations services offered by Forum to his advertising clients while he offered it for free as part of the advertising package. But Forum did it nevertheless, and, in addition, took portions of the advertising budget. Eshkol (2002) explained that, while they did not intend to deal with advertising, the client insisted on receiving advertising and public relations services from the one firm: "It started with Shemen and then we decided to employ an advertising person in Forum as well. Advertising was a bigger source of income but our focus and identity was always public relations."

To put the rivalry into the context of the Israeli market, it is useful to quote Professor Michael Perry's (1988) article about marketing thinking in Israel:

> During the first twenty years of the state [1948–1968] the concept of "marketing" and whatever was connected to it was almost unknown in industry and commerce, and this because of the feeling that there was no need for it at all. At this period the demand increased at a very fast pace, because of the growth in population size and also because of the rise in the standard of living, while the supply did not have the time to match it. Moreover, the local industry enjoyed very high protection by customs and administrative barriers to import, so it did not need to persuade the customer to prefer its products. The result was that marketing activities seemed superfluous, sometimes even negative, as they have not "produced" any product or any direct benefit for the customer, and therefore were perceived as "Air Deals" [Luftgesheften] causing a waste of resources.
>
> (p. 24) [ATH]

In such a small market, the competition in the private sector between advertisers and the new public relations practitioners over clients and jobs was, understandably, bitter and intense. However, different relations existed between advertisers and spokespeople of government ministries and state-owned enterprises. Since these spokespeople were often in charge of the advertising budget of the organization, advertisers courted the spokespeople, sometimes offering personal bribery (Amitai, 2002).

The lack of marketing thinking in Israel, which lasted till the end of the 1960s (Perry, 1988), was reflected in the minimal public relations activity in the private sector. The membership list published in the annual report of the Israeli Public Relations Association in 1965 mentioned ten firms, including one-person firms, and advertising firms with a public relations department which were not employed by a specific organization (out of 83 members in the Association of Tourism Centers and Public Relations Tel Aviv).

Early public relations firms

The entertainment sector

Arie Geldblum, a well-known journalist on the daily newspaper *Haaretz*, was actually the first practitioner specializing in public relations in the Israeli market. According to his widow, the actress Miriam Zohar (2005), he joined the advertising agency Tal-Arielli in 1957 as a partner, responsible for the public relations function. Three years later, in 1960, he opened his own public relations agency, which he managed for 20 years. He served clients in the entertainment business (the Habima Theater, Gudik musical productions), as well as industry and government (the Israeli Electricity Corporation, Klin) and politicians (Shlomo Lahat, the mayor of Tel Aviv: "Lahat is good for Tel Aviv" was his slogan). Geldblum's agency offered public relations as well as advertising services and marketed his service as a new concept: "advertise without paying anything to the media." This concept of public relations was described by his colleague Shmuel Shai (2002) as a "novelty" in those days.

Nitzozt

Nitzozt was founded in 1957 in a business collaboration with the advertising company Dahaf, which was owned by Eliezer Zurabin and was the first to offer paid public relations services in a separate firm. The firm's name, Nitzotz (Spark), was inspired by Lenin's magazine *Iskra*, also meaning "Spark," and hinted at two of its allegiances. Its founders, Alex Masis and Uri Sela, were radical left-wingers connected with the Communist Party and the Matzpen group, which promoted the idea of peace with the Arab world, a dissident idea at that time. A third partner, Willy Gafni, was an entertainment impresario, and the focus of Nitzozt was on artists, theatres, movies, and entertainment. According to Shmuel Shai (2002), Nitzotz brought the Red Army Choir to Israel via its Party connections, and the income from that successful performance was paid to the Israeli Communist Party.

During the early 1950s, Sela and Masis were prominent participants in *Haolam Hazeh*, the only critical magazine at the time in Israel that exposed corruption and scandals. Uri Sela was widely recognized for his exceptional communication talents: "His communication skills were brilliant. He was a perfect dilettante: light, floating over the surface, shining and blessed with a thousand talents" (S. Cohen, 1973, p. 31) [ATH]. While also managing a public relations firm, Sela published articles and columns in *Yediot Ahronot*, edited books, wrote speeches and slogans, and translated and published joke books. Following his Nitzozt experience, Sela joined Arie Geldblum in the second half of the 1960s and worked as a public relations practitioner till his death in the early 1980s.

Shmuel Shai

Shmuel Shai (2002) founded his independent practice in 1958 with the admission that he had no idea about journalism, let alone public relations, but succeeded easily: "Newspapers were interested in the theatre, and usually news releases were attached to the advertisements. I just looked for a story that would interest journalists and when there was none, I invented it." He recalled his first show promotion for "A Spark of a Poet" by Eugene O'Neill and his news release claiming that Habima would organize a free show for poets, though it actually never intended to. The news release was published first page. Another news item announced that Habima has invited Charlie Chaplin, which never happened, but got publicity anyway" (Shai, 2002).

For the show *An Apartment for Rent*, he used the press agency model of a news release describing people who were calling to ask if the apartment had two or three rooms: "Serious journalists such as Natan Dunevitch in *Haaretz*, Shaike Ben-Porat in *Yediot Ahronot*, and Tomy Lapid in *Maariv* published my imaginary materials and were not angry at me when they realised it was spin" (Shai, 2002) and observed that they "depended on my materials as the entertainment world at the time was very limited and could not provide them with a lot of stories." Shai (2002) explained why the entertainment sector was the first to employ public relations in the Israeli business sector: "They were the only ones with a real need to sell. The socialistic market of these days had nothing to sell and did not court consumers. Theatre and entertainment needed to sell tickets."

This motivation also linked entertainment with public relations in the United States. Shai may not have known about P. T. Barnum, the most famous and successful of 19th-century press agents, but his style of work was similar to that of the circus promoter: "[I]n fact the PR tactic of press agentry grew up with the entertainment business in the nineteen century, a flamboyant era of road shows and circuses" (Newsom et al., 1996, p. 38). Another major characteristic that binds Barnum with Shai is that neither would meet current public relations professional codes of ethics, which demand that practitioners "adhere to the highest standards of accuracy and truth in advancing the interests of those we represent and with communicating with the public" (Public Relations Society of America, 2012). Some of Shai's (2002) firm's first clients were world-famous artists who knew and respected the function: "I met John Gielgud, Margot Fontaine, and Frank Sinatra, and learned from them what kind of service public relations should be."

Political–economic connections

Forum

On June 1, 1960, David Eshkol and Yohanan Goldberg (Dobje Kidon) founded Forum with Alter Welner. This was the first professional firm in Israel that had clients with a long-term retainer, a professional concept of public relations, and a full range of services (including consultancy, production, media relations, events, lobbying, and advertising). Forum might be considered the founder of professional public relations services in the Israeli private sector, and the firm that led the field's development for two decades.

David Eshkol, like most of the practitioners, came to public relations from journalism. He and Dobje (Yohanan Goldberg) worked for *Lamerchav*, a political daily of the left-wing party Achdut Haavoda. The third founder, Welner, was also a reporter for *Lamerchav* but in 1964 he left and was replaced in Forum by Yosef Fetman-Golan, yet another ex-*Lamerchav* reporter. Eshkol had been immersed in political ideology since his high school days. He was a member of the secretariat of the Hanoar Haoved (Labor) youth movement (Shimon Peres was the secretary), editor of the movement magazine *Bamale* and editor of a book, *Hanoar Haoved*. Then, in his last year of high school, he joined the Palmach [pre-state military combat units] and served as a politruk or commissar (education officer), involved in the establishment of the first Hebrew radio station. After the independence war, Eshkol worked as a night editor for *Al Hamishmar*, a left-wing party newspaper. In 1954, Eshkol became political reporter for *Lamerchav* and served as the London correspondent for *Lamerchav* from 1958 to 1960, where he was first exposed to professional public relations. He took a public relations course, thereby becoming the first Israeli to study public relations formally, and upon his return from London joined forces with Dobje, the military correspondent of *Lamerchav*, because "The newspaper was run by the party and editors were appointed by party decision. There was no place for us to get promoted there" (Eshkol, 2002).

Dobje, who died in 1986, immigrated to Israel from Poland as a young boy and studied in a Zionist Youth Aliyah agricultural school, where he had to defend his "civilized" appearance against the tough and thorny Sabra (Israeli-born) youngsters who made fun of new immigrants. They used the Polish word for "okay," *dobrze*, or "Dobje," as a nickname for the young Yohanan, but Dobje reacted with early signs of public relations skills by adopting his negative nickname and turning it into a positive. Dobje became his only name, and was written on his tomb. Dobje served in the British Army as a high-ranking officer and became a journalist prior to his *Lamerchav* experience. He also covered Israel for European military magazines, and this was his first exposure to professional public relations. He went with David Eshkol to Europe to cover the Air Salons exhibitions and they both started to contemplate the idea of a European-style public relations firm in Israel:

> We studied the public relations materials that were sent to us when we were journalists and were well prepared. Our first client was achieved thanks to a family connection with the management of the Israel Electricity Corporation. The second client arrived via a political contact – Moshe Carmel, the Minister of Transportation (Achdut Haavoda), recommended Forum services for Autocars-Shubinski, the producers of the first and only Israeli car, Susita, that was made of fibreglass ("the only car that can be eaten by a camel").
>
> (Eshkol, 2002)

Three years after starting Forum, Eshkol and Dobje went to London and Geneva to check the field there. They discovered that public relations services included, in addition to media relations, such tools as posters, films, and brochures. These inspired them, so that in the mid-1960s they organized events and produced cinema commercials for their clients. "No other public relations firm in Israel offered these services with a public relations focus at that time" (Eshkol, 2002).

The major client that gave Forum the big push forward was Koor, Israel's largest industrial holding company, which had factories all over the country. Koor belonged to Israel's Trade Union Federation and had a lot of influence on the Israeli market. In 1968, Major-General Meir Amit, former head of Israel's intelligence services, was appointed Koor's director. With an MA in Business Administration from Columbia University, New York, and his exceptional commanding skills, Amit modernized the old-fashioned company and opened it to dialogue with the public. In Moshe Teomim's (2002) account, he was the first Israeli corporate manager who "consumed public relations in a systematic way . . . [and] understood the importance of symbols and used the Koor logo in many creative ways. He paid attention to the employees and developed internal communication with the help of Forum."

Amit knew Dobje from their army service and retained Forum's services. The involvement of Forum with Koor's many factories grew, and Forum had an office within Koor's headquarters building so that they "were part of the Koor's kitchen [dominant coalition of decision makers]" (Eshkol, 2002). For Koor's different companies, Forum produced newsletters and leaflets, catalogues, events, and advertising materials in addition to media relations services.

Eshkol (2002) practised political public relations with total identification with the political clients he represented: "In my 41 years in public relations I never represented anyone who was not on the left side of the map." He also observed that this was not always the case with his colleagues.

Forum dissolved in 1987, when Dobje introduced his family to the company and Eshkol did not want to become a minority in a family business. Dobje created a new advertising and public relations firm in the same year called Gitam with his nephew Moshe Teomim, and Eshkol opened his own public relations firm, Logos, which he managed till his death in 2006.

One of the major explanations for Forum's success was its political connections and personal political involvement that translated into clients. This formula was successfully adopted by Moshe Teomim, who developed the political–economic connection into an art later in Gitam during the 1980s and 1990s. Political connections with the people in power proved to be an asset for public relations in Israel because it is such a highly politicized society. The major role played by government in the economy and the strong involvement of politicians in the market advantaged people such as Eshkol and Teomim, who used their political connections to develop their firms and to help their clients with lobbying functions. For other practitioners, who were not so heavily involved in politics, this became a problem, as will be demonstrated in the case of Moshe Triwax.

The consumer market

Until 1965 the Israeli market belonged to the manufacturers. The size of the market was very small and the few consumer goods were grabbed by the consumers.

158 *The emergence of private consultants*

The media were not interested in consumer issues and there was no effort to satisfy consumers. Shimshoni (1982) wrote that because Israeli consumers lacked organization, and belief in their influencing power, they did not persist, and so the "general consumer has second priority to the demands of the workers in the government-owned electric company, or of those of the driver-owners of the bus cooperatives, or to those of a foreign investor tempted by promised monopoly rights" (p. 261) [ATH].

This situation started to change with investigative journalism by Baruch Nadel in *Yediot Ahronot* in the 1965–1975 period. But the media were very careful and avoided the risk of upsetting advertisers. Gradually public relations services were employed to deal with criticism, and the practitioners became involved in management decisions. This development became more significant in the 1980s and 1990s.

Moshe Triwax: the discovery of the niche

The success of the Triwax public relations firm in the Israel market for almost 50 years could not be credited to political connections. Moshe Triwax was not involved politically, and this deficiency presented difficulties when he first started to practice public relations in 1963. In Triwax's (2002) view,

> Forum had accessibility to ministers and blocked my options. In some cases they were connected to my client via a minister for certain projects that I just lost. During the 1960s this presented a major problem but in the 1970s the market changed and I discovered the consumer commercial niche, which became the focus of my firm.

Prior to practising public relations, Moshe Triwax was a journalist, and the son of a journalist. His father was the Israeli reporter for the Polish Jewish newspaper *Heint*. Triwax studied journalism in Syracuse University in the United States and worked as a military reporter for *Bamachane* (IDF magazine) and an editor for *Yediot Ahronot*. In 1963, Triwax decided to move from journalism to public relations to increase his income. The first three years he worked from his house with the help of his wife. The Israel Flight Club and the Israel Council for Road Safety were the first clients for media relations and print publications. The NGO Ilan, which raises support for polio victims, became a client for 20 years, a connection that involved a lot of fundraising work, including the annual "March of Dimes." This is where Triwax (2002) used, for the first time in Israel, celebrity testimonials for fundraising:

> My major difficulty then and now was to explain to clients what public relations was about. Many companies felt anxious about publicity and did not want to attract the tax authorities' attention. In the 1990s there were few that kept this attitude. Many more became publicity addicts. It was always difficult to deal with the expectation that public relations should not be paid for. There

was also a problem with the pressure from the media to connect editorial publicity with advertising. This connection between advertisement and editorial publicity exists today as well.

Triwax's breakthrough happened in the 1970s, when the market started to become more interested in the consumers, and the standard of living improved along the lines described by Perry (1988):

> During the seventies it became clear that the competition in the market was increasing and it was not possible to rely on higher demand than supply or on administrative protection. At the same time the increased demand in the local market stabilized and the effort to look for export markets, in which the rules of the game were different, began.
>
> (p. 24) [ATH]

The consumer role in the Israeli market developed gradually. In 1958 the first department store, Kol Bo Shalom, opened in Tel Aviv and caused a sensation; in 1962 the international companies Helena Rubinstein and Revlon started marketing cosmetics in Israel; and in 1968 Israeli Television started broadcasting (as a public service, with no commercial advertising).

In the 1970s, Triwax participated in the Israeli market shift into improved lifestyles: he organized media tours abroad for Olympic Airlines; inaugurated the new plant of Helena Rubinstein and promoted its cosmetic products; promoted wines (Carmel, Eliaz) and good foods; and organized fashion shows. In serving these commercial private companies, Triwax was not dependent on political connections. Triwax (2002) described the environment as follows:

> The media started to be interested in fashion and consumer information and "the women's section" space increased. The consumer issues were the light, disregarded part of the newspaper. Consumer journalism developed only later in the 1980s with Nitza Holzman in *Maariv*, Nurit Arad and Shoshana Hen in *Yediot Ahronot*, and Lea Porat in *Haaretz*.

Moshe Dayan: customer education and professional ethics

Moshe Dayan, who opened his firm in Tel Aviv in 1974, developed the customer focus of public relations firms. He was well prepared for this new market orientation by his six years of work (1967–1973) as the in-house advertising and public relations manager of Helena Rubinstein in Israel (while Moshe Triwax was its consultancy firm). Dayan entered public relations via advertising, which he studied in 1960 in a six-month course run by the Advertisers' Association of Israel, and some practice in Tel Aviv advertising agencies. Dayan (2002) described the environment as follows:

> At the beginning of the 1960s there were offices of "advertising, public relations, and real estate" that operated like small shops. I worked for Gordon,

Levinson, Eilon, the advertising agency of Helena Rubinstein, and moved to manage the advertising effort of HR in-house. Helena Rubinstein and Revlon introduced cosmetics to Israel while competing with each other. Before 1962, the year they arrived in Israel, there were only two local modest cosmetic companies – Taya and Helen Curtis – and imports of Max Factor, which were sold in 500 perfumeries. Helena Rubinstein introduced the role of beauty stewardess, something they learned from the company in France, and my first job was to train the stewardesses to become not just salespeople but customer representatives. This was a novelty. The stewardesses were sent all over the country to teach young people to use perfume and treatment creams. We met with soldiers in the army camps, with women in clubs, customers in shops. When we made a special effort to educate the Israeli macho soldier to use deodorant, the company headquarters in France were angry because Helena Rubinstein should not be politically associated with an occupier army [after the 1967 war].

Dayan's experience represents the challenges of public relations practitioners of the private sector in two particular aspects. First, the introduction of new products that were considered to promote self-indulgence in luxury was not consistent with the Zionist puritan values of austerity and a modest lifestyle. This created a need to educate the consumer and legitimize the marketing effort. Second, Israel had become isolated in the world market because of the Arab boycott. Y. Elizur (1992) described how international companies entered the Israel market while keeping a very low profile:

It is not a coincidence at all that multinational corporations prefer to act "low-profile" in Israel. This behaviour is part of a general phenomenon, which starts with the Arab boycott, and with the avoidance, because of it, of publicity for any connection with Israel. As years went by, this "silent connection" became accepted also by the Israeli companies. . . . When the American soft drinks company Coca-Cola responded to the American Jewish community pressure in 1966 and agreed to produce its soft drinks in Israel, the "low-profile" boycott was broken somehow. The opening of the Hilton hotel in Tel Aviv in 1967 was another breakthrough. Very slowly and carefully, some other multinationals, including Pepsi-Cola, infiltrated the Israeli market and were accepted with sympathy by the Israeli consumer, who was longing for "international recognition."

(p. 17) [ATH]

Public relations practitioners who started to promote international products were caught in the paradoxical position of doing so while keeping a low profile – a unique professional challenge imposed by Israel's political-economic situation.

Dayan's firm initially served clients in the fashion industry and other consumer products. His reputation, though, is associated with his role for 15 years (1975–1990) as spokesperson for Magen David Adom (MDA, the Israeli organization doing the same work as the Red Cross but not affiliated with it). He received a lot of exposure and credit for MDA via intensive media relations. However, in 1990 he was fired following a highly publicized scandal. It arose in August 1990 while preparations for the Gulf War were very intense, and Dayan (2002) was asked by the media about the MDA situation:

> I could not lie about such an important matter. The general director, who was a new appointee, instructed me to tell the media "everything is fine," and I refused. I knew the MDA was not prepared. He fired me immediately and responded to the journalists himself. But people in MDA branches leaked the truth when I was already out of the picture. The cover-up was published and the scandal did not help MDA's image.

Dayan stayed on as spokesperson for the MDA employee committee for 11 more years and commented on this affair in a press interview:

> One of the rules of the Israeli Public Relations Association [adopted in 1987] says that there is information that belongs to the client exclusively to which the public should not have access. Unlike journalists, public relations practitioners have not sworn to the right of the public to know. They did swear not to lie.
>
> (cited in Duek, 1990, p.12)

Koteret: a public relations firm owned by an advertising agency

At the same time as Amnon Arielli separated from Eliyahu Tal and formed his advertising agency, in January 1966, he established a public relations firm called Koteret. Arielli asked Dalia Magnat to head Koteret, which was owned by Arielli Advertising but functioned as an independent company, serving its own public relations clients and some of Arielli Advertising's clients. Later on, the formula changed and the Koteret executives Dalia Magnat, Niso Cohen, and Shosh Kinamoni enjoyed 50% of Koteret's revenues. Although it was still highly dependent on advertising, these kinds of arrangements between advertising and public relations signified a change in recognizing the value of public relations as a profession.

Koteret eventually became a leading public relations firm during the 1970s and 1980s. According to Dalia Magnat (2002), who headed Koteret till 1991, the major function of the firm was media relations built on fair and honest relationships with journalists. In addition, she also personally set professional and ethical standards so as to maintain her "integrity and reputation" by refusing to work for clients that she felt were expecting her to mislead public opinion in their favour or to fake events (Magnat, 2002). Her commitment fits well with a broad interpretation of Christensen's (1994) definition of profession as "an occupation where taking advantage of the customer is against the rules" (p. 28). She also "refused to work for a political party that I could not identify with" (Magnat, 2002).

162 *The emergence of private consultants*

Her account (Magnat, 2002) of one incident reveals the kind of relationship problems between advertising and public relations in the joint venture:

> In 1986 I managed a very successful campaign for Epilady, a new product of Mepro, Kibbutz Hagoshrim. It was an innovative depilator that promised to revolutionise the international hair removal market, and our public relations campaign resulted in an overwhelming exposure in the media. The publicity achieved enabled successful marketing and export deals and the company decided to cancel the planned advertising campaign. Arielli Advertising was not very happy about it.

The competitive relationship between public relations and advertising existed even when they worked together, and income was still often a major issue.

Public relations firms and consultants in the 1980s and 1990s

As Strawczynski and Zeira (2002, p. 64) observed, the turning point for Israel's economy, albeit with fluctuations, was 1985:

> The stabilization program of July 1985 reduced the annual rate of inflation from more than 400 percent to an average of 20 percent. The years 1985–1989 are therefore years of stabilization. . . . In 1990 a large wave of immigration from the former Soviet Bloc began, which started a period of high economic growth. . . . In 1993–1996 economic growth was further spurred by the peace process, which was revitalized by the Oslo Accords in September 1993.

The success of high-tech industry and the move towards nearly total exposure to foreign trade by the end of the century had a further positive impact on the Israeli economy in the 1990s. The process of opening to the world was gradual but was certainly occurring during these two decades. In addition, the increased exposure to anti-trust legislation in 1989 resulted in a much more competitive market.

The political developments of the 1990s were no less dramatic. A gradual change in the dominance of the government over the socio-economic system led to a radical change in the election process. The competition over voters, and the new relationships between the elected politicians and the voters, created a need for specialized public relations services and involved practitioners in lobbying and political consultancy.

For public relations firms the growth in economic activity and the increased competition was very good news. The 1980s and 1990s brought a mushrooming in numbers of practitioners in the Israeli private sector. If the 1960s saw fewer than ten public relations firms in Tel Aviv, the end of the 1990s saw about 200 firms all over the country. In 2006, according to Israel's largest information corporation, the Ifat Media Information Center, there were 376 public relations agencies in Israel (a 30% increase compared to 2005) and 545 spokespeople, of whom 148 were employed by municipalities and city councils, 137 by associations and NGOs, 50 by national and government institutions, 17 by government enterprises, 31 by army and police bodies, 30 by commercial corporations, 10 by banks, 30 by the health sector, 33 by education institutions, 25 by art and culture organizations, 13 by media (print, radio, and television channels), 11 by political parties, and ten by transportation (Boltanski, 2006, pp. 695–749). On the negative side, many of the new firms became involved in public relations without any training in and understanding of the field, merely because the opportunity for work and income was there. Not surprisingly, the level of professionalism and ethical standards were compromised.

Breaking boundaries: the rise in international affiliations

The Israeli market developed without an open connection with international corporations for reasons that included the lack of political stability, the dependence on significant support from the United States and from the Jewish world, the government intervention in the market, and the Arab boycott. These helped weaken the Israeli economy in terms of keeping foreign investment away.

International public relations was practised in this environment by one practitioner in the private sector, Burton Halpern, who, from 1965, helped promote Israeli products such as diamonds, fashion, irrigation systems, and technologies abroad. Halpern, a graduate of Syracuse University, gained experience as an editor and publicist in New York before migrating to Israel. He served in US Army public information and in 1982 he published a guide to international public relations in which he presented himself on the cover as "a specialist in the practical exploitation of the public relations weapon in the global arena" (Halpern, 1982). Despite these claims, according to David Eshkol (2002), while "Halpern was the only practitioner with international practice during the 1960s and the 1970s, when there were few English speakers in the public relations sector," he "did not integrate into the Israeli environment and had no effect on the practice of the profession in Israel."

In the other direction – the promotion of international imports into Israel – nothing happened till 1979. In that year, Moshe Triwax met with the local representative of Edelman Public Relations in London and became the first affiliated agency in Israel:

> It happened actually very easily. At that time I did not know what "affiliation" meant but, following the connection with Edelman, I initiated contacts with other American firms and we represented six of them in Israel, including Hill & Knowlton, Burson Marsteller, Fleishman Hillard, and others. Until the 1990s I was the only representative of foreign public relations firms in Israel. We received clients via these connections but we were quite passive – we translated and distributed the news releases that were prepared abroad. The real partnerships developed later.
>
> (Triwax, 2002)

The real breakthrough came in the second half of the 1990s. Following the peace process, international corporations became interested in Israel as a market and as a door to the Middle East. The Arab boycott became insignificant. The government promises regarding privatization encouraged new initiatives, and Israeli advertising agencies became targets for international agencies. These agencies started to form all kinds of affiliations and partnerships to compete in the Israeli market.

Public relations followed the advertising model. The international advertising agency BBDO became a partner in Gitam Advertising, and Gitam's public relations department became affiliated with Porter Novelli public relations; Kesher Barel Advertising became partners of McCann Erickson, and its public relations firm became affiliated with Shandwick. Stern-Arielli public relations signed a representation contract with GCI public relations international, and MS communication, which was headed by Nissan Balaban, became part of Burson Marsteller. Wagner-Greenstein affiliated with Golin/Harris International, and Triwax, now headed by Moshe's daughter, Dafna, had to give up most of the international firms it represented in the 1980s because of exclusivity issues.

Working with leading international public relations companies had a dramatic effect on the Israeli public relations firms. The exposure to professional standards and expectations meant that Israeli practitioners now had to prove their value and measure their results. They had to submit business plans and communicate professionally with colleagues abroad.

The 1990s were also buoyant years for the Israeli stock exchange market and saw, for the first time, the appearance of public relations firms specialising in investor relations. In several cases, journalists who were covering the stock exchange and financial affairs identified opportunities for income by serving companies in the process of issuing stocks to the public. Company image and recognition is a major factor in successfully selling stocks and information became a financial asset.

Lobbying: changes and policy in the 1990s

The 1990s were characterized not only by increasing activity in the Israeli market and stock exchange but also by political change. What Peri (2004) called a "political revolution" (p. 52) happened as part of the relative decline in the level of state power in all advanced democracies (p. 54). In Israel, a decline in the dominance of the "party state," and increased dissatisfaction with government, reached a peak in the coalition crisis of 1990 and led to changes in the political system:

> Until the 1990s voters in general elections put one slip in the ballot box, bearing the name of the party. Each party's list was voted on by the party's appointment committee or by a broader party forum after being handed down by the party leaders and political bosses. During the1980s the number of people involved in composing the list of candidates grew until almost all

parties adopted the primary system whereby all the members of the party share in choosing the candidates.

(Peri, 2004, pp. 64–65)

The introduction of the primaries system to Israel's democracy was one of the aspects of the political revolution that resulted in increased dependency of the elected decision makers on voters and on public opinion: "Politics does not exist in a vacuum. Out of the ruins of the old party system, something new emerged: mediapolitik, or media-centered democracy" (Peri, 2004, p. 72).

Although the function itself had deep roots in the *shtadlan* role in the Jewish society of the Diaspora (see Chapter 7), this political revolution helps explain the emergence of professional lobbying firms as a form of expertise in 1990s Israel.

From the early years of the State of Israel, lobbying was executed by representatives of organizations. The religious interest groups, the agricultural interest groups, the Histadrut, and its rival, the Industrialists' Association, were all very present in the Knesset. This was particularly noticeable before budget decisions, and they developed lobbying into a real power. Yet all these efforts were organized by employees of the organizations, without involving specialist professional lobbyist firms.

The pioneering professional lobbying firm in Israel was Boris Krasney's Policy. Krasney was active behind the scene in major Labor Party projects for many years. He migrated to Israel from the Soviet Union and was sometimes nicknamed "Rasputin" in the party. In 1987 he formed Policy-Political Communication Consultancy in partnership with the journalist Menachem Golan. In 1990 they employed nine people, representing clients such as the tobacco company Philip Morris against a law that was going to limit advertising of cigarettes, and they provided media training to Members of the Knesset and ministers (Pearl, 1991, p. 18) [ATH].

High-tech: Doran Communication and MS Business Communication

The 1990s were also the years of the high-tech revolution "which placed Israel at the forefront of economic activity in the information technology sector, especially in communications equipment and software" (Justman, 2002, p. 446). The buoyant high-tech market valued information as a major asset: images of new, innovative companies translated into investor interest and helped recruit skilful employees. The high-tech industry opened a new speciality for Israeli public relations practitioners with expertise in international communication, marketing, internal communication, and reputation management. The two leading firms specializing in the high-tech sector were Doran Communication and MS Business Communication.

Both were established in 1988. Doran was founded by Raanan Rogel, the son of a well-known broadcaster. Rogel was the editor of the high-tech weekly *People and Computers* and the Doran firm's mission was "promoting business opportunities for customers and investors throughout our network of contacts and our strategic partners around the world" (www.doran.co.il).

MS Business Communication was co-founded by Nissan Balaban and developed brand awareness and media relations programmes. It also included crisis management for clients in the high-tech and defence industries: "10 out of my 14 clients are foreign companies working in Israel" (Balaban, 2003). The intensive exposure to the international business world led Balaban (2003) to identify a "huge gap between Israel and the developed countries in the level of public relations professionalism," with the major difference being ethics: "In Israel you can buy most of the journalists and there is no respect for precise information. I see ethical problems in the business world all over . . . but bribery of journalists in Israel has reached a very low level."

Conclusion

Public relations firms in Israel began gradually and developed slowly. In the first two decades of the state, the few public relations practitioners who were active in the business sector struggled to be recognized as a separate function from advertising and to be paid for their services. Advertisers provided public relations services for free and did not welcome the independent public relations offered by a few firms in the 1960s. The rivalry mainly concerned very limited resources in a small, underdeveloped, and isolated market.

As consumer affairs were not on the public agenda, the early Israeli public relations practitioners were not engaged in any struggle against media attacks and were more focused on promoting new products. In the US history, early practitioners supported big business as a key part of the development process of the profession: "For the most part, big business hired former reporters to counter the muckrakers with whitewashing press agentry" (Cutlip et al., 1999, p. 116). In Israel the major challenge facing the early practitioners was to promote a consumerism that was incompatible with the basic ideology of the state, and to promote public relations itself as an essential service. A specific Israeli issue was the challenge to promote imported products while keeping a low profile for international producers who for political reasons did not wish to be identified with Israel.

The early Israeli public relations practitioners focused their services on the entertainment industry. Political connections and professional knowledge helped Forum to develop the first professional services for the manufacturing and business sector and to become the leader of the public relations function in the early stage. The power of political connections, which translated into clients, or enabled client satisfaction, was also a major characteristic of Israel business in general and Israeli public relations in particular.

The 1980s and 1990s were the years of a big leap forward for the Israeli economy. The government gradually relaxed its control over the market, and competition through imports increased the need for marketing, promotion, and public relations services. The changes in the political sphere introduced competition over voters, and public opinion became a valuable asset for candidates, thus creating the need for specializations in political public relations services and lobbying. The dramatic growth of high-tech industry and stock exchange activity stimulated the rise of public relations firms specializing in high technology and investor relations. The new specialities were developed to answer the new needs of the changing Israeli socio-economy and were inspired by services that existed abroad – in the United States and in Europe.

All these new developments happened in just few years at the end of the 1980s and the 1990s, and many practitioners, seizing the opportunity, became public relations practitioners without appropriate training. This contributed to the growth of ethical issues that have yet to be resolved.

The public relations function is still perceived by many Israeli managers as focused on media relations and mainly for the purpose of covering up organizational faults and for publicizing organizational achievements. In a 2007 New Year congratulations video clip message emailed by the Israeli PR agency Gitam-Porter Novelli to its clients, the director sends the agency's employees out to cut a negative story from all newspapers. The explicit message to the client is "Wishing You a Year of Good News" and the implicit message is "We will use any method possible to protect your reputation." There is no regard given to the ethical implications of the message.

12 Conclusion

Representing nations and influencing Israel

Public relations has never had the field of nation building to itself, either in Israel or in other countries. Particular challenges to its jurisdiction in the area come from two fields: the long-established field of public diplomacy; and the currently popular field of nation branding. In relation to public diplomacy, Cull (n.d.) notes that despite an 1856 British use of the term, the phrase is usually associated with Edmund Gullion, a dean at Tufts University and "a distinguished retired foreign service officer," for whom public diplomacy "deals with the influence of public attitudes on the formation and execution of foreign policies . . . [and] encompasses dimensions of international relations beyond traditional diplomacy." As that and most subsequent definitions suggest, public diplomacy is more oriented to looking outside a nation rather than inside.

Nevertheless, there are overlaps between public diplomacy and public relations concerning representations of nations. Public relations scholars themselves have recognized the efforts of governments from one nation to send messages directly to "people" in another country as public diplomacy or cultural diplomacy (Coombs & Holladay, 2010, p. 299). In acknowledging that, this book has not described Israel's public diplomacy as such, but followed Coombs and Holladay's (2010) position that "public relations is strongly akin to public diplomacy" and that "essentially public diplomacy would benefit from being treated as public relations" (p. 299).

We see public relations as having the potential to offer a more holistic focus, one that goes beyond traditional international relations and public diplomacy, and a greater understanding of nation building. This book does not make a general separation between the Israeli public relations targeting external publics and campaigns targeting internal constituents. We focus on analyzing the concepts and values inspiring any Hasbara activities, while treating external and internal publics as part of the whole picture.

Israel's *raison d'être* is to serve as refuge and cultural centre for the Jewish people, and every Jew has the right, by the Law of Return, to become a citizen upon arrival in Israel. In these circumstances, Diaspora Jews should not be considered as an external public, but they are not an internal public either. The new communication technologies and global access to information have made it impossible to separate external and internal publics. Accordingly, we relate to public relations in the most inclusive sense as a function in charge of building and maintaining relationships between organizations and all their internal and external constituents.

Support for a more holistic and public relations-centred approach can be found in the field's literature. Taylor and Kent (2006), for example, find that all "nation-building campaigns include large communication components that are essentially public relations" (p. 304). In addition to domestic applications, L'Etang (2008b) contends that "states need PR to manage public opinion in foreign countries" (p. 241) and identifies similar tools and techniques used by diplomacy and public relations.

Since the early 1990s, marketing and branding agencies have made big moves into the business of promoting nations, so that the professional struggle over who should best represent nations has widened beyond diplomats and governments. It may be premature to name this a jurisdiction dispute – in Abbott's (1988) sense of professions defining themselves against occupational territory held by other professions – but public relations will definitely need to work to hold space in an increasingly crowded field.

Branding nations: Anholt and beyond

The second challenge to the jurisdiction of public relations is nation branding. Simon Anholt is widely credited with originating "the concept of national branding in 1996" (The Economist, 2009, p. vii) and has been called "the leading authority on managing and measuring national identity and reputation" (p. vii). Anholt has written a number of relevant books – for example, *Brand America: The Making, Unmaking and Remaking of the Greatest National Image of All Time* (Anholt & Hildreth, 2005) and *Competitive Identity: The New Brand Management for Nations, Cities, and Regions* (Anholt, 2007) – and edits the journal *Place Branding and Public Diplomacy*.

In that journal's first editorial, Anholt (2004) sees place branding, which includes the branding of nations and public diplomacy, as "a new field, standing at the intersection of several other well-established fields (marketing, public policy, trade and tourism promotion, economic development and international relations, to name only the principal ones)" (p. 4). Anholt does not include public relations, although the journal does publish articles from a public relations perspective.

It is interesting to compare this list and rationale with Kunczik's (1997) view that because of the interdisciplinary nature of the nation, "findings made in the public relations, advertising research, prejudice research and other fields" (p. ix) also need to "be taken into account" (p. ix) and that a difficulty in drawing any "boundaries concerning the actors influencing the images of nations" (p. ix) occurs because it is even difficult "to distinguish between the image of the nation-state and the images of big enterprises like Krupp, Ford or Coca Cola" (p. x). Such factors will make it very difficult for any one profession to claim control over nation building and national image cultivation. From a base in marketing and tourism, for example, the Israeli scholars Avraham and Ketter (2008) have created an interesting niche by researching media strategies for marketing places in crisis.

It is salutary to look at more recent events in Israel and relate them to earlier Hasbara efforts that approximate to contemporary nation branding and consulting. International criticism over the way Israel handled such events as the 2006 invasion of Lebanon after Hezbollah rocket attacks on Israel, and the death of nine Turkish activists on the flotilla trying to break the blockade on Gaza, reactivated challenges about the effectiveness of Hasbara. Even before these events, Akiva Eldar (2005), a *Haaretz* reporter, noted limits to Hasbara:

> For 57 years, we've been told that the world is against us due to poor hasbara and unpolished (to put it mildly) spokespeople. We've heard that it would be a totally different picture if we only produced more explanatory movies about Arab terror and more documents proving the anti-Semitic incitement in their textbooks.... An in-depth study by the marketing research institute of the giant Young & Rubicam ad agency pulls the rug out from under the basic assumption that has been dictating Israeli hasbara policy for years ... it shows that Americans are not lacking information on "the Israeli case."
>
> Most of them have simply lost interest in the country, and most of those who think that they are capable of discerning the uniqueness of the "Israel brand" don't like what they see.
>
> [*Haaretz* in English]

That Young & Rubicam agency advice to the Israeli Ministry of Foreign Affairs was to shelve Hasbara pamphlets and propaganda films dealing with the conflict. Instead, they were advised to replace them with a trusty old classic: the "Light unto the Nations" [ATH] brand (i.e. narratives of cultural and technological excellence) (Eldar, 2005).

Rebranding Israel?

Chapter 9 described how the post-Six Day War consultancy report on a "Coordinated Communication Program for the State of Israel," submitted in 1967 by Ruder & Finn, ended up raising a secretary's seat height for fear that Menachem Begin would find the suggestion that Israel take responsibility for the Palestinian refugees issue. This time, the Young & Rubicam consultancy advice seems to have had an impact in a "Branding Israel" project. Recent nation branding, which ignored conflicts with the Palestinians and the Arab countries, contributes to a Hasbara strategy focusing instead on Israeli accomplishments in business, science, and technology.

Rami Hasman, a strategic marketing and research fellow at the Harold Hardog School of Government and Policy at Tel Aviv University, published a report entitled *Branding Israel: Political Marketing in a Continuing Conflict Situation* (2008) [ATH]. On the basis of an overview of different models for branding nations, Hasman (2008) suggested a brand that used the concept of *tikkun olam*, meaning "repairing the world." For liberal Jews, this old Jewish value means that Jews are not only responsible for creating a model society among themselves but also responsible for the welfare of the society at large. In line with that tradition, Hasman (2008) recommends that Israel build a brand associated with contributions to developing countries and humanitarian assistance in health and education (p. 53).

Hasman (2008) sees the main Israeli national narrative as the pioneering heroism story from the establishment of the state till the war of 1967, and the romantic historical-religious narrative since then. Calling it "the crusaders' narrative" (p. 51) – because of its emphasis on the use of military power to defend religion – Hasman (2008) saw this narrative as damaging to the national brand. His research found that in the United States the current brand was associated with militarism, religious fanaticism, and machismo (p. 52), and that the world questioned the legitimacy of a Jewish state claiming to be both Jewish and democratic at the same time. Hasman (2008) proposed an alternative story stressing technological innovation, science, education, healing, and medical services to give Israel the brand advantage through "the Jewish brain, science and technology" (p. 53) (ATH).

This is not new. A major part of the Masbirim Israel campaign has intermittently sought, and still seeks, to deliver this message. For example, the concept was partly implemented by the Israeli Ministry of Foreign Affairs from the late 1950s with the Mashav Center for International Cooperation project as a way of building relationships with developing countries. It provided training courses in health and agriculture to over 200,000 people from Africa and Asia.

As recently as November 2009, Senor and Singer's (2009) *Start-Up Nation* (see Chapter 8), published under the sponsorship of the Council on Foreign Relations in the United States, promotes a story that is "on message" with Hasman's (2008) suggested narrative. Senor and Singer (2009) update the story with praise of Israeli innovative culture in general and innovative Israeli companies and entrepreneurs in particular. Their supporting statistics note that "[i]n 2008, per capita venture capital investments in Israel were 2.5 times greater than in the United States, more than 30 times greater than in Europe, 80 times greater than in China, and 350 times greater than in India" (pp. 11–12).

Despite its being on message, some critics identified the book's exaggerated "press agentry" style, noting that in 2009, just one year after Senor and Singer had lauded Israel's venture capital success, the funding they had referred to fell sharply: "Ruth Schuster, senior business and finance editor for *The Marker*, a financial paper distributed with the Israel daily *Haaretz*, says . . . there are great lessons to be gleaned from Israel's high-tech success" but that "*Start-up Nation* engages in too much cheerleading for its own good. 'The book is filled with a gasping sense of wonder, which weakened the authors' arguments'" (Prusher, 2010).

Nation branders and nation builders alike would do well to remember Kunczik's (1997) warning not just that many different actors are involved but also that this process is "long and demanding . . . [and a] positive image cannot be forced nor bought, and once it has been built it needs continuous cultivation" (p. ix).

Hasbara and realities

On April 15, 2012, just two years after the Masbirim Israel campaign leaflets at Ben Gurion Airport that we describe in the first chapter, the same airport featured a very different scene. Hundreds of international pro-Palestinian activists were refused entry into Israel in a large-scale security operation. According to the Israeli police spokesperson, activists were arrested or deported "to prevent any major incidents taking place. These are not terrorists, but they could be a threat to Israel's security" (*Haaretz*, April 15, 2012).

In fact, the risk was to Israel's reputation rather than its security. The activists, mostly from Europe, had been planning to travel to Bethlehem in the Palestinian West Bank for a week-long programme of educational and cultural activities under the banner of "Welcome to Palestine." They had to fly via Ben Gurion Airport as Israel controls all entry points to the West Bank. However, hundreds of ticket-holders were told hours before their flight that they would not be permitted to board planes. Israel had distributed a list of about 1,200 names, each of them *persona non grata* to airlines, and demanded that they be barred from flights regardless of the fact that they had not committed any crime.

The 2012 "no-fly" operation followed the higher-profile 2010 "Flotilla" campaign, in which international pro-Palestinian activists attempted to break the Israeli–Egyptian blockade on the Gaza Strip. During the struggle between Turkish activists and Israeli soldiers, nine activists were killed. The violent Israeli response was condemned internationally, and severely damaged Israel's relationship with Turkey, its only former ally in the Middle East. In both these cases – and in many other violent responses to what are perceived by the Israeli government as threats, or risks to its reputation – the Hasbara professionals use similar narratives. These present Israel as the victim, put the blame on the Palestinians, and argue for self-defence against those who refuse to recognize Israel's right to exist.

The "no-fly" operation eventually developed into a public relations disaster for Israel nicknamed – after the earlier "Flotilla" episode – "Flytilla." Flytilla "ensured a high profile for the pro-Palestinian protesters' attempted show of solidarity with the people of the West Bank" (*Haaretz*, April 15, 2012). The operation only showcased how the West Bank has become a prison for Palestinian residents, who, without permission from the Israeli authorities, were clearly able neither to travel nor to accept visitors from abroad.

Hasbara's blind spots

Israeli government and military institutions rarely make an apology, or any admission of a mistake, or any recognition of Palestinians' rights as human beings, let alone as a nation. Typically, officials use one-way communication that makes no attempt to develop a dialogue despite the fact that although dissenting voices "by definition bring views and ideas to the table that are at times difficult to consider . . . they may also have a critical message to convey – a message that can save lives and change history" (Ben-Ami, 2011, p. 30). Critics from the international community are frequently accused of anti-Semitism, and liberal Israelis who criticize the government are often labelled "self-hating Jews" and called "over-righteous." In the United States, Ben-Ami (2011) and the J Street advocacy and political action group, which is openly pro-Israel and pro-peace, found themselves called "fanatics, anti-Semitic, extremists and self-hating Jews" (p. 42) because "today's mainstream leaders tell us to stay quiet, respect unity and avoid dissent" (p. 42). In recent years, Israeli activists who protest against the government's policies on Palestinians have been persecuted – and not only by the government but also by (often well-funded) non-profit organizations and student organizations claiming to protect Israel's reputation. Ben-Ami (2011) sees that "attacks against human rights organizations are steady, harsh and growing" (p. 240), and points to organizations such as the Jerusalem-based NGO Monitor, which "launched ads and billboards attacking progressive organizations such as the New Israel Fund for their support to groups that provided critical information on the conduct of the Israeli military in Gaza to international investigators" (p. 240), and the student group Im Tirtzu, which acts as a form of thought police in attacking individual academics, artists, and what it claims are biased curricula for being insufficiently Zionist: "In 2009, Im Tirtzu's largest donor was the John Hagee Ministries (JHM) via the Christian-Zionist organization Christians United for Israel (CUFI). Im Tirtzu received US$100,000 from JHM and $34,000 from other sources" (http://en.wikipedia.org/wiki/Im_Tirtzu).

In the United States, "friends" of the State of Israel "consistently suggest that Israel has a 'PR problem' – that it hasn't done an adequate job of explaining itself, or making its case in the court of public opinion" (Ben-Ami, 2011, p. 121). As a result, Ben-Ami continues, when "news media run stories critical of Israel, the ensuing discussion in the community isn't about whether Israel should look more closely" (p. 121) at its actions but "about the underlying anti-Israel bias in the media" (p. 121) when the problem may lie in "the policies of the State of Israel and the behavior of parts of the Jewish community in Israel" (pp. 120–121).

Shenhav et al.'s (2010) study of Israeli public diplomacy argues that Israel's failure to defend its international reputation is a result of a reactive, rather than proactive, strategy, and of "incompleteness of messages in terms of major framing functions, and of incoherence in the basic narrative structure of complication-resolution" (p. 157). As Eldar (2005) and other Hasbara critics observe, it could equally be argued that Israel's reactive and proactive narratives cannot cover up the basic faults of unjustified and unmeasured violent actions, 45 years of occupation, and denials of basic human rights for the Palestinians.

We see the absence of such basic contemporary public relations efforts as listening to the other side in this conflict over territories and freedoms; consulting; conducting a sincere dialogue; building relationships; and negotiating – with a prior willingness to compromise – a fair deal. Nonetheless, no public relations professional in today's Israel is able to consult with the government on choosing more up-to-date public relations over the traditions of Hasbara. One-way communication and the absence of negotiations and dialogue create a problem for constructing credible narratives. To gain credibility, the best way for nations remains Kunczik's (1997) three actions: "be democratic," "observe human rights," and "pursue policies of openness" (p. 283).

As Eldar (2010) observes, "it is necessary not to dismiss the increasing delegitimization of Israel in foreign countries . . . instead of whining and blaming the messengers, the captains of the ship of state would do well to change its direction." It is significant that from 1993 to 2000, following the Oslo peace agreement and Israel's commitment to compromises on territory and to a Palestinian self-controlled autonomy, there was a significant change. During that period the international community turned towards Israel with political support and involvement in peaceful projects, foreign investments and economic cooperation, and acceptance of Israel as a legitimate member of the international community. Once the peace process stopped, Israel's image in the world deteriorated.

This book offers our explanation of the overreaction and intolerance of Israel to any criticism of its policies, and its undemocratic activities in seeking to shut down Palestinian and pro-Palestinian voices. By examining the narratives and myths developed by leaders and professional communicators since the early days of the Zionist movement, and throughout almost 66 years of existence as the State of Israel, we have sought to clarify the logic, the emotions, and the history that underpin contemporary Israeli public relations. Those public relations origins are located in deeply rooted fear inherited from 2,000 years of Jewish persecution experiences living without a territory and dependent on the non-Jewish community, in the sacrifices demanded from immigrant people for the sake of building a nation, and in the conviction that a modern Jewish democratic state has the right to exist in the traditional Jewish "Promised Land." This right is in spite of the fact that for many generations this land has been inhibited by Palestinian Arabs – Muslims and Christians who make up about 20% of the Israeli population today. In Yiftachel's (2006) terms, Israel is an "ethnocracy," which he explains as a regime promoting "the expansion of the dominant group in contested territory while maintaining a democratic façade" (p. 5)

The occupation of Palestinian territory in the West Bank and its control over Gaza since the 1967 war intensified the challenge to Israeli democracy. Gorenberg (2011) brings this home in describing the specifics of Elisha, "an illegal outpost, one of about a hundred small settlements established" (p. 2) since the Oslo Accord in 1993:

> Ostensibly, the settler activists who established the outposts defied the government and laws in force in Israeli-occupied territory. In reality, multiple state agencies lent a hand, while elected officials ignored or helped the effort. The Housing Ministry spent over $300,000 on infrastructure and buildings at Elisha alone. The army provides soldiers to guard the spot. The purpose of the outpost enterprise is to fill the gaps between larger existing settlements, to extend Jewish control over West Bank land, to fragment the territory left to the Palestinians. It is actually a massive rogue operation making a mockery of the rule of law.
>
> (p. 2)

The Elisha settlement represents for Gorenberg a "crossroads – not on the map, but in Israeli history. The ongoing occupation, the fostering of religious extremism, the undercutting of the law by the government itself all threaten Israel's future. In particular, they place its aspiration to democracy deeply at risk" (p. 4). Gorenberg's book *The Unmaking of Israel* (2011) argues for going beyond Hasbara explanations. This is because by keeping the territories, Israel crippled its democracy and to save itself needs to "end the settlement enterprise, end the occupation, and find a peaceful way to partition the land between the Jordan and the Mediterranean" (p. 222).

Israel's public relations and democracy

Israel's ethnocratic features do not stand up well in the international court of public opinion. Building the Israeli nation on ethnicity rather than on citizenship entails other problematic issues (e.g. lack of separation between state and religion, and the lack of a constitution to protect human rights). Those issues are a challenge for the practice of modern professional public relations, which needs an environment respectful of freedoms of speech and movement, and of individual citizens' rights.

We have described how professional Hasbara practitioners were employed by the pre-state Zionist institutions, and later by government agencies, to promote and educate the old-new nation. Their task was to create a new identity, and design new narratives, myths, events, songs, films, and other mediated communication, in order to unify Jews from 70 different countries into one nation. They also attempted to achieve consensus and support for the Zionist and Israeli leadership. The survival of the small Jewish community in the pre-state era under the British Mandate depended on voluntarism and enthusiastic consensus. Professional communicators were needed to enlist and motivate the people to meet difficult challenges.

Practitioners managed intensive Hasbara campaigns that involved the education system in constructing a new Israeli culture. Their work in the service of Zionist institutions helped create and promote new national traditions, and supported the revival of the Hebrew language in a unique campaign through which it became "a major vehicle in creating a new and more uniform national culture that propagated Zionist ideology and pioneering values" (Zerubavel, 1995, p. 80). The first Hebrew newspapers and the media in the first two decades of the State of Israel were expected to function as unifying agents, to boost the people's morale, and to support the national cause as defined by the leadership. The mass media were tools for the movement and its organizations to use in order to achieve the goal of building a nation.

In many cases, journalists functioned as Hasbara practitioners themselves as part of the dominant political coalition. Historically, too, from early pre-state days there were financial deals between Hasbara practitioners and news agencies. Hasbara practice in national institutions involved financial support also to film production companies and press photographers. All these took place without transparency and without respect for the function of independent journalism in a democratic system.

After the decentralization following the crisis of 1973, Peri (2004) noted key changes in journalists' self-perception and the redefinition of their role on the spectrum as subservient to the government at one end and, at the other, developing "a profession that is supposed to provide checks and balances to the national leadership – the perception of the political media as representative of the citizenry facing up to government" (p. 89). The post-1973 expansion of the journalistic spectrum aided the collapse of consensus in Israeli society and opened a door of opportunity for public relations practitioners.

It can safely be concluded that public relations in the Israeli context did not divorce itself from journalism. The book traces the blurring of boundaries between these two occupations from before the state to the present. Journalists in Israel today advertise commercial products and services, take public relations jobs, and are deeply involved socially with politicians and public relations practitioners.

Hasbara, society, and culture

The collapse of centralized consensus and the changing role of journalism from the mid-1970s stimulated a process of change in many aspects of Israel's value system. The effort to build a collective identity for the new nation was replaced by individualism and a shift towards "a civil society bubbling with action and vitality" (Yishai, 1998, p. 160) where people were "no longer mobilized to endorse a national cause but eagerly demand that their interest be considered and then realized" (p. 160). The privatization of politics and the economy gave rise to many activists who competed for public support for their cause. This process gave voice also to groups who represented a threat to democracy and who increased social divisions. The diversity of voices struggling to be heard, and the competition between them for public support, fuelled an increase in the demand for professional public relations services.

In the new millennium, Israeli public relations practitioners still hold attributes of their predecessors. This still persists in spite of the post-1990s growth in the number of practitioners, and despite exposure to professional concepts from the international public relations community – and especially their growing consensus that public relations should contribute to "a fully functioning society" (Heath, 2006, p. 94). Ironically, Heath's (2010) more recent proposal on best practice cites Martin Buber: "Entities working to foster mutually beneficial relationships seek what Buber (1965) called an I–Thou relationship. . . . Beneficial relationships exhibit a workable and mutually beneficial balance of control, trust and positive regard" (p. 3).

Heath (2010) continues that, in championing dialogue, Buber (1965) "set the standard as depending on whether the participants have "'in mind the other or others in their present and particular being and turn to them with the intention of establishing a living mutual relationship' (p. 19)" (p. 3). Maureen Taylor (2010) takes this in a new definition that *"Public relations' role in society is to create (and re-create) the conditions that enact civil society"* (p. 7; italics in the original) that is grounded in civil society, and civil society theory, which in "the ancient and Enlightenment epochs were characterized by a growing awareness of public deliberations and decision making" (p. 7). Significantly, in sentences extremely relevant to the Israeli context, she concludes that "civil society was not about having one common idea; it was about a tolerance of debating different ideas" (p. 7) and that "[c]ivil society is a communicative process grounded in information, communication, and relationships" (p. 7).

As our narrative shows, little of this has been internalized or adopted by Israeli practitioners. The practice's major professional focus remains on media relations, on one-way communication, and on "engineering acceptance." Israeli practitioners in general do not see themselves as responsible to the stakeholders, let alone stakeseekers, or for upholding the integrity of the organizations they represent, or for creating the conditions for civil society.

Influencing Israel: continuities

Neither public relations practitioners nor journalists went through a full transition of their professional role definition. Partly because of this, Israeli media, in spite of some dramatic changes, have retained some inherited values. The Israeli media magazine *Hayin Hashveet* (The Seventh Eye), produced by the Israel Democracy Institute, devoted an issue to the question: "Are the media cooperative?" and the editor, Uzi Benziman, concluded:

> Israeli media (of course, with some exceptions) have always backed prime ministers. This was the situation in the first years of the state, when the relationship between the leadership and senior reporters was similar to that of members in an aristocratic order, and this was the situation in later years, when the media seemingly wakened up, developed antidotes against the virus of excessive closeness to the establishment, and became a power in themselves. Even the lessons learned from the [1973] Yom Kippur war, which exposed their opportunism and its readiness to adopt the establishment's version, have been burned out. Today's media reveal the same tendency to give credit to the establishment and to identify with its moves.
>
> (2005) [ATH]

In fact, it could be argued that the approach of Israeli public relations practitioners' predecessors, who practised one-way communication in the service of Zionism, was replaced by an approach that practised one-way communication in the service of businesses, even in cases that claimed to demonstrate corporate social responsibility. The Diaspora heritage and the Zionist ideology may still be traced in the Israeli public relations practitioners' approach to the role of communication as the glue that connects the people and builds a nation, especially in time of national crisis.

Postscript

Our book aims to make a contribution to scholars who study the phenomenon called public relations, its evolution as a profession, and its role in society. At the same time, it seeks to help public relations practitioners – in Israel and elsewhere by comparison and contrast – to recognize their own professional history and better understand the influence of their contexts. As Adelman (2008) notes, any "state, no matter how exceptionalist, has much in common with the 200 states in the world" (p. 42).

Our account tracks how public relations has been intertwined with national circumstances, changes, and events, and we illustrate elements of a history more hidden than even Cutlip's (1994) "unseen power" history of US public relations. Our evidence and analysis lend support to those who presume the existence of different national models of public relations development in different environments.

The new realities and political changes that followed during the 1980s and 1990s provided a more appropriate environment for the development of the profession. However, a change towards a closed, centralized, and less democratic state in the new millennium poses new challenges for human rights and freedoms. And it poses serious risks for the profession. Since 2009, the right-wing and religious-influenced government led by Prime Minister Netanyahu has used that power to launch a wave of anti-democratic legislation initiatives that have led the Association for Civil Rights in Israel to fear

> intensifying infringements on democratic freedoms in Israel. Of particular concern is the fact that two of the central arenas from which these threats arise are the very ones charged with safeguarding democracy: The Knesset (Israeli parliament) and the government. Senior officials have voiced harsh and unprecedented statements against human rights organizations, political groups, and minorities, and have made various attempts to narrow their operations; . . . the basic principles of the Israeli democratic system are being undermined. There is an ongoing infringement on issues such as freedom of expression, and human dignity and equality; on the possibility of upholding the pluralism of views and thoughts; on freedom of assembly and protest; and on the very legitimacy of certain views and positions.
>
> (Association for Civil Rights in Israel, 2011)

Yet, while finishing on that pessimistic note, we are not without hope. Israeli newspapers still publish investigative journalism and books critical of Israel still appear; indeed, we happily acknowledge using a number of them. But an active and vibrant public sphere and the spaces for activists, radicals, and other voices need to be expanded rather than contracted. What happens in Israel is unique but it is not unlike what is happening to the public sphere of many other countries. Moloney (2006) has argued that "PR will spread more widely through the civil societies and political economies of liberal democracies" (p. 176); that "[a]s citizens and consumers we will support, reject and question its 'voices' as suits our interests" (p. 176); and that

> after reform, with all "voices" who want to speak audible to all who want to listen, and that listening done in a sceptical way in person or via a diverse media, liberal democracies and markets will have more varied and informed public debates. In this way, the positive effects of PR will outweigh the negative ones – just.
>
> (p. 176)

We hope our narrative will encourage public relations practitioners and scholars everywhere to make their histories visible, to learn from them, and to share them widely. More than that, our hope is that we can work together as forces for democracy. We see an urgent need to make the future activities of public relations, rather than only "just" outweigh the negative effects, contribute positively and transparently to more "fully functioning societies" in Israel and elsewhere.

References

Abadi, J. (1993). *Israel's leadership: From Utopia to crisis.* Westport, CT: Greenwood Press.
Abbott, A. (1988). *The system of professions: An essay on the division of expert labor.* Chicago, IL: University of Chicago Press.
Adelman, J. R. (2008). *The rise of Israel: A history of a revolutionary state.* London, UK: Routledge.
Aharoni, Y. (1991). *The political economy in Israel.* Jerusalem, Israel: Am Oved, Eshkol Institute and the Hebrew University.
Aldoory, L. (2005). Women in public relations. In R. L. Heath (Ed.), *Encyclopedia of public relations* (Vol. 2, pp. 899–902). Thousand Oaks, CA: Sage.
Almagor, D. (2000). Dress rehearsal for independence: The foundation of the Hebrew University of Jerusalem 75 years ago. *Ariel, 111,* 25–37.
Almog, O. (1997). *The Sabra: A profile.* Tel Aviv, Israel: Am Oved.
Amit, Z. (2002, October 30). Personal communication with the lead author in an interview in Tel Aviv.
Amitai, Y. (2002, October 7). Personal communication with the lead author in an interview in Lod.
Anderson, B. (1991). *Imagined communities: Reflections on the origins and spread of nationalism.* London, UK: Verso.
Anholt, S. (2004). Editor's foreword to the first issue. *Place Branding and Public Diplomacy, 1* (1), 4–11.
Anholt, S. (2007). *Competitive identity: The new brand management for nations, cities, and regions.* Basingstoke, UK: Palgrave Macmillan.
Anholt, S., & Hildreth, J. (2005). *Brand America: The making, unmaking and remaking of the greatest national image of all time.* London, UK: Cyan Communications.
Arnon, M. (2002, October 22). Personal communication with the lead author in an interview in Jerusalem.
Association for Civil Rights in Israel. (2011). Anti-democratic initiatives. Retrieved December 8, 2011 from http://www.acri.org.il/en/?cat=64
Avineri, S. (1981). *The making of modern Zionism.* New York, NY: Basic Books.
Avisar, A. (1990, March 23). 24 hours in the service of the boss and the media: Women conquer state spokesperson roles. *Maariv,* p. 10.
Avnion, E. (Ed.). (1997). *The Hebrew–Hebrew concise Sapir dictionary.* Or-Yehuda, Israel: Hed Artzi.
Avraham, E. (2001). *The hidden Israel: Kibbutzim, Jewish settlements, development cities and Arab towns in the Israeli press* [ATH]. Jerusalem, Israel: Academon Press.

References 181

Avraham, E., & Ketter, E. (2008). *Media strategies for marketing places in crisis.* Oxford, UK: Butterworth-Heinemann.

Balaban, N. (2003, July 23). Personal communication with the author in an interview in Tel Aviv.

Barak, R. (2012, February 8). Ethics? An editor of *Makor Rishon* [Primary Source] writes speeches for Netanyahu [ATH]. *Globes,* 8 February. Retrieved July 22, 2012 from http://www.globes.co.il/news/article.aspx?did=1000723017

Bar-Gal, Y. (1999). *An agent of Zionist propaganda: The Jewish national fund 1924–1947.* Jerusalem, Israel: Haifa University and Zmorah Bitan Publishing.

Barnea, N. (1999). *Bibi time: Political columns, 1993–1999.* Tel Aviv, Israel: Zmorah.

Bar-On, M. (1999). The Bithonism and its critics: 1949–1967. In M. Bar-On (Ed.), *The challenge of sovereignty: Creativity and philosophy in the state's first decade* (pp. 62–103). Jerusalem, Israel: Yad Ben Zvi.

Beilin, Y. (1987). *Israeli industry: Roots.* Jerusalem, Israel: Keter.

Beilin, Y. (1999). *The death of the American uncle.* Tel Aviv, Israel: Yediot Aharonot.

Ben-Ami, J. (2011). *A new voice for Israel: Fighting for the survival of the Jewish nation.* New York, NY: Palgrave Macmillan.

Ben-Ari, D. (1993, December 13). The ministers called him by his first name. *Laisha,* pp. 60–61.

Ben-Bassat, A. (Ed.). (2002). *The Israeli economy, 1985–1998: From government intervention to market economics.* Cambridge, MA: MIT Press.

Bendix, R. (1996). *Nation-building and citizenship: Studies of our changing social order.* New Brunswick, NJ: Transaction.

Ben-Meir, D. (2002, November 11). Personal communication with the lead author in an interview in Tel Aviv.

Bentele, G., & Junghänel, I. (2004). Germany. In B. van Ruler & D. Verčič (Eds.), *Public relations and communication management in Europe: A nation-by-nation introduction to public relations theory and practice* (pp. 153–168). Berlin, Germany: Mouton de Gruyter.

Bentwitch, N. (1954). *For Zion's sake: A biography of Judah L. Magnes, first Chancellor and first President of the Hebrew University of Jerusalem.* Philadelphia, PA: Jewish Publication Society.

Ben-Yehuda, N. (2002, December 18). Personal telephone communication with the lead author in an interview.

Benziman, U. (2005, May). The media does not detach itself from the establishment. *The Seventh Eye, 56.* Retrieved September 2, 2005 from http://www.the7eye.org.il/Section Archive/EditorsSay/Pages/article5601.aspx?RetUrl=/WRITTERS/Pages/uzi_benziman.aspx

Benziman, U. (2011). The freedom to oppress [ATH]. *The Seventh Eye.* Retrieved December 26, 2011 from http://www.the7eye.org.il/DailyColumn/Pages/251211_Freedom_of_oppression.aspx

Berkhofer, R. F., Jr. (2008). *Fashioning history: Current practices and principles.* New York, NY: Palgrave Macmillan.

Berkhofer, R. F., Jr. (1995). *Beyond the great story: History as text and discourse.* Cambridge, MA: Belknap Press of Harvard University Press.

Bernays, E. L. (1947). The engineering of consent. *Annals of the American Academy of Political and Social Science, 35,* 113–120.

Bettelheim, A. (1990). *The merchants.* Tel Aviv, Israel: Tel Aviv and Jaffa Chamber of Commerce.

References

Biran, A. (1997). Israel Museum. In Keter Publishing House (Ed.), *Encyclopedia Judaica*. Jerusalem, Israel: Judaica Multimedia.

Bistritzki, N. (1980). *The hidden myth*. Tel Aviv, Israel: Yachdav.

Blau, U. (2011, December 2). A fund existing for itself. *Haaretz*, weekend supplement. Retrieved December 6, 2011 from http://www.haaretz.co.il/magazine/1.1580636

Boltanski, O. (2006). *Infor2006*. Tel Aviv, Israel: Kodaf.

Broom, G. M. (2009). *Cutlip and Center's effective public relations* (10th ed.). Upper Saddle River, NJ: Prentice Hall.

Brown, R. E. (2006). Myth of symmetry: Public relations as cultural styles. *Public Relations Review, 32* (3), 206–212.

Brown, R. E. (2010). Symmetry and its critics: Antecedents, prospects, and implications for symmetry in a postsymmetry era. In R. L. Heath (Ed.), *The Sage handbook of public relations* (pp. 277–292). Thousand Oaks, CA: Sage.

Buber, M. (1963). *Israel and the world: Essays in a time of crisis*. New York, NY: Schoken Books.

Buber, M. (1965). *Between man and man* (R. G. Smith, Trans.). New York, NY: Macmillan.

Carmon, A. Z. (1994). *Beyond exile and return: Redefining the concept of peoplehood*. Tel Aviv, Israel: Institute for Democracy and Hakibbutz Hameuchad Publishing.

Caspi, D. (2006). The nonstop institutionalization of mass media in Israel. In U. Cohen, E. Ben-Refael, A. Bareli, & E. Ya'ar (Eds.), *Israel and modernity: For Moshe Lisak's Jubilee* (pp. 241–281). Tel Aviv, Israel: Israeli Institute in Jerusalem, and the Institute for Zionist and Israeli Research at Tel Aviv University.

Caspi, D. (2010). Masbirim for Israel or for the Minister. YNET – opinions. Retrieved December 2, 2011 from http://www.ynet.co.il/articles/0,7340,L-3854453,00.html

Caspi, D., & Limor, Y. (1992). *The mediators: The mass media in Israel, 1948–1990* [ATM]. Tel Aviv, Israel: Am Oved.

Caspi, D., & Limor, Y. (1998). *The mediators: The mass media in Israel, 1948–1990*. Tel Aviv, Israel: Am Oved.

Chen, E. K. (2012.) *Historiography: An introductory guide*. New York, NY: Continuum.

Christensen, B. (1994, January). What is a profession? *Journal of the American Society of CLU and ChFC*, pp. 28–30.

Cohen, K. (2002, December 4). Personal telephone communication with the lead author in Jerusalem.

Cohen, H. (2004). *An army of shadows: Palestinian collaborators in the service of Zionism*. Jerusalem, Israel: Ivrit-Hebrew Publishing House.

Cohen, R. (2009). *Israel is real: An obsessive quest to understand the Jewish nation and its history*. New York, NY: Farrar, Straus & Giroux.

Cohen, S. (1973). *Haolam hazeh*. Tel Aviv, Israel: Tfachot Publishing.

Coombs, W. T., & Holladay, S. J. (2010). *PR strategy and applications: Managing influence*. Malden, MA: Wiley-Blackwell.

Cull, N. J. (n.d.). What is public diplomacy? Retrieved June 7, 2012 from http://uscpublicdiplomacy.org/index.php/about/what_is_pd/

Curtin, P. A., & Boynton, L. A. (2001). Ethics in public relations: Theory and practice. In R. L. Heath (Ed.), *The handbook of public relations* (pp. 411–421). Thousand Oaks, CA: Sage.

Curtin, P. A., & Gaither, T. K. (2007). *International public relations: Negotiating culture, identity, and power*. Thousand Oaks, CA: Sage.

Cutlip, S. M. (1994). *The unseen power: Public relations, a history*. Hillsdale, NJ: Lawrence Erlbaum.

Cutlip, S. M., Center, A. H., & Broom, G. M. (1999). *Effective public relations* (8th ed.). Upper Saddle River, NJ: Prentice Hall.

Dankner, A., & Tartakover, D. (1996). *Where we were and what we did: An Israeli lexicon of the fifties and sixties.* Jerusalem, Israel: Keter.

Davis, A. (2002). *Public relations democracy: Public relations, politics and the mass media in Britain.* Manchester, UK: Manchester University Press.

Day, K. D., Dong, Q., & Robins, C. (2001). Public relations ethics: An overview and discussion of issues for the 21st century. In R. L. Heath (Ed.), *The handbook of public relations* (pp. 403–409). Thousand Oaks, CA: Sage.

Dayan, M. (2002, December 10). Personal communication with the lead author in an interview in Tel Aviv.

Donovan, J. (2002). Hadassah. *Nightline, 21 December.* [From Ohayon Helaine's transcription in an email to Hadassah Boston Chapter, March 28, 2002].

Dor, D. (2001) *Newspapers under the influence.* Tel Aviv, Israel: Babel.

Dozier, D. M. (1984). Program evaluation and roles of practitioners. *Public Relations Review, 10* (2), 13–21.

Duek, N. (1990, August 21). MDA moved him out. *Yediot Ahronot,* p. 12.

Duhé, S. C., & Sriramesh, K. (2009). Political economy and public relations. In K. Sriramesh & D. Verčič (Eds.), *The global public relations handbook: Theory, research, and practice* (rev. ed., pp. 25–51). New York, NY: Routledge.

Economist, The. (2009). *Brands and branding* (2nd ed.). London, UK: Profile Books.

Editorial Staff Encyclopedia Judaica. (1997). Pearlman, Moshe. In Keter Publishing House (Ed.), *Encyclopedia Judaica.* Jerusalem, Israel: Judaica Multimedia.

Edwards, L. (2010). "Race" in public relations. In R. L. Heath (Ed.), *The SAGE handbook of public relations* (pp. 205–221). Thousand Oaks, CA: Sage.

Einstein, A. (1925, March 8). The mission of our university. *The New Palestine, 27,* 294.

Eisenstadt, S. N. (1985). *The transformation of Israel society: An essay in interpretation.* London, UK: Weidenfeld & Nicolson.

Eisenstadt, S. N. (1997). *Comments on the continuity of some Jewish historical forms in Israeli society.* Jerusalem, Israel: Shazar Library.

Elam, Y. (1984). *A dream that came through: Central problems in the history of Zionism* (2nd ed.). Tel Aviv, Israel: Israel Ministry of Defense and Tel Aviv University.

Eldar, A. (2005, May 6). A brand from the burning. *Haaretz.* Retrieved May 10, 2005 from http://www.haaretz.com/a-brand-from-the-burning-1.157923

Eldar, A. (2010, November 29). For Israel, "delegitimization" is becoming an excuse. *Haaretz.* Retrieved 20 December, 2011 from http://www.haaretz.com/print-edition/opinion/for-israel-delegitimization-is-becoming-an-excuse-1.327551

Elizur, J. (1976). *Commercial broadcasts on Israeli television.* Jerusalem, Israel: Hebrew University.

Elizur, Y. (1992). *The shekel and the olive branch.* Haifa, Israel: Gestlit.

Ellul, J. (1965). *Propaganda: The formation of men's attitudes* (K. Kellen & J. Lerner, Trans.). New York, NY: Vintage Books.

Elon, A. (1983). *The Israelis: Founders and sons.* New York, NY: Viking Penguin. (Original work published 1971)

Eshet, E. (2003, August 7). Personal communication with the lead author in an interview in Tel Aviv.

Eshkol, D. (2002, October 10). Personal communication with the lead author in an interview in Tel Aviv.

Felber, M. (1996). *Industry in Israel*. Jerusalem, Israel: Merkaz Haasbara, Ministry of Education.

Finer, H. (1931). Officials and the public. *Public administration, 9*, 23–26.

Fontana, A., & Frey, J. H. (2005). The interview: From neutral stance to political involvement. In N. K. Denzin & Y. S. Lincoln (Eds.), *The handbook of qualitative research* (3rd ed., pp. 695–727). Thousand Oaks, CA: Sage.

Fraser, N. (1992). Rethinking the public sphere: A contribution to the critique of actually existing democracy. In C. Calhoun (Ed.), *Habermas and the public sphere* (pp. 109–142). Cambridge, MA: MIT Press.

Freitag, A. R., & Stokes, A. Q. (2009). *Global public relations: Spanning borders, spanning cultures*. New York, NY: Routledge.

Ganor, A. (1993, March 5). The public does not know what public relations is. *Haaretz*, p. 10.

GAR (Government Annual Report). (1949/1950). Jerusalem, Israel: Government of Israel.

GAR (Government Annual Report). (1950/1951). Jerusalem, Israel: Government of Israel.

GAR (Government Annual Report). (1953). Jerusalem, Israel: Government of Israel.

Gazit, S. (1991, June 26). IDF spokespeople – non political. *Maariv*, p. 7.

Geary, P. J. (2003). *The myth of nations: The medieval origins of Europe*. Princeton, NJ: Princeton University Press.

Gilbert, M. (1998). *Israel: A history*. New York, NY: William Morrow.

Gineo, V. (2003, January 1). Personal communication with the lead author at an interview in Jerusalem.

Golan, M. (2012, July 20). The council for corruption of the press: Speechwriting for the PM is against all the sacred principles of the press. [ATH]. *Globes*. Retrieved July, 22, 2012 from http://www.globes.co.il/news/article.aspx?did=1000767494

Goren, A. A. (1996, Spring). The view from Scopus: Judah L. Magnes and the early years of the Hebrew University. *Judaism*, pp. 203–224.

Gorenberg, G. (2011). *The unmaking of Israel*. New York, NY: HarperCollins.

Gower, K. K. (2007). Preface. In D. S. Straughan (Ed.), *Women's use of public relations for Progressive-era reform: Rousing the conscience of a nation* (pp. i–iv). New York, NY: Edwin Mellen Press.

Grunig, J. E., & Hunt, T. (1984). *Managing public relations*. New York, NY: Holt, Rinehart & Winston.

Grunig, L. A., Toth, E. L., & Hon, L. C. (2001). *Women in public relations: How gender influences practice*. New York, NY: Guilford Press.

Haaretz (2012, April 15). Israel blocks entry to pro-Palestinian activists at airport. Retrieved June 15, 2012 from http://www.haaretzdaily.com/israel-blocks-entry-to-pro-palestinian-activists-at-airport/

Habermas, J. (1976). *Legitimation crisis* (T. McCarthy, Trans.). London, UK: Heinemann.

Hadary, A., & Ernest, S. (1997). Jewish Agency. In Keter Publishing House (Ed.), *Encyclopedia Judaica*. Jerusalem, Israel: Judaica Multimedia.

Hadassah. (1962, April 5). Letter with the contract of Hadassah with the Gillons. New York, NY: Hadassah Archives (retrieved May 4, 2002).

Hadassah NY. (1929, December 7). News release. New York, NY: Hadassah Archives (retrieved May 3, 2002).

Hadassah Women's Zionist Organization. (1984–1985). *How Hadassah gratefully acknowledges gifts: A certificates and devices catalogue*. New York, NY: Hadassah Women's Zionist Organization.

Halpern, B. (1982). *Tell it to the world: A guide to international public relations*. Jerusalem, Israel: Gefen.

Harris, L. (1973). Text of presentation made to the HMOIC in 1973 by Mr. Lucian Harris, Director of Hadassah Services in Israel. CZA Serial Alef 341 file 28.

Harshav, B. (1993). *Language in time of revolution*. Stanford, CA: University of California Press.

Hasman, R. (2008, April). *Branding Israel: Political marketing in a continuing conflict*. Tel Aviv, Israel: Harold Hardog School for Government and Policy, Tel Aviv University.

Hatalgi, T. (2002, December 3). Personal communication with the lead author in an interview in Jerusalem.

Hattis Rolef, S. (Ed.). (1988). *Political dictionary of the State of Israel*. Jerusalem, Israel: Keter.

Heath, R. L. (2001). Shifting foundations: Public relations as relationship building. In R. L. Heath (Ed.), *Handbook of public relations* (pp. 1–10). Thousand Oaks, CA: Sage.

Heath, R. L. (2006). Onward into more fog: Thoughts on public relations' research directions. *Journal of Public Relations Research, 18* (2), 93–114.

Heath, R. L. (2010b). Mind, self, and society. In R. L. Heath (Ed.), *The SAGE handbook of public relations* (pp. 1–3). Thousand Oaks, CA: Sage.

Hever, H. (2002). *Producing the modern Hebrew canon: Nation building and minority discourse*. New York, NY: New York University Press.

Hiebert, R. (1996). *Courier to the crowd*. Ames, IA: Iowa State University Press.

Hobsbawm, E. J. (1990). *Nations and nationalism since 1780: Programme, myth, reality*. New York, NY: Cambridge University Press.

Holtzhausen, D. R. (2012). *Public relations as activism: Postmodern approaches to theory and practice*. New York, NY: Routledge.

Hon, L. C., Grunig, L., & Dozier, D. (1992). Women in public relations: Problems and opportunities. In J. Grunig (Ed.), *Excellence in public relations and communication management* (pp. 419–438). Hillsdale, NJ: Lawrence Erlbaum.

Honig, E. (2003, January 1). Personal communication with the lead author in an interview in the Hebrew University.

Horowitz, D., & Lissak, M. (1978). *Origins of the Israeli policy* (C. Hoffman, Trans.). Chicago, IL: University of Chicago Press. Published in Hebrew by Am Oved, 1977.

Hua, N. (2003). Diasporic Asian feminism: Bridging ties. *Politics and Culture, 3*. Retrieved July 2, 2005 from http://www.politicsandculture.org/2010/08/10/anh-hua-diasporic-asian-feminism-bridging-ties-2/

Izkovitch, G. (2010, July 26). Ten years after "temporary" appointment, controversial Government Press Office head may be forced out of office. *Haaretz*. Retrieved January 2, 2012 from http://www.haaretz.com/print-edition/news/ten-years-after-temporary-appointment-controversial-government-press-office-head-may-be-forced-out-of-office-1.304023

Justman, M. (2002). Structural change and the emergence of Israel's high-tech sector. In A. Ben-Bassat (Ed.), *The Israeli economy 1985–1998: From government intervention to market economics* (pp. 445–483). Cambridge, MA: MIT Press.

Katriel, T. (1986). *Talking straight: Dugri speech in Israeli Sabra culture*. Cambridge, UK: Cambridge University Press.

Katz, E., Hass, H., Weitz, S., Adoni, H., Gurevitch, M., Schiff, M., & Goldberg-Anabi, D. (2000). *Leisure patterns in Israel: Changes in cultural activity 1970–1990*. Tel Aviv, Israel: Open University of Israel.

Katz, J. (1963). *Tradition and crisis: Jewish society at the end of the Middle Ages* (2nd ed.). Jerusalem, Israel: Bialik Institute.

Kellen, K. (1962). Introduction. In J. Ellul, *Propaganda: The formation of men's attitudes* (K. Kellen & J. Lerner, Trans.) (pp. v–viii). New York, NY: Vintage.

Keller, A. (2012, June 17). Nine killed, two reports, and one siege. Retrieved June 18, 2012 from http://adam-keller1.blogspot.co.il/2012/06/blog-post_17.html

Khoury, R. (2011). The conflict of narratives. In M. Raheb (Ed.), *The invention of history: A century of interplay between theology and politics in Palestine* (pp. 259–268). Bethlehem, Palestine: Diyar.

Kimmerling, B. (1973). *The struggle over the lands*. Jerusalem, Israel: Hebrew University of Jerusalem Papers in Sociology Series.

Kimmerling, B. (2001). *The end of Ashkenazi hegemony*. Jerusalem, Israel: Keter.

Kimmerling, B. (2005). *The invention and decline of Israeliness: State, society, and the military*. Berkeley, CA: University of California Press.

Kirshenblatt-Gimblett, B. (1997). Making a place in the world: Jews and the Holy Land at World's Fairs. In J. Shandler & B. Wenger (Eds.), *Encounter with the Holy Land: Place, past and future in American Jewish culture* (pp. 60–82). Philadelphia, PA: National Museum of American Jewish History.

Kohn, H. (1965). *Nationalism: Its meaning and history* (rev. ed.). New York, NY: Van Nostrand.

Kouts, G. (1998a). Zionism and the Jewish press: Between propaganda and "objective journalism." In J. Wilke (Ed.), *Propaganda in the 20th Century: Contributions to its history* (pp. 99–112), Cresskill, NJ: Hampton Press.

Kouts, G. (1998b). The Zionist movement, the Hebrew press and the pattern of "national responsibility." *Am Vesefer, 10*, 199–212.

Kouts, G. (1999). *Studies in the history of the Hebrew press*. Tel Aviv, Israel: Yaron Golan.

Krantz, H. (1987). *Daughter of my people: Henrietta Szold and Hadassah*. New York, NY: E. P. Dutton.

Kunczik, M. (1997). *Image of nations and international public relations*. Mahwah, NJ: Lawrence Erlbaum.

Lamme, M. O., & Russell, K. M. (2010). Removing the spin: Toward a new theory of public relations history. *Journalism and Communication Monographs, 11* (4), 281–362.

Laniado, E. (2002, December 23). Personal communication with the lead author in Tel Aviv.

Laqueur, W. (1972). *A history of Zionism: From the French Revolution to the establishment of the State of Israel*. New York, NY: MJF Books.

L'Etang, J. (2004). *Public relations in Britain: A history of professional practice in the twentieth century*. Mahwah, NJ: Lawrence Erlbaum.

L'Etang, J. (2008a). Writing PR history: Issues, methods, and politics. *Journal of Communication Management, 12* (4), 319–335.

L'Etang, J. (2008b). *Public relations: Concepts, practice and critique*. London, UK: Sage.

Lebel, U. (2005). Confrontation or co-dependency? The relationship between security and communication at war and in routine times: Theoretical framework. In U. Lebel (Ed.), *Security and communication: Dynamics of relationships* (pp. 13–48). Beer Sheva, Israel: Ben-Gurion University, Ben-Gurion Institute for Israel Research.

Levin, M. (1997). *It takes a dream: The story of Hadassah*. Jerusalem, Israel: Gefen.

Levin, R. (2011, November 9). The help of the public is requested: Should bloggers be granted with a press ID card? [ATH]. *The Marker*. Retrieved January 2, 2012 from http://www.themarker.com/advertising/digital/1.1562174

Lineal, S. (1965). Presentation in a member's panel, "What is allowed and forbidden in public relations." *Annual Report of the Israeli Public Relations Association 1965*. Tel Aviv, Israel: Israel Printing.

Lineal, S. (2002, November 28). Personal communication with the lead author in an interview in Haifa.

Lis, Y. (2011, December 4). Likud MK Akunis: Every word Senator Joseph McCarthy said was right. *Haaretz*. Retrieved December 18, 2011 from http://www.haaretz.com/news/national/likud-mk-akunis-every-word-senator-joseph-mccarthy-said-was-right-1.399517

Lory, A. (2002, December 27). Fear, they are taking photos. *Haaretz Magazine*, p. 26.

McKie, D., & Munshi, D. (2007). *Reconfiguring public relations: Ecology, equity, and enterprise*. London, UK: Routledge.

Magnat, D. (2002, December 9). Personal communication with the lead author in an interview in Tel Aviv.

Mann, R. (2011, December 27). Kol Israel from Jeruslaem. *Seventh Eye*. Retrieved December 30, 2011 from http://www.the7eye.org.il/The_Analog_Age/Pages/271211_The_voice_of_Israel_from_Gerusalem.aspx?RetUrl=/THE_ANALOG_AGE/Pages/The_Analog_Age_Lobby.aspx

Marchand, R. (1998). *Creating the corporate soul: The rise of public relations and corporate imagery in American big business*. Berkeley, CA: University of California Press.

Mearsheimer, J. J., & Walt, S. M. (2006). The Israel lobby. *London Review of Books, 28* (6), 3–12. Retrieved January 29, 2011 from http://www.lrb.co.uk/v28/n06/john-mearsheimer/the-israel-lobby

Mearsheimer, J. J., & Walt, S. M. (2007). *The Israel lobby and U.S. foreign policy*. New York, NY: Farrar, Straus & Giroux.

Meyer, M. (2002, December 3). Personal communication with the lead author in an interview in Jerusalem.

Meyers, N. (2002, October 27). Personal communication with the lead author in an interview in Rehovot.

Meyers, O. (2005). Israeli journalism during the state's formative era: Between ideological affiliation and professional consciousness, *Journalism History, 31* (2), 88–97.

Mishori, A. (2000). *Look and behold: Zionist icons and visual symbols in Israeli culture*. Tel Aviv, Israel: Am Oved.

Moloney, K. (2006). *Rethinking public relations: PR propaganda and democracy*. London, UK: Routledge.

Morrison, S. E. (1935). *The founding of Harvard College*. Cambridge, MA: Harvard University Press.

Moss, D., Verčič, D., & Warnaby, G. (2003). Preface. In D. Moss, D. Verčič, & G. Warnaby (Eds.), *Perspectives on public relations research* (pp. xvi–xvii). London, UK: Routledge.

Munshi, D., & Kurian, P. (2005). Imperializing spin cycles: A postcolonial look at public relations, greenwashing, and the separation of publics. *Public Relations Review, 31* (4), 513–520.

Mushkin, B. (2002, October 23). Personal communication with the lead author in an interview in Jerusalem.

Negbi, M. (2011). *Freedom of journalists and freedom of the press: Media law and ethics*. Ra'anana, Israel: Open University.

Neiger, M. (2005, May 1). In the battlefield of the images. *Pnim, the Israel Teachers Union Magazine, 32*. Retrieved November 27, 2011 from www.itu.org.il

Neumann, D. (2002, October 21). Personal communication with the lead author in an interview in Jerusalem.

Newsom, D., Turk, J. V., & Kruckeberg, D. (1996). *This is PR: The realities of public relations* (6th ed.). Belmont, CA: Wadsworth.

OECD (Organization for Economic and Co-operation and Development). (2002, September). OECD investment policy review: Israel overview. Retrieved from http://www.oecd.org/general/searchresults/?q=iSRAEL&cx=012432601748511391518:xzeadub0b0a&cof=FORID:11&ie=UTF-8

Oren, R. (1997, Autumn). Building a location: Propaganda and Utopic space in Zionist landscape photography 1898–1948. *Dvarim Acherim, Magazine for Communication, Culture and Society Issues, 2*, 13–30.

Parag, N. (2010, June). Israelis 2nd most active in internet usage. *Globes, Israel's Business Arena*. June, 2010. Retrieved December 9, 2011 from http://www.globes.co.il/serveen/globes/docview.asp?did=1000569406&fid=1725

Patterson, T. E. (1998, July). Introduction. In N. Shai, *The spokesperson – in the crossfire: A decade of Israeli defense crisis from an official spokesperson's perspective*. Discussion Paper D-29. Cambridge, MA: Joan Shorenstein Center, Harvard University.

Pearl, M. (1991, July). Krasney, Drori and Kremer are lobbying. *Hadashot Hashavua*, p. 18.

Pearson, R. (1992). Perspectives on public relations history. In E. L. Toth & R. L. Heath (Eds.), *Rhetorical and critical approaches to public relations* (pp. 111–130). Hillsdale, NJ: Lawrence Erlbaum.

Peri, Y. (2004). *Telepopulism: Media and politics in Israel*. Stanford, CA: Stanford University Press.

Perlmuter, A. (1969). *Military and politics in Israel: Nation-building and role expansion*. London, UK: Frank Cass.

Perry, M. (1988). Thoughts about the marketing thinking in Israel. *Otot, 100*, 24–25.

Pieczka, M. (2011). Public relations as dialogic expertise? *Journal of Communication Management, 15* (2), 108–124.

Pieczka, M., & L'Etang, J. (2001). Public relations and questions of professionalism. In R. L. Heath (Ed.), *Handbook of public relations* (pp. 223–235). Thousand Oaks, CA: Sage.

Postal, B. (1997). Public relations. In Keter Publishing House (Ed.), *Encyclopedia Judaica*. Jerusalem, Israel: Judaica Multimedia.

Prusher, I. R. (2010, March 9). Innovation center? How Israel became a "Start-Up Nation." *Christian Science Monitor*. Retrieved November 21, 2011 from http://www.csmonitor.com/World/Middle-East/2010/0309/Innovation-center-How-Israel-became-a-Start-Up-Nation

Public Relations Society of America (PRSA). (2012) Member code of ethics. Retrieved February 6, 2012 from http://www.prsa.org/AboutPRSA/Ethics/CodeEnglish/

Raheb, M. (Ed.). (2011). *The invention of history: A century of interplay between theology and politics in Palestine*. Bethlehem, Palestine: Diyar Publishing.

Raupp, J. (2004). Public sphere as central concept of public relations. In B. van Ruler & D. Verčič (Eds.), *Public relations and communication management in Europe: A nation-by-nation introduction to public relations theory and practice* (pp. 309–316). Berlin, Germany: Mouton de Gruyter.

Reinharz, J. (1993). *Chaim Weizmann: The making of a statesman*. New York, NY: Oxford University Press.

Rivlin, P. (2011). *The Israeli economy from the foundation of the state through the 21st century*. New York, NY: Cambridge University Press.

Rosolio, D. (1999). *System and crisis: Crises, adjustments and changes in the Kibbutz movement*. Tel Aviv, Israel: Am Oved.

Rosolio, D. (2002, December 1). Personal communication with the lead author in the Western Galilee College.

Samuel, R. (1997). Weisgal, Meyer Wolf. In Keter Publishing House (Ed.), *Encyclopedia Judaica*. Jerusalem, Israel: Judaica Multimedia.

Sand, S. (2009). *The invention of the Jewish people*. London, UK: Verso.

Segev, T. (2001). *The new Zionists*. Jerusalem, Israel: Keter.

Seitel, F. P. (2001). *The practice of public relations* (8th ed.). Upper Saddle River, NJ: Prentice Hall.

Senor, D., & Singer, S. (2009). *Start-up nation: The story of Israel's economic miracle*. New York, NY: Twelve.

Shahar, N. (1994). *The Eretz Israel song and the Jewish National Fund*. Israel: Research Institute for the History of the Keren Kayemet leIsrael, Land and Settlement Research Series (1).

Shai, N. (1998, July). *The spokesperson – in the crossfire: A decade of Israeli defense crisis from an official spokesperson's perspective*. Discussion Paper D-29. Cambridge, MA: Joan Shorenstein Center, Harvard University.

Shai, S. (2002, December 31). Personal communication with the lead author at an interview in Tel Aviv.

Shalev, M. (2005, January 14). Prime education leader. *Yediot Aharonot*, p. 7.

Shalit, E. (2004). *The hero and his shadow: Psychological aspects of myth and reality in Israel*. Lanham, MA: University Press of America.

Shamgar, I. (1999, April 18). The Israeli version of *Pravda*. *Maariv*, p. 10.

Shapira, A. (1973). *The disappointing struggle: Hebrew Labor, 1929–1939*. Tel Aviv, Israel: Tel Aviv University.

Shapira, A. (1992). *Land and power: The Zionist resort to force, 1881–1948* (W. Templer, Trans.). Stanford, CA: Stanford University Press.

Sharpe, M. L., & Pritchard, B. J. (2004). The historical empowerment of public opinion and its relationship to the emergence of public relations as a profession. In D. J. Tilson & E. C. Alozie (Eds.), *Toward the common good: Perspectives in international public relations* (pp. 13–36). Boston, MA: Pearson Education.

Shatz, Y. (2002, November 19). Personal communication with the lead author in an interview in Jerusalem.

Shatz, Y., & Ariel, S. (1998). *The lexicon of the state of Israel* (3rd ed., Vol. 2). Tel Aviv, Israel: Dvir.

Shavit, O. (2001, March 9). A senior official in his plane. *Haaretz Magazine*, pp. 32–38.

Shenhav, S. R., Sheafer, T., & Gabay, I. (2010). Incoherent narrator: Israeli public diplomacy during the disengagement and the elections in the Palestinian Authority. *Israel Studies, 15* (3), 143–162.

Shimshoni, D. (1982). *Israeli democracy: The middle of the journey*. New York, NY: Free Press.

Shochat, D. (2002, November 19). Personal communication with the lead author in an interview in Jerusalem.

Shtrasman, G. (1961, April 21). The "Treaty Center" for foreign reporters has opened its gates. *Maariv*, p. 4.

Shvika, Y. (1997). *Rav-Milim: The complete new Hebrew dictionary*. Tel Aviv, Israel: MTH, the Center for Educational Technology.

References

Smythe, R. (2001). The genesis of public relations in British colonial practice. *Public Relations Review, 27* (2), 149–161.

Sofer, R. (2011). *Mass communication in Israel*. Ra'anana, Israel: Open University.

Sriramesh, K. (2003). Introduction. In K. Sriramesh & D. Verčič (Eds.), *The global public relations handbook: Theory, research, and practice* (pp. xxv–xxxvi). Mahwah, NJ: Lawrence Erlbaum.

Sriramesh, K. (2009). The relationships between culture and public relations. In K. Sriramesh & D. Verčič (Eds.), *The global public relations handbook: Theory, research, and practice* (rev. ed., pp. 47–61). New York, NY: Routledge.

Sriramesh, K., & Duhé, S. C. (2009). Political economy and public relations. In K. Sriramesh & D. Verčič (Eds.), *The global public relations handbook: Theory, research, and practice* (rev. ed., pp. 25–51). New York, NY: Routledge.

Sriramesh, K., & Verčič, D. (Eds.). (2003a). *The global public relations handbook: Theory, research, and practice*. Mahwah, NJ: Lawrence Erlbaum.

Sriramesh, K., & Verčič, D. (2003b). A theoretical framework for global public relations theory and practice. In K. Sriramesh & D. Verčič (Eds.), *The global public relations handbook: Theory, research, and practice* (pp. 1–19). Mahwah, NJ: Lawrence Erlbaum.

Sriramesh, K., & Verčič, D. (Eds.). (2009). *The global public relations handbook: Theory, research, and practice* (rev. ed.). New York, NY: Routledge.

Sternhell, Z. (1995). *Nation-building or new society? The Zionist labor movement (1904–1940) and the origins of Israel*. Tel Aviv, Israel: Am Oved.

Straughan, D. S. (Ed.). (2007). *Women's use of public relations for Progressive-era reform: Rousing the conscience of a nation*. New York, NY: Edwin Mellen Press.

Strawczynski, M., & Zeira, J. (2002). Reducing the relative size of government in Israel after 1985. In A. Ben-Bassat (Ed.), *The Israeli economy 1985–1998: From government intervention to market economics* (pp. 61–81). Cambridge, MA: MIT Press.

Tal, E. (2002a, November 26). Personal communication with the lead author at an interview in Tel Aviv.

Tal, E. (2002b). *A tribute to a lone wolf*. Tel Aviv, Israel: TalPeter.

Tauber, G. E. (1997). Einstein, Albert. In Keter Publishing House (Ed.), *Encyclopedia Judaica*. Jerusalem, Israel: Judaica Multimedia.

Taylor, M. (2000). Toward a public relations approach to nation building. *Journal of Public Relations Research, 12* (2), 179–210.

Taylor, M. (2010). Public relations in the enactment of civil society. In R. L. Heath (Ed.), *The SAGE handbook of public relations* (pp. 5–15). Thousand Oaks, CA: Sage.

Taylor, M., & Kent, M. L. (2006). Public relations theory and practice in nation building. In C. H. Botan & V. Hazleton (Eds.), *Public relations theory II* (pp. 299–315). Mahwah, NJ: Lawrence Erlbaum.

Teomim, M. (2002, December 16). Personal communication with the lead author in an interview in Tel Aviv.

Terry, V. (2005). Postcard from the steppes: A snapshot of public relations and culture in Kazakhstan. *Public Relations Review, 31*, 31–36.

Tevet, S. (1985). *Ben-Gurion and the Palestinian Arabs: From peace to war*. New York, NY: Oxford University Press.

Toledano, M. (2010). Military spokespeople and democracy: Perspectives from two Israeli wars. In R. L. Heath (Ed.), *The Sage handbook of public relations* (pp. 585–598). Thousand Oaks, CA: Sage.

Toledano, M. & McKie, D. (2009). The Israeli PR experience: Nation building and professional values. In K. Sriramesh & D. Verčič (Eds.), *The global public relations handbook: Theory, research, and practice* (rev. ed., pp. 243–265). New York, NY: Routledge.

Triwax, M. (2002, November 26). Personal communication with the lead author at an interview in Tel Aviv.

Tryster, H. (1995). *Israel before Israel: Silent cinema in the holy land.* Jerusalem, Israel: Steven Spielberg Jewish Film Archive.

Tzur, J. (1997). Jewish national fund. Jewish Agency. In Keter Publishing House (Ed.), *Encyclopedia Judaica*. Jerusalem, Israel: Judaica Multimedia.

Tzur, M. (2008). (Ed.). *Zionism: Selected writers on Zion.* Tel Aviv, Israel: Miskal Publishing House of Yediot Aharonot and Hemed Books.

Van Leuven, J. K. (1996). Public relations in South East Asia: From nation-building campaigns to regional independence. In H. M. Culbertson & N. Chen (Eds.), *International public relations: A comparative analysis* (pp. 207–222). Mahwah, NJ: Lawrence Erlbaum.

van Ruler, B. (2004). The Netherlands. In B. van Ruler & D. Verčič (Eds.), *Public relations and communication management* (pp. 261–275). Berlin, Germany: Mouton de Gruyter.

van Ruler, B., & Verčič, D. (2002). *The Bled manifesto on public relations.* Ljubljana, Slovenia: Pristop.

van Ruler, B., & Verčič, D. (Eds.). (2004a). *Public relations and communication management in Europe: A nation-by-nation introduction to public relations theory and practice.* Berlin, Germany: Mouton de Gruyter.

van Ruler, B., & Verčič, D. (2004b). Overview of public relations and communication management in Europe. In B. van Ruler & D. Verčič (Eds.), *Public relations and communication management in Europe: A nation-by-nation introduction to public relations theory and practice* (pp. 1–11). Berlin, Germany: Mouton de Gruyter.

Venkataswaran, A. (2004). The evolving face of public relations in Malaysia. In D. Tilson & E. Alozie (Eds.), *Toward the common good: Perspectives in international public relations* (pp. 405–425). Boston, MA: Pearson Education.

Watson, T. (2012). Editor's introduction: Bournemouth University's 2011 history conference. *Public Relations Review, 38* (3), 339–340.

Weaver, K., Motion, J., & Roper, J. (2006). From propaganda to discourse (and back again): Truth, power, the public interest and public relations. In J. L'Etang & M. Pieczka (Eds.), *Public relations: Critical debates and contemporary practice* (pp. 7–21). Mahwah, NJ: Lawrence Erlbaum.

Webb, A., & Salmon, C. T. (2005). United States government and public relations. In R. L. Heath (Ed.), *Encyclopedia of public relations* (Vol. 2, pp. 877–880). Thousand Oaks, CA: Sage.

Wechsberg, J. (1967). *A walk through the garden of science.* London, UK: Weidenfeld & Nicolson.

Weisgal, M. (1971). *Meyer Weisgal . . . so far: An autobiography* [lead author translation from Hebrew]. Jerusalem, Israel: Weidenfeld & Nicolson.

Wilcox, D. L., Cameron, G. T., Ault, P. H., & Agee, W. K. (2003). *Public relations: Strategies and tactics* (7th ed.). Boston, MA: Allyn & Bacon.

Xifra, J., & McKie, D. (2012). From realpolitik to noopolitik: The public relations of (stateless) nations in an information age. *Public Relations Review, 38,* 819–824.

Yaari, A. (1997) *Shluhei Eretz Israel: The history of emissaries from Haaretz to the Diaspora from the destruction of the Second Temple to the nineteenth century.* Jerusalem, Israel: Harav Kuk Institute Publishing.

Yaron, R. (2009, October 19). Personal communication with the lead author at Modyin, Israel.
Yatziv, G. (2002). *Social lexicon* (3rd ed.). Jerusalem, Israel: Academon.
Yiftachel, O. (2006). *Ethnocracy: Land and identity politics in Israel/Palestine.* Philadelphia, PA: University of Pennsylvania Press.
Yishai, Y. (1998). Civil society in transition: Interest politics in Israel. *Annals of the American Academy of Political and Social Science, 555*: *Israel in Transition* (G. Ben-Dor, Ed.). Thousand Oaks, CA: Sage.
Yitzhaki, S. (2002). Personal communication with the lead author in an interview in Tel Aviv, December 9, 2002.
Zaharna, R. S., Hammad, A. I., & Masri, J. (2009). Palestinian public relations: Inside and out. In K. Sriramesh & D. Verčič (Eds.), *The global public relations handbook: Theory, research, and practice* (rev. ed., pp. 236–260). New York, NY: Routledge.
Zameret, Z. (1993). *The melting pot.* Jerusalem, Israel: Keter Press Enterprise and Ben-Gurion Research Center.
Zameret, Z. (1999). Ben-Zion Dinur between "statehood" and "the movement." In M. Bar-On (Ed.), *The sovereignty challenge* (pp. 52–56). Jerusalem, Israel: Yad Ben Zvi.
Zameret, Z., & Yablonka, H. (1997). At the era opening. In Z. Zameret & H. Yablonka (Eds.), *The first decade* (pp. 7–10). Jerusalem, Israel: Yad Ben Zvi.
Zerubavel, Y. (1995). *Recovered roots: Collective memory and the making of Israeli national tradition.* Chicago, IL: University of Chicago Press.
Zohar, M. (2005, July 4). Personal communication with the lead author in a telephone interview.

Index

Abbott, A. 7, 8, 97, 149, 151, 169
Academy for the Hebrew Language 5
Adams, Samuel 39, 50,
Advertisers' Association of Israel 151, 159
advertising 1, 4, 8, 15, 65, 71, 74, 117, 134, 138, 150, 151–154, 155, 157, 159–160, 161–162, 164, 165, 166, 169
agriculture 12, 44, 76, 80, 104, 105–108, 119, 135, 146, 171
Ahdut ha-Avoda 133
Akunis, Ophir 28
Aldoory, L. 140
Aliyah 42–43, 106, 156
Almog, O. 43, 54, 115,
Alon, Yigal 57, 133
American Jewish Joint Distribution Committee 76
American Jewish Physician Committee 86,
American Jews 41, 72, 86,
American National Association of Manufacturers (NAM) 117
American Revolution 11, 39, 50,
Amit, Major General Meir 157
Amit, Zvi 110–111, 117, 118, 119
Amitai, Yechiel 78, 79, 133, 135, 136–137
Anderson, Benedict 22
Anholt, Simon 169
anti-democratic 27, 138, 178
anti-Semitism 40–41, 48, 51, 54, 72, 173,
Arab: countries 1, 44, 45, 57, 62, 91, 122, 126, 141, 170; Jewish 47, 87, 99; national movement 45, 46; nations 42, 56, 123; Palestinian 39, 44–45, 47, 174; problem 44, 53
Arab Bureau of the Jewish Agency 46
Aran, Zalman 128
Arielli, Amnon 154, 161
Arnon, Mike 123
Ashkenazi 113

assimilation 28, 41
Association of Industry Owners 109, 114. 116, 117; (see also Industrialists' Association)
Australia 16, 88, 105
Avineri, Shlomo 49
Avoda Ivrit [Hebrew Labour] 112–113, 114, 115

Babylonian 25,
Baitar Zionist 76
Balaban, Nissan 164, 166
Balfour Declaration 42, 50, 51, 52, 69, 87
Baltianski, Gadi 138–139
Bar-Gal, Y, 70, 71, 73, 74, 75
Bar-On, M. 57
Barak, Ehud 138–139
Begin, Menachem 126, 131, 170
Beilin, Yossi 78, 83, 108, 109, 114, 115, 116, 118
Ben-Ami, J. 36, 172, 173
Ben-Gurion, David 26, 46–47, 50, 57–58, 61, 62, 98, 122, 127, 128, 132, 142
Ben-Horin, Moshe 125
Ben-Meir, Dov 130
Ben-Shitrit, Nisim 136
Ben Yehuda: Eliezer 43, 132; Netiva 132, 133
Benayahu, Avi 145–146
Benei Akiva 76
Benziman, Uzi 66, 177
Berger, Alfred 88
Berger, Julius 71, 72
Berkhofer, R. F. 21–22
Bernays 10, 13–14, 15, 18, 150
Beth Hadin 27
Bettelheim, Avi 109, 119
Bialik, Chaim 87
Bing-Lineal 152

Bistritzki, Natan 72, 74, 75, 76, 77, 80
Bithonism 56, 57–58, 122, 142
Blau, Uri 66
Blumenfeld, Kurt 88
branding 12, 14, 50, 168, 169–170
Brendman Institute for Public Opinion Research 5
Britain 15, 17, 39, 42, 50, 69, 88, 92, 121, 135, 146, 148, 150
British Mandate 42, 51, 52, 60, 61, 64, 69, 71, 80, 109, 110, 121–124, 175
Brit Shalom 41, 47, 87, 99
Broadcasting Authority 3, 33, 62, 63, 125, 138, 144
Brown, R. 13, 18
Brug, Avinoam 146
Buber, Martin 47, 87, 99, 100, 176
Bundists 41
Burson, Harold 54, 149, 163, 164

Canada 67, 93, 105
Carmon, Arye 122
Caspi, D. 9, 60, 61, 62, 63, 124, 148
Central Zionist Archives 71
Chamber of Commerce 108, 110, 114–115, 116, 117–119
Chamberlain, Joseph 49
Cherrick, Bernard 88–89, 94, 97, 101, 102,
Christensen, B. 161
citizenship 129, 130, 175
coalition 35, 58, 77, 109, 114, 157, 164, 175
Cohen, H. 46
Cohen, Israel 138, 161
Cohen, Niso 161
Cohen, R. 58
collaboration 31, 34, 96, 101,103, 128, 133, 137, 142, 154
communication: organizational 19; persuasive 2, 9, 37, 42, 53, 65, 70, 81, 121, 146, 147; practitioners 11, 69; strategic 10, 27, 44, 121; strategies 19; two-way 18; Zionist 24, 50–51
consultants: private 12, 149–167
Coombs, W. T. 11, 168
culture 2, 14, 19, 27, 29, 33, 34, 56, 60, 62, 84, 120, 129, 163, 171; Arab 99; Diaspora 28; Dutch 6; European Yiddish 94; Hebrew culture 62, 70, 80; Israeli 35, 41, 43, 57, 68, 70, 83, 114, 121, 127, 175; Jewish 40, 100; national 28, 32, 44, 175; Sabra 115
Curtin, P. A. 23

Cutlip, S.M. 150, 178

Dachlan, Mohammed 47
Dankner, A. 106–107
Dayan, Moshe 159–161
democracy 9, 12, 17, 20, 31, 34, 58, 65, 122, 124, 127, 129, 134, 175; Israel's 56, 66, 165, 174, 177
Dershowitz, Alan 36
Diaspora 1, 10, 11, 25–32, 34–38, 43, 54, 57–59, 74, 80, 83, 84–85, 87, 95, 105, 106, 108, 109, 120, 122, 124, 129, 165, 167, 177; Jewish 25–30, 35, 38, 57, 59, 83, 84
Dinur, Ben-Zion 127, 142
diplomacy: professional 42; public 1, 9, 12, 124, 129, 168, 169, 173
discourse 4, 24. 30, 53, 55, 85, 109, 113; development of 45; political 67; public 11, 25, 30, 37, 59, 60, 61, 122, 146, 147; Zionist 26, 43
discrimination 40, 64, 112
Donovan, J. 100
Dor, Daniel 139
Doran Communication 165–166
Duhé, S. C. 104
Durkheim, Émile 6

Eastern Europe 29, 35, 41, 43, 50, 53
Economic Stabilization Program 111, 162
Egypt 58, 91, 99, 131, 141, 172
Einstein, Albert 86, 89, 90, 91
Eisenstadt, S. 27
Elam, Y. 41
Eldar, Akiva 170, 173, 174
Elisha 174–175
Elizur, Dr Judy 62
Elizur, Y. 160
Ellul, Jacques 14–15
Elon, Amos 29, 44, 50–51, 57, 105, 113
emancipation 27, 28, 40–41, 123,
emissaries 11, 36, 37, 73, 81, 84, 85–103
Empire Marketing Board (EMB) 71
Epstein, A. M. 72
Eretz Israel 36–37, 58, 70, 72, 74, 80, 82, 84, 85, 87, 90,98, 103, 109, 115, 122
Eshed, Eti 136, 139, 140
Eshkol, David 111, 117, 118, 125, 126, 153, 155, 156–157, 163
European Enlightenment movement 27
European Jews 28, 40, 41
European Public Relations Education and Research Association (EUPRERA) 16

Faisal, King of Iraq 45
Falcor 80, 82, 97
Fetman-Golan, Yosef 156
Folk, Adolf 71
Ford, Henry 72, 169
Foreign Journalists' Association 124
Forum 153, 155–157, 158, 166
Foundation Fund 71, 73, 74, 75, 86, 88
France 76, 98, 99, 160; French 21, 76, 89, 90, 98, 124
Fraser, N. 33
freedom of the press 30, 60, 66
French Revolution 28, 40
fundraising 84–89, 100, 158; agencies 73; campaigns 31; efforts 42, 88, 95, 101; methods 37, 72–74; professional 36; prominence of 25; and public relations 84–85, 93, 98, 101, 103

Gafni, Willy 154
Gaither, T. 23
Galili, Israel 125–126
Ganani, Deborah 139
Gaza 47, 62, 124, 126, 141, 145, 170, 172, 173
Gazit, Shlomo 125, 143
Geary, P. J. 21
Geldblum, Arieh 76, 77, 154
General Bureau of Statistics 134, 135
gentile 26, 28
Germany 5, 6, 13, 42, 71, 74, 76, 109
Gillerman, Dan 110, 111, 117–118, 119
Gillon, Philip and Hadassah 97
Gineo, Vicky 132, 133
Gitam Advertising 157, 164
Golan Heights 58
Goldberg, Yohanan (Dobje) 155–156, 157
Golman, Eric 18
Gordon, David 40
Goren, A. A. 90, 91,
Government Press Office 3, 121, 123–125, 129
Greek 26
Grunig, James E. 10, 18, 150
Grunig, L. 140
Gulf War 143–144, 161
Gutman Institute for Applied Social Research 33

Haber, Eitan 131
Habermas 33, 59,
Hadassah Medical Organization 84, 95–98, 99–100, 101,

Hadassah Women's Zionist Organization of America 95, 98
Haezrachi, M. 72
Hagira 43
Hallaha 27
Halpern, Burton 163
Hamilton, Alexander 39
Hammer, Zevulun 138
Haolam Hazeh 154
Harman, Abe 88, 123
Harman, Leo 71
Harris, Lucian 96–97, 99, 101
Harshav, B. 43
Harvard University 85, 114, 144
Harzfeld, Avraham 132
Hasbara 9, 11, 15, 20, 24, 31, 34, 46, 57, 61, 62, 65, 68, 69, 70–72, 76, 77, 80–83, 89, 121, 123, 125, 130, 136, 141, 143, 147, 151, 168, 170, 172, 173, 175–176; Center 129; challenges 126–127; Department 78–79, 101, 128, 135, 142; and Israel 2–3; Israeli military 141; and public relations 4–7
Haskala movement 40–41, 100
Hasman, Rami 170–171
Hatalgi, Theodor 76–77, 78, 79, 135
Heath, R. L. 10, 11, 103, 121, 176
Hebrew 4, 9, 15, 26, 35, 41, 43, 49, 51, 64, 73, 74, 89, 94, 105, 115, 116, 122, 132, 133, 151, 152; coinage 57; culture 62, 70, 80; language 32, 43–44, 57, 60, 80, 175; Labour 112–113; literature 32; media 30, 31, 82, 94, 113, 156,176; nation 61; press 30, 31, 81, 82, 113
Hebrew University 50, 51, 64, 79, 84, 85–92, 94, 95, 96–97, 100,101, 102, 123
Hebron 36
Helman, Oran 124
Hen, Zalman 132–133, 135
Herzl, Theodore 39, 42, 44, 48–51, 53, 90, 100, 128
Hever, H. 32
Histadrut 3, 64, 104, 107–109, 111–114, 119, 133, 134, 165
historiography 18, 21, 25
Hitler, Adolf 15
Hobsbawm, Eric 22–23, 24, 25
Hofein, Eliezer 109
Holladay, S. J 11, 168
Holocaust 29, 42, 54, 128, 130
Holtzhausen, D. 6, 17, 18, 19, 39
Hon, L. 140

Honig, Eliyahu 86, 88, 89, 92, 101
Horowitz, D. 69, 118
Hua, N. 28
Hunt, Todd 10, 18, 150
Hushi, Abba 115

identity: collective 27, 29, 59, 176; creation of 43, 175; cultural 26–27, 34, 44; Jewish 26, 28, 52; national 9, 20, 29, 47, 56, 71, 122, 127, 169; professional 2, 8, 150, 152; public relations 2, 4, 10
ideology 12, 14, 20, 21, 24, 45, 48, 50, 51, 54, 58, 70, 76, 83, 105, 107, 114, 115, 122, 127, 129, 131, 135, 147, 148, 156, 166; Zionist 40, 41, 44, 64, 90, 103, 104, 105, 107, 120, 132, 175, 177
Iggeret Klalit [General Letter] 37
Iggeret Le-Nedivim [Letter to Philanthropists] 37
immigration 3, 29, 32, 34, 42, 45, 53, 61, 64, 69, 80, 82, 83, 107, 109, 122, 129, 162
Independence Day 125, 127–128, 129, 130, 142
Independence War 123, 127, 156
Industrialists' Association 110, 111, 117, 118, 119, 165; (see also Association of Industry Owners)
infrastructure 35, 38, 40, 50, 56, 63, 112, 116, 121, 174
International History of Public Relations Conference 17
interprofessional competition 6, 81, 97, 151, 153
Iraq 45, 99, 144, 145
Israel Defense Forces (IDF) 3, 10, 33, 121, 141–144, 145–146, 158
Israel Museum 84, 98, 100–101
Israel: State of 1, 2, 6, 9, 14, 25, 26, 29, 32, 35, 36, 39, 42, 50, 51, 53, 61, 72, 75, 77, 78, 80, 82, 84, 85, 88, 89, 94, 121–122, 126, 165, 170, 173, 174, 175
Israeli Advertising Association 5, 151
Israeli government 1, 4, 12, 14, 65, 67, 77, 79, 82, 83, 108, 114, 120, 121, 127, 128, 130, 135, 139, 147, 149, 172
Israeli Public Relations Association 61, 153, 161
Italy 76

Jabotinsky, Zeev 52–53, 128

Jefferson, Thomas 39
Jerusalem 26, 36, 37, 58, 69, 71, 72, 85, 86, 87, 90, 91, 95, 97, 98, 99, 100, 101, 102, 109, 114, 118, 123, 124, 136, 137, 173
Jerusalem Temple 26, 36, 37, 85, 102
Jewish 4, 5, 11, 24, 25–38, 39–61, 64, 69, 70, 72–74, 76, 78–80, 82, 95–100, 103, 105, 108–110, 112–115, 121–123, 127, 135, 138, 143, 152, 158, 163, 173, 174, 175; community 27, 35, 59–60, 69, 74, 84–85, 160, 173; history 36, 44; identity 26, 28, 52; people 4, 11, 24, 25, 26, 38, 40–43, 45, 47, 49, 50, 52, 70, 79, 90, 100, 122, 129, 142, 168; public sphere 6, 9, 11, 26, 28–29, 37; religion 23, 29; society 28–30, 34, 37, 40, 165; state 11, 20, 25–29, 38, 41–42, 45, 48, 50–51, 96, 122, 171
Jewish Agency 3, 46, 64, 70, 78, 80, 82, 83, 97, 112–114, 121, 123, 152,
Jewish Diaspora 24, 25–26, 29, 30, 35, 38, 57, 59, 83, 84
Jewish Hebrew press 30–31, 40, 59,
Jewish National Fund (JNF) 32, 70–77, 78–79, 90 88–89, 90, 97, 121, 123, 127, 135
Jordan 58; River 46, 62, 175
journalism: profession 8, 65, 81, 124; competition with public relations 97, 134, 147, 176
Journalists' Association 30, 61, 66, 78, 79, 101, 124
Justman, M. 106, 119

Kamm, Anat 66
Katriel, T. 133
Katz, E. 33–34
Katz, Israel 132
Katz, J. 28, 29
Katz research group 33, 34
Katzenelson, Berl 50, 113
Katzir, Ephraim 27
Kazakhstan 16
Keller, A. 126
Kent, M. 19–21, 169,
Khoury, R. 21
Knesset (Israeli parliament) 28, 59, 61, 62, 66, 125, 128, 136, 140–141, 165, 178
Kimmerling, B. 113, 128, 141
Kinamoni, Shosh 161
Kishon, Ephraim 76

Kohn, H. 26
Kol Israel 3, 61, 78, 79, 123, 129, 130, 136, 138
Kollek, Teddy 61, 99, 101
Koor 157
Koteret 161
Kouts, G. 30–31, 59
Krasney, Boris 165
Ku Klux Klan 72
Kunczik, M. 4, 19, 169, 171, 174
Kurian, P. 19

L'Etang, J. 15, 17, 71, 121, 137, 147, 150, 169
Labor Party 58, 59, 165
Lain, F. 72
Lamme, M. 19
Landor, David 124
Laniado, Eli 117–118, 119
Laqueur, W. 45, 53,
Lautman, Dov 111, 118, 119
leadership 30, 88, 95, 110, 112, 121; Arab 46; political 32, 34, 37, 61, 62, 64, 147; Zionist 31, 42, 44, 45, 53, 84, 86, 92, 175
League of Nations 42, 69, 121
legitimacy 22, 34, 53, 58, 69, 107, 117, 126, 145, 171, 178
Likud 24, 28, 131, 140,
Lilienblum, Moshe 40,
Limor, Y. 124, 148
Lineal, Shimon 151, 152–153
Lissak, M. 69
lobbying 42, 49, 52, 110, 155, 157, 162, 165; and fundraising 10, 25, 37–38; campaign 42; lobbyist 34, 42, 46, 51–52, 165; shtadlan 46, 165
Logos Public Relations 117, 157
Lory, A. 124

Magen David Adom (MDA) 160–161
Magnes, Judah L. 85, 86–88, 91, 99
Magnat, Dalia 161–162
Malaysia 17
Moloney, K. 178–179
Mamlachtiut 56–58, 122
Mann, R. 61
Mapai Party 58, 61, 106, 107, 113, 132, 133
marketing 110, 152, 166; efforts 63, 160; political 65; tactics 74
Marchand, R. 117
Marx, Karl 6

Masbirim 1, 3, 9, 65, 68, 124, 126, 131, 171, 172
Masis, Alex 154
mass media 59, 82, 94, 150, 175
McCarthy, Joseph 28
McKie, D. 7, 17–19
Mearsheimer, J. 35–36
media 43, 66, 152, 158–159, 165, 170; control over 47, 51, 59–60, 68, 80, 124, 139, 145; Hebrew 30, 94; Israeli 30, 60–63, 65, 79, 94, 123, 177; Jewish 37; politics 65; power of 41, 94; role of 30; social 1; use of 31, 37, 49, 54
media relations 6, 10, 38, 59, 76, 83, 89, 93, 101, 117, 123, 130, 136, 140, 145, 147, 152, 155, 156, 157, 158, 161, 166, 167, 177
mediapolitik 65, 165
Meir, Golda 82, 125, 132
Menorah 24, 26–27
Merkaz haHasbara 128–131, 142
Meyer, Meyer 101–102
Meyers, Nechemia 94–95
Middle East 4, 36, 42, 52, 56, 95, 99, 127, 164, 172
military 36, 41, 53, 64, 66, 93, 108, 120, 133, 141, 143, 145, 156, 158, 171, 173; British 82; leaders 58, 62; occupation 4; operations 64, 124, 126, 141, 145; service 142; spokespeople 12, 135, 1 44; struggle 41, 93, 142
Milosevic, Slobodan 21, 22
Ministry of: Defense 125, 142, 143, 144; Education 3, 33, 118, 121, 127–128, 129, 138, 142; Environment 139; Finance 3, 110, 111, 117; Foreign Affairs 3, 82, 101, 123, 125, 136, 143, 145, 170, 171; Hasbara and Diaspora 1; Health 96, 139; Interior 61; Internal Security 143; Justice 28, 136, 139, 140; Labour 131, 132, 133; Public Diplomacy 1, 129; Tourism 3; Transportation 78, 133, 134, 135, 156
Modai, Yitzhak 118
Modoux, Alain 131
MS Business Communication 165, 166
Munshi, D. 17–19, 20
Mushkin, Benny 79, 89
Mushli, Harriet 126
Muslim 24, 42, 46, 174

Nadel, Baruch 158

Index

narrative 1, 2, 6, 12, 17, 21, 23, 27, 32, 44, 53, 55, 64, 104, 123, 128, 145, 170, 173, 175, 177, 179
nation building 13, 72, 79, 100, 108, 112, 127, 141, 169; challenges 61–62, 149; effort 23, 24, 104, 120, 147; and media 60, 62; process 84, 147; and public relations 19–21, 103, 168
National Front 21
nationalism 21, 23, 28, 40, 46, 50, 53, 112
Nave, Dani 143
Navon, Yitzhak 61
Nazi 6, 69, 72, 76; Germany 13; propaganda 71
Negbi, Moshe 66
Neiger, M. 3
Netanyahu, Bibi 138, 178
Netherlands 5, 6, 123; Dutch 6, 16, 123
Neumann, David 137
newspapers: *Al Aharam* 91; *Al Hamishmar* 156; *Davar* 113, 115, 133; *Haaretz* 64, 66, 76, 79, 88, 125, 154, 155, 159, 170, 171; *Hamevaser* 30; *Hayin Hashveet* 176; *Jerusalem Post* 97; *Lamerchav* 156; *Social Lexicon* 4; *The Jewish State* 48, 49; *Yediot Ahronot* 118, 154, 155, 158, 159
Nissim, Moshe 118
Nitzotz 154
Nordau, Max 100

Oren, Ruth 75
Organization for Economic and Co-operation and Development (OECD) 104–105
Ottoman 69; Empire 48; Palestine 44

Paine, Tom 39
Palestine 4, 9, 11, 21, 39, 41–48, 50, 51, 52, 53, 69, 71, 72, 74, 75, 80, 83, 86, 88, 90–91, 95, 96, 99, 121, 122, 141, 172
Patterson, Thomas E. 144
Pearlman, Moshe 123
Pearson, R. 2
Peled, Elad 126
Perlmuter, A. 141
Peres, Shimon 58, 111, 156
Peri, Y. 58–59, 64, 65, 164, 176
Perry, Michael 153, 159
Pieczka, M. 15, 47, 121
Policy-Political Communication Consultancy 185

practitioners 4, 6, 12, 19, 20, 34, 40, 59, 71, 72, 83, 120, 130, 147, 151, 156, 158, 162, 175; communication 11, 69; government 12, 121, 134, 135; Hasbara 175; public relations 2, 6, 7–9, 11, 22, 23, 30, 38, 53, 55, 63, 65, 68, 74, 76, 81, 84, 87, 94, 96, 103, 104, 117, 121, 127, 138, 141, 148, 153, 160, 165, 166, 176; Zionist 94
propaganda 2, 4, 10, 11, 12, 13–15, 18, 32, 36, 47, 48, 49, 52, 54, 58, 60, 62, 69, 70, 72, 75, 78, 83, 91, 93, 100, 105, 112, 127, 129, 142, 147, 170; and public relations 4, 12, 13, 14, 15, 18, 123, 135; Jewish National Fund 70–71, 72–73, 74, 75, 76, 78, 80; methods 74–75; of agitation 14; of integration 14, 15, 131; Palestinian 126; Propaganda, Press, and Youth Department 70, 72, 73; techniques 51; Zionist 31, 42, 43, 45
Proper, Dan 119
public diplomacy 9, 168–169
public relations: campaign 1, 20, 109, 111, 112, 121, 162; definition of 4–5; Hasbara 4–6; history 7, 11, 13, 16–22, 85; Israeli 2, 8, 11, 16, 22, 30, 31, 34, 39, 48, 55, 61, 83, 92, 96, 142, 153, 164, 166, 174, 177; literature 7, 11, 13, 16, 48, 59; practitioners 7–9, 11, 22, 23, 30, 38, 53, 55, 63, 65, 68, 74, 76, 81, 84, 87, 94, 96, 103, 104, 117, 121, 127, 138, 141, 148, 153, 160, 165, 166, 176; profession 2, 13, 68, 102, 117, 121, 131, 155, 166, 173; propaganda 4, 12, 13, 14, 15, 123, 135; theory 11, 16, 47

Rabin, Yitzhak 128, 131
Raheb, M. 21
Raucher, Alan 18,
Raupp, J. 59
Regev, Miri 145–146
Reinharz, J. 52
religion: Arab–Christian 46; Arab–Muslim 46; Christian 24, 46, 174; Christian–Zionist 173; Jewish 23, 25, 29; Muslim 24, 42, 46, 174; Roman Catholic Church 18
Reporters without Borders' Freedom of the Press 66
Rivlin, P. 120
Rogel, Raanan 165

Rome 26, 82
Rubinstein, Helena 159, 160
Rosenthal, Miriam Freund 98
Rosolio, Dani 125–126
Rothberg, Sam 88,
Ruder & Finn 126, 170
Rupin, Arthur 87
Russell, K. 19
Russia 49, 50, 53, 74, 125, 142

Sabra 43, 54, 115, 133, 156
Sadat, Anwar 141
Safed 36, 85,
Salmon, C. T. 131, 146
Sand, S. 4, 23, 25
Sapir, Pinchas 107–108
Seaman, Dan 124
Second Authority for Radio and Television 63
Sela, Uri 154
Senor, Dan 120, 171
Serbian history 21
Shabak [Intelligence Services] 66
Shai, Dr Nachman 66, 143, 144
Shai, Shmuel 154–155
Shalit, E. 29
Shamgar, I. 32
Shamir, Yitzhak 108, 140, 144
Shamis, Giora 94
Shapira, A. 42, 45, 46, 112
Sharon, Ariel 135
Shatz, Yakov 2, 3, 129, 130, 131
Shavit, O. 139
Shemen 152–153
Shenkar, Arie 109, 114
Shertok, Moshe 113
Shochat, Doron 129–130, 142
Shoken, Zalman 88,
shtadlan 35, 165
Shtrasman, Gabi 124
Silbert, Harvey 89,
Sinai Desert 58
Singer, Saul 120, 171
Six Day War 58, 77, 83, 99, 126, 131, 17
Smolenskin, Pertz 40
socialism 41, 50, 113
Sofer, R. 62, 63, 64, 67
Sokolow, Nahum 31, 97
sovereignty 41, 83, 122, 127
Spigel, Malka 88
Sriramesh, K. 11, 16, 17, 56, 59, 104
Star of David 26
State Controller Office 63, 126, 104, 143

Straughan, D. 19
Strawczynski, M. 162
synagogues 26, 37, 72
Syria 58,
Szold, Henrietta 87, 95, 96, 99,

Tal, Eliyahu 151–152, 154, 161
Tartakover, D. 109–110
Taylor, M. 19–21, 169, 176
Teachers' Association 73, 126
Tel Aviv 31, 109, 116, 117, 123, 151, 153, 154, 159, 160, 162, 170
Teomim, Moshe 157
Tevet, S. 46
theory: civil society 20, 177; coorientation 20; critical 14; dialogic 20; political economy 104
Tiberia 36
Titus 85; Arch 26
Toledano, Margalit 16, 145–146
Toth, E. 140
Tozeret haAretz campaign 109, 110, 114–115, 117, 119, 152
Triwax, Moshe 157, 158–159, 163
Tryster, H. 71
Tukan, Haidar 46
Turkey 31, 42, 172
Tzimuki, Arye 133

Ukraine 72
UNESCO 131
United Nations 42, 50, 121–122
United States 3, 6, 11, 13, 14, 15, 16, 17, 19, 23, 35, 36, 39, 41, 42, 48, 51–52, 59, 67, 68, 72, 74, 83, 86, 87, 91, 93, 95, 96, 99–100, 105, 111, 129, 135, 137, 146, 149, 150–151, 155, 158, 163, 167, 171, 173
Ussishkin, Menachem 72, 73

Vaadat Haorhim 64
Valish & Machner 74
Van Leuven, J. 19
Van Ruler, B. 5, 6, 16, 123,
Venkataswaran, A. 17
Verčič, D. 11, 16, 17, 56, 59
Victor Emmanuel, King 49

Walt, S. 35–36
Watson, Tom 17,
Webb, A. 131, 146
Webber, Max 7
Wechsberg, J. 93–94

Index

Weisgal, Meyer 86, 91–94, 102
Weizmann: Chaim 44, 45, 46, 51–52, 84, 85, 86, 87, 88, 89, 90, 91–93, 99, 128; Institute 92–94, 95, 100
Welner, Alter 155–156
West Bank 58, 62, 79, 99, 141, 172, 174
Western Wall 37, 91
World War I 13, 42, 50, 52, 69
World War II 9, 29, 42, 81, 150, 152
World Zionist Organization 3, 31, 51, 69, 70, 73, 76, 80, 83, 86, 87, 92, 100

Yaalon, Bugi 145
Yaari, Avraham 36–37
Yablonka, H. 122
Yaron, Ruth 145
Yeshiva 36, 85, 88
Yiddish 31, 43, 76, 92, 94,
Yishuv 11, 42, 43, 47, 57, 58, 60–61, 69–70, 71, 73, 87, 106, 107, 108, 109, 112, 114, 115, 121, 122, 123, 152
Yitzhaki, Sara 140
Yom Kippur War 58, 62, 64, 144, 177

Zambia 16
Zameret, Z. 122
Zeira, J. 162
Zimbabwe 16
Zimerman, Sari 139
Zinder, Zvi 61
Zionism 24, 26–28, 40–42, 47, 48–50, 52, 53, 77, 95, 100, 107, 109, 119, 122, 177
Zionist Congress 45, 49, 85, 100
Zionist movement 9, 10, 11, 23–26, 27, 29, 30, 32, 35, 38, 40, 41, 44, 45, 46, 49, 50, 51, 52, 53, 54, 69, 70, 73, 74, 75, 78, 81, 82, 85, 86, 87, 88, 89, 91, 100, 106, 107, 113, 174
Zionist Organization of America 91, 95
Zionist revolution 11, 14, 26, 39, 40, 43, 48, 50, 55, 69
Zionist, socialist 32, 41, 45–46, 50, 112, 113, 132, 133, 155
Ziv-Av, Yitzhak 142
Zohar, Miriam 154